CAVALRY & GUARDS

A LONDON HOME

CAVALRY & GUARDS

A LONDON HOME

Edited by Val Horsler

Advisory Editor Charles Webb

© Authors, The Cavalry and Guards Club
  and Third Millennium Publishing Limited

First published in 2009 by
Third Millennium Publishing Limited,
a subsidiary of Third Millennium Information Limited.

2–5 Benjamin Street
London
United Kingdom
EC1M 5QL
www.tmiltd.com

ISBN 978 1 906507 02 2

British Library Cataloguing in Publication Data
A CIP catalogue record for this book is available from the British Library.

Edited by Val Horsler
Designed by Susan Pugsley
Production by Bonnie Murray
Reprographics by Studio Fasoli, Italy
Printed by Gorenjski Tisk, Slovenia

III THIRD MILLENNIUM
PUBLISHING, LONDON

Illustrations have been commissioned from and provided by a number of professional
agencies and individuals; we are much indebted to the quality of their work:

1st The Queen's Dragoon Guards: Colonel Savill, p 98.

© Amoret Tanner/Alamy: Eton v Harrow match tickets July 1938, p 163.

Bridgeman Art Library: General Sir Samuel James Browne, p 56.

Scott Collier: pp 105,107, 109, 149, 184–5.

**Collins & Brown, The Gentleman's Clubs of London, by permission of the author
and publisher (photographs Malcolm Lewis):** pp 32, 41, 42, 102.

Corbis: Field Marshal Earl Haig, p 59.

Getty Images: 'Manners and Customs of Ye Englyshe in 1849', p 15; Field Marshal
Sir P Chetwode, p 90; Queen Salote, p 94; Coronation of HM Queen Elizabeth II,
p 94; West Piccadilly, p 112; Pig Stickers, p 171.

© Lordprice Collection/Alamy: Ascot Royal Enclosure 1895, p 164.

Annabel McEwan: pp 7, 48–9, 76, 77, 104–5, 143, 159, 175, 176–7, 184–5.

Mary Evans: 2nd Duke of Cambridge, p 54; Vortix Vermouth/Naval & Military Club,
p 127; Eton v Harrow 1864, p 162; Lord Byron, p 162; Goodwood, p 167.

National Portrait Gallery: Frederick Lambart 10th Earl of Cavan, p 28; Robert
Stephenson Smyth Baden-Powell, p 81; Michael Power Carver, p 137; Charles Lennox
3rd Duke of Richmond and Lennox, p 166.

The Royal Air Force Club: p 131.

Shooting Times & Country Magazine, © Copyright IPC Media Ltd: p 153.

Sotheby's: Portrait of Colonel Daniel Mackinnon, p 16.

TopFoto: Pig-sticking, p 171.

© Trinity Mirror/Mirrorpix: HM Queen Elizabeth The Queen Mother 1981
Sandown Park, p 164.

Andrew Wood: pp 2–3, 6, 10, 39, 51, 89, 110–11, 120, 125, 132–3, 139, 141, 147, 154,
158–9.

Photographs of many of the Club's works of art by Roy Fox copyright © TMI.
All other images copyright © The Cavalry and Guards Club.

Contents

ACKNOWLEDGEMENTS   7

FOREWORD BY THE PRESIDENT, HRH THE DUKE OF KENT KG   8

INTRODUCTION   10

THE GUARDS CLUB 1810–1975   12

     LADIES AND LADY MEMBERS   46

THE CAVALRY CLUB 1890–1975   52

     CLUB STAFF   102

127 PICCADILLY   110

     CLUBS IN PICCADILLY   126

THE CAVALRY AND GUARDS CLUB   132

     SPORTING OCCASIONS   160

APPENDIX A: THE BRITISH ARMY   174

APPENDIX B: WINNERS OF THE KADIR CUP, 1869–1939   178

APPENDIX C: PATRONS, PRESIDENTS AND CHAIRMEN   180

APPENDIX D: CLUB SECRETARIES   182

INDEX OF SUBSCRIBERS   186

INDEX OF NAMES   190

Acknowledgements

When the idea of a book on the Club and '127' Piccadilly was first aired some three years ago, the Club Committee was at first doubtful as to how such a major project could be undertaken with the very limited archive material that appeared to be available, at least on first inspection.

However, we are indebted to Major General Jonnie Hall for his introduction to Julian Platt of Third Millennium Publishing who was quick to establish that there was indeed ample material for the sort of book in which they specialise and which is presented here. As a result, the Committee was convinced that, albeit with a great deal of effort, a thoroughly worthwhile and timely publication could be brought to the presses.

Since that initial meeting, the Club has been fortunate that a number of people took up the challenge of producing this excellent volume and I would like to thank them all.

Firstly thanks are due to the small Committee who steered the project – namely, Charles Webb, William Peto and the current Club Secretary, David Cowdery - for their dedication and commitment to producing this book. The latter in particular has been tireless not only in his search for material dating back nearly 200 years, but also in his enthusiasm in ensuring that no stone has been left unturned in all aspects of the project.

I would also like to thank the team at Third Millennium who have done such a sterling job in putting the book together and particularly Christopher Fagg, Susan Pugsley, Michael Jackson and Joel Burden.

Credits for the many pictures and other archive material can be found on page 4, but I would also like to take this opportunity to thank the many members of the Club – both past and present - whose various tales and reminiscences bring the book and it's story to life. My particular thanks must go to Lord Monteagle, who as the sole survivor of the last Guards Committee not only undertook to provide his own reminiscences, but also very kindly read through the chapter on the Guards Club to ensure its accuracy.

We are also fortunate to have had each of the Club's recent Chairmen provide an insight and 'View from the Chair', which helps to illuminate the contemporary history.

Finally I wish to thank the author –Val Horsler – for her wonderful writing and editing which has managed to turn the Clubs' archive material, together with all the more up to date offerings, into this excellent book which I trust will provide much interest and enjoyment.

CHRISTOPHER MACKENZIE-BEEVOR
CHAIRMAN – BOOK COMMITTEE

For over two hundred years London Clubs have provided for their Members a refuge from the world outside their doors and a meeting place for men of like-minds. It is perhaps a novelty to the 21st century observer that such places not only exist but continue to go from strength to strength, supported and encouraged by new generations of Club men – and now, indeed, Club ladies.

One of the original Members' Clubs was that formed by the Guards in 1810 and their story written here provides an absorbing record of the vicissitudes of Club life in general. Equally the Cavalry Club, formed much later in 1890, has had its share of dramatic changes over the years.

Members of my family have been associated with both Clubs over their long histories and as President of the Cavalry Club since 1975 and subsequently of the Cavalry and Guards Club, I have witnessed both the negotiations for the merger of the two Clubs in 1976 and the tremendous struggle for the purchase of the freehold in 1987.

These two defining moments in the history of the Clubs are recounted here in engrossing detail, together with profiles and contributions from Members. Whether you are a longstanding Member who wishes to appreciate your connection with the Club, or indeed a visitor or just a reader with a friendly interest in this fascinating corner of London Clubland, I am sure you will find something worthwhile to detain you in this admirably produced book.

HRH The Duke of Kent, KG
President
The Cavalry and Guards Club

Introduction

The years 2009 and 2010 are two milestones in the long history of the Cavalry and Guards Club. The second is the double centenary of the foundation of the Guards Club in 1810; the first marks 100 years from 1909, when the Cavalry Club reconstructed its building at 127 Piccadilly, resulting in today's classic interior which epitomises everything that a London club ought to be.

The century since then witnessed many vicissitudes in the history of both institutions, notably the effect on their military membership of two devastating world wars, as well as the ups and downs of rapidly changing times. There were occasions during those decades when both Clubs contemplated the possibility of closure as finances failed to keep pace with the demands of the modern world. Changes in society too had their effect, as manners and customs relaxed and what were seen by many as old-fashioned ways of doing things – for example, attitudes towards lady members – looked increasingly out of place.

Yet the Cavalry and Guards Clubs have not only survived; they are stronger than ever in their merged form and in their splendid clubhouse at 127 Piccadilly. Their history is full of the momentous events of the last two centuries, and their headquarters exudes that history and that immediate connection to so many of the world-changing happenings of which their members were part. And yet the Club is now thoroughly modern too, alive and well at the beginning of yet another century and still combining a strong sense of its military pedigree with a relaxed, family atmosphere fully at ease in the contemporary world.

This book celebrates both the history of these two remarkable institutions, now become one, and the strength and value of the Cavalry and Guards Club today

Above: Edward VII.

Left: A Christmas dinner on the heights before Sebastopol.

THE GUARDS CLUB
1810 to 1975

'London clubs are a law unto themselves. Each is partially different. Some are unique. Clubland is a purely English invention. The Travellers' in Paris, the Oglethorpe in Savannah, the Knickerbocker in New York, the St James's in Montreal, the Rand in Johannesburg would never have seen the light of day if Francesco Bianco had not started White's, and if two Coldstream Guards officers had not invented the first members' club in St James's.'

CHARLES GRAVES, *LEATHER ARMCHAIRS*

The Guards Club – motto *Tria Juncta in Uno* – was the oldest members' club in London when it finally closed its doors in October 1975, having been founded originally in 1810, with the encouragement of the Prince Regent, by officers of the Foot Guards. As the pioneer, it led the way for the formation of similar clubs throughout the West End of London and elsewhere in the Commonwealth; and although there are older clubs in London, such as White's (1693) and Boodle's (1762), they are, or were, proprietary clubs – started by businessmen as businesses that could be bought and sold. At the time the Guards Club was founded, these places were called 'subscription houses'.

It was a war that created the Guards Club, just as subsequent wars helped to sustain it. England's efforts to help win back the continent of Europe from Napoleon saw an increase in the size of the British army – and a corresponding increase in the number of officers. About 1808, when the Peninsula campaign got under way, London saw an influx of officers, some gentlemen who had adopted the army as a profession and others who had not. The London they saw was a city of extremes, of luxury and squalor. On the one hand there were the ultra-fashionable haunts whose main source of income was from gambling, such as Almack's – the smartest – and White's – the more powerful. On the other hand there were the chophouses and taprooms with their poor appointments and seedy clientele.

The Prince Regent found his conscience stirred by a sense of responsibility; his own excesses did not prevent him from appreciating the value of good conduct and homely virtues. He was concerned that officers on leave or awaiting posting had nowhere to go and were frequently embroiled in unseemly drunken brawls. The Duke of Wellington shared this concern. He is reported as stating that the Guards were the most troublesome people when there was nothing to be done, and he had constant occasions to be vexed with them when in quarters and in the intervals of active operations; but when these were recommenced, they were the best soldiers in the army.

Jack Talbot, gazetted from Eton into the Coldstream Guards in 1808, was a moving spirit in early discussions about setting up a facility for Guards officers in London. He was backed by Colonel Daniel Mackinnon of the same regiment, who was one of the ablest and best known officers in the army. They talked the problems over with the Prince Regent and the Royal Dukes, and the recommendation was that they should initially establish a general meeting place with the aim, once support had been raised, of setting up their own home. The Prince Regent cautioned them against excessive luxury and suggested that the ideal would be a combination of the comforts of a gentleman's house with the facilities of a select hotel.

Original document establishing the Guards Club, signed by founder members.

Carriages and their occupants are objects of curiosity for passers by in St James's Street. Drawn by Richard Doyle, 1849.

Previous pages: The Roll Call, *after Lady Butler.*

which spells of foreign service had made the officers familiar; they were determined to avoid the ambience of pothouses which, with their sanded floors and seedy appearance, seemed more intolerable than ever when they returned to London after time spent abroad. In passing, the amusing chronicler Captain Gronow records that 'Bordeaux gave particular pleasure to the Guards who found the delicate and refined bouquets of their wine much to their liking after the rough Spanish stuff, quite apart from the tables and the daughters of the merchants which and whom they loved equally'.

The house had a dining room, a card room, some bedrooms and a drawing room looking on to the street and facing the bow window of White's. There was undoubtedly some rivalry with this close neighbour, which was perceived to be the most important club in London and the citadel of the establishment of those days (a claim which it retains in the early twenty-first century).

So in 1810 arrangements were made for a room to be set aside for the officers of the Foot Guards in St James's Coffee House at the bottom of St James's Street, opposite Lock's the hatter. From this room they could exclude such taproom frequenters as 'Irish bullies and persons of fashionable exterior but not of good birth and breeding'. Captain Gronow, Etonian, Grenadier, Member of Parliament and member of the Guards Club from 1813 to 1821, wrote in later life that this first room was 'a miserable little den with the floor sanded over as if it were a taproom'. Even so, the Dukes of York and Cambridge and nearly all the field officers in London put in an appearance there. The experiment proved a great success, and in 1815 the members of the Guards Club were ready and able to set up their first home. In that year a lease was taken of 49 St James's Street.

This house was at the top end of the street opposite White's and next to Hoby the boot maker, who had the top shop on the Piccadilly corner. The first lease, for a period of only three years, was taken out on the members' behalf by the Club's bankers Messrs Cox and Greenwood, those staunch friends of the hard-up soldier and predecessors of the firm of Cox and Kings. The Club subscription of £5 per year was paid direct to them by the members.

The clubhouse was an unpretentious building, and the members paid heed to the Prince Regent's warning not to indulge in excessive luxury. The emphasis was on comfort and was inspired by the standard and refinements of the continental restaurants with

JACK TALBOT

Jack Talbot was captain of the Oppidans at Eton and from there was gazetted into the Coldstream Guards on 17 November 1808. He was the kindliest of human beings and both the idol of women and their champion. Captain Gronow reminisced that wherever Jack was, at the Guards Club or elsewhere, he would be surrounded by a circle of friends, amused by his witty conversation and cheered by his good humour. He was a bold and skilful leader in the field: in one attack on 5 March 1811 at the Barrosa heights, twenty-five kilometres from Gibraltar, he was wounded. His failings were common to the time rather than personal to himself. He loved good wine, and it was said of him that if he were tapped for blood it would run pure claret. His end was abrupt. One day his good friend the Duke of Cambridge enquired of his servant how the Captain fared, and was shocked to receive the reply that the Captain was in a poor way, wanting to see neither doctor nor parson, but only to die. The Duke immediately sent for Doctor Keate, then headmaster of Eton and a strong moral force, who went to Jack's rooms in Mount Street, only to find him in his armchair, dead, with a half-empty sherry bottle beside him. He was twenty-seven.

COLONEL DANIEL MACKINNON 1791–1836

Daniel Mackinnon, whose grandfather was chief of the Clan Mackinnon in the western Highlands, was the nephew of General Mackinnon who was killed during the Peninsular War. He joined the Coldstream Guards as an ensign at the age of fourteen, and saw service in Germany and Denmark before distinguishing himself in the campaigns against Napoleon in Spain. He achieved rapid promotion, first to Lieutenant and then to Captain, before becoming Aide-de-Camp to General Stopford. His coolness under fire was remarkable and a great encouragement to his men, and by 1814 he had attained the rank of Captain in the Guards and Lieutenant Colonel in the army.

He played an important role at the Battle of Waterloo in 1815, where he had three horses shot under him. Despite receiving a shot in the knee which killed his horse, he remounted and continued to advance at the head of his men. Later in the day he was ordered by the Duke of Wellington to occupy the farm of Hougoumont, a position of enormous strategic importance which he defended with about 250 men of the Coldstream Guards and the first regiment of the Grenadier Guards. Napoleon directed assault after assault against the farm, with huge loss of life on both sides, but Colonel Mackinnon, despite the pain and disability of his wounded leg, continued to hold it against the French. When the battle was won at the end of the day, he collapsed from exhaustion and loss of blood, and was sent to Brussels to recover. In 1826 he became a full Colonel in the British army and commander of the Coldstream Guards regiment to which he had been attached for the whole of his military career. His book on the regiment, *The Origin and Services of the Coldstream Guards*, was published in 1833.

His powerful and athletic figure was much admired; and by contrast he was also a great practical joker. The famous clown Grimaldi said of him, 'If the Colonel would don motley and show himself on the boards of Sadlers Wells, my occupation would be gone'. One of his jokes is said to have inspired Byron's harem scene in *Don Juan*: learning while on the staff of the Duke of Wellington in Spain that the Duke had expressed a desire to visit a famous nunnery, he managed to insinuate himself among the nuns and took Wellington by surprise when he spotted his delicate features and smooth-shaven face among them. He narrowly escaped a court martial for that exploit.

Colonel Mackinnon worked hard for the Guards Club, running the first committees, ensuring that the food was good and the cellars first rate, and keeping the whist points in the card room discreetly low!

Portrait of Daniel Mackinnon, by George Dawe RA, sold by the Club in 1988 to fund the purchase of the freehold.

DUKE OF WELLINGTON'S DISPATCH FROM SPAIN TO WHITEHALL, AUGUST 1812

Gentlemen:

Whilst marching from Portugal to a position which commands the approach to Madrid and the French forces, my officers have been diligently complying with your requests, which have been sent by HM ship from London to Lisbon and thence by dispatch rider to our headquarters.

We have enumerated our saddles, bridles, tents and tent poles, and all manner of sundry items for which His Majesty's government holds me accountable. I have dispatched reports on the character, wit and spleen of every officer. Each item and every farthing has been accounted for, with two regrettable exceptions for which I beg your indulgence. Unfortunately the sum of one shilling and ninepence remains unaccounted for in one infantry battalion's petty cash and there has been hideous confusion as to the number of jars of raspberry jam issued to one cavalry regiment during a sandstorm in western Spain. This reprehensible carelessness may be related to the pressure of the circumstances, since we are at war with France, a fact which may come as a bit of a surprise to you gentlemen in Whitehall.

This brings me to my present purpose, which is to request elucidation of my instructions from His Majesty's government, so that I may better understand why I am dragging an army over these barren plains. I construe that perforce it must be one of two alternative duties, as given below. I shall pursue either one with my best ability but I cannot do both.

1. To train an army of uniformed British clerks in Spain for the benefit of the accountants and copy-boys in London, or, perchance
2. To see to it that the forces of Napoleon are driven out of Spain.

Your most obedient servant,
Wellington

Portrait of the Duke of Wellington, by Henry Perronet Briggs.

However, among the frequenters of White's were 'a number of pot-bellied, raddled old men who ogled the ladies in the street from their window vantage point'. No lady would, of course, walk down St James's Street, but they were caught in their carriages in traffic jams, as frequent then as now. A writer in 1853 recorded of the previous years that on a 'Drawing Room' day the window of the Guards Club 'formed a battery no less formidable for the fairer portion of creation than the celebrated bay window itself'. In the estimation of many it was a more dangerous citadel for the ladies to pass, the eyes of the young Guardsmen being far more trenchant than the glasses of the antiquated beaux at White's.

At the time when the Guards Club first arrived in St James's Street, the owner of White's was a fellow called George Raggett, who himself waited at the high play gaming tables in the evening and augmented his wealth in the morning by sweeping up the counters left by the befuddled players. The Guards Club, however, was run by the members for the members, and started as a kind of cooperative, non-profit-making enterprise – an approach which was to continue throughout its history, with some dire consequences. In these early days Captain Gronow was able to write that the Club was 'composed of the best men that England could boast of'. But there were some legal problems innate in this sort of institution, particularly in how the property was to be held. A solution was found in the decision that persons would be appointed by the members to act as Trustees on their behalf; the first Trustees took office in 1827.

During these early years of the nineteenth century, the Guards Club attracted many imitators, who were quick to recognise a clear and identified need; as a result a rash of service clubs broke out across the West End, starting with the United Service Club in a building in Charles Street in 1815. By the middle of the century there were nearly half-a-dozen of them. Meanwhile, the house at St James's Street had proved sufficiently to their liking for the members of the Guards Club, through the Trustees, to take out a further twenty-one-year lease to commence from 1 July 1828.

Then a minor disaster occurred. Both now and later in its history, it seems that the Guards Club was not to prove terribly lucky in its property transactions. Just after the new lease had been taken, the clubhouse fell down – although it was not the members' fault.

What happened was that William Crockford, a successful London fishmonger and gambler, had bought 50–53 St James's Street in 1825 and was having them pulled down so that a great

CROCKFORD'S

Crockford's, on the south side of the Guards Club, opened for business in 1828 and was instantly a roaring success; the grandeur and elegance of the rooms were unlike anything then in London – thronged with anyone who was anyone, but especially with those who had money in their pockets or lands they could turn into cash. The place became the major gaming establishment of London, and when Crockford died he was worth over £1 million. Of him Captain Gronow wrote, 'One might safely say without exaggeration that Crockford won the whole of the ready money of the then existing generation'.

After Crockford's death, his club started a slow descent in reputation, and by the time the Guards Club left St James's Street in 1848, 'Crockey's' was regarded as a 'refuge for the destitute, a cheap dining house for Irish buckeens, spring captains, welshers from Newmarket and suspicious looking foreigners'. The building went on to house the Devonshire Club and then later the Jamaican High Commission. It has latterly returned to its original use as a gaming house and club –'50' St James's; Crockford's still exists as a gaming club in Curzon Street.

new house of luxurious gambling rooms could be built. Nearly the whole of the upper end of St James's Street from Bennett Street to Piccadilly was in a state of confusion, with the contractors excavating deep into the soil to build an underground icehouse for cooling the champagne. The members of the Guards Club were exceedingly alarmed by all the work, fearing that their own foundations might be endangered.

Their alarm was well founded. On 9 November 1827 the Club fell into the hole. The entire side fell down with a fearful crash, leaving the interior of the house with the beds and furniture of the different apartments in a ludicrous state of exposure and in a most perilous position. The subsequent nocturnal operations of the many workmen, working by torchlight on overtime to restore the damage, gave the scene an extraordinary appearance. There was much sarcastic comment in the press, and a lyric attributed to the brilliant T Moore went the rounds.

> What can these workmen be about
> Do Crockford let the secret out
> Why thus our houses fall?
> Quoth he: 'Some folks are not in town
> I find it better to pull down
> Than have no pull at all.'

> See, passenger, at Crockford's high behest
> Red-coats by black legs ousted from their nest;
> The arts of peace o'ermatching reckless war
> And gallant Rouge outdone by wily Noir.

> Fate gave the word – the King of dice and cards
> In an unguarded moment took the Guards;
> Contriv'd his neighbours in a trice to drub
> And did the trick by – turning up a Club.

> 'Tis strange how some will differ – some advance
> That the Guards' Club House was pulled down by chance;
> While some, with juster notions in their mazard,
> Stoutly maintain the deed was done by hazard.

Left: Crockford's Club at the top of St James's with the Guards Club to the right.

Not much else is known of those early days in St James's, though we do know that the members decided that *The Times* newspaper was not to be allowed in the Club. This was because they were greatly loyal to Queen Caroline, and such was the horror that pervaded the Club at the time of her trial, when *The Times* used disrespectful language towards Her Majesty, that a meeting was convened by Sir Henry Hardinge at which a resolution was passed that the newspaper be 'expelled' from the Club. It is not known when it managed to get back in.

A few years before the lease at 49 St James's Street was due to expire in 1848, the members decided that the Club should

HOBY

The other neighbour of the Guards Club was Hoby, the boot maker at number 48 on the corner of Piccadilly. Hoby was the greatest and most fashionable boot maker of his time and employed as many as 300 workmen. He was so great a man in his own estimation that he was apt to take an insolent tone with his customers, although they tolerated him and not only overlooked his impertinence but even considered it rather a joke. He was a bumptious fellow with a considerable vein of sarcastic humour, and one can imagine that at the Guards Club tables the latest Hoby story would be recounted with relish.

One of those tales had Horace Churchill, an ensign and a member of the Guards Club, walking into the shop and telling Hoby that his boots were so ill fitting that he would never employ him again. Hoby adopted a most pathetic look and said to his shopman, 'John, close up the shutters. I must shut up shop. Ensign Churchill withdraws his custom.' Then there was the story of Sir John Shelley, who told Hoby that his boots had split and, when Hoby asked how it happened, replied that it was while walking to his stable. Hoby answered with a sneer, 'I made those boots for riding, not for walking'. And a story well illustrative of his conceit was that about the time when the Duke of Kent (father of Queen Victoria) was trying on some boots and an equerry came in to tell him of the Duke of Wellington's victory at Vittoria, Hoby remarked, 'If Lord Wellington had had any other boot maker than myself he never would have had his great and constant success, for my boots and prayers bring his Lordship out of his difficulties'.

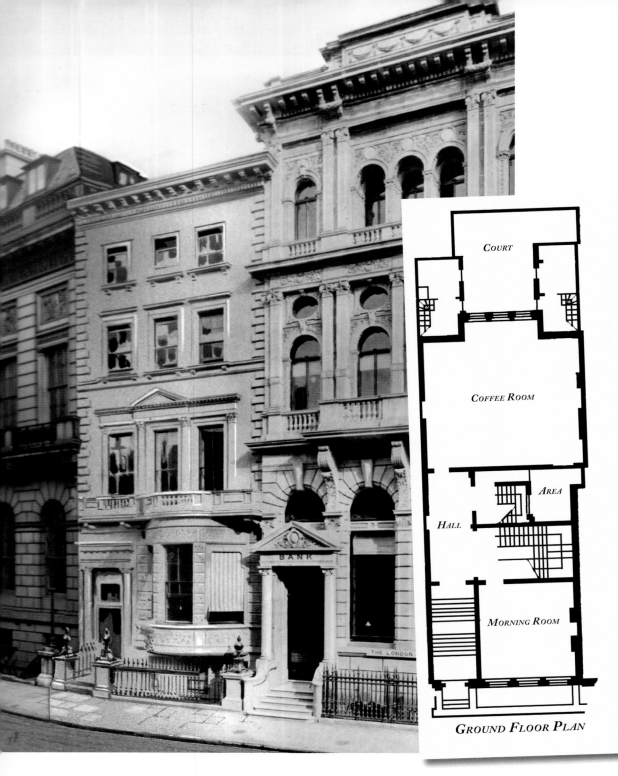

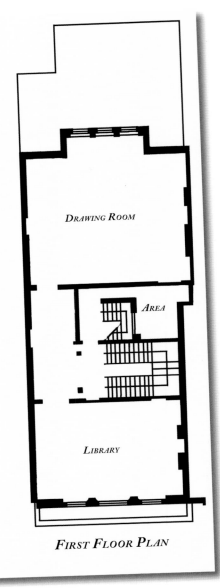

COURT

COFFEE ROOM

DRAWING ROOM

AREA

HALL

AREA

MORNING ROOM

LIBRARY

GROUND FLOOR PLAN

FIRST FLOOR PLAN

build its own clubhouse. An eminent architect, Henry Harrison, was commissioned to prepare designs for a site at 70 Pall Mall, where the new building replicated a smart private house, modest in its architectural pretensions but admirably designed for convenience and comfort. However, it seems that before the move to these auspicious new premises, the members and Trustees made a ghastly mistake in a property transaction (a mistake that was to be repeated in the twentieth century) and the designs were scaled down. Although there is no record of this transaction in the Club records, it appears in a book on London clubs that was published in 1853: 'A few years ago the members of the Guards Club, finding their former premises inconveniently small, erected a new clubhouse in Jermyn Street adjacent (*sic*), and in this they carried simplicity to

extreme in opposition to the profusion lavished in ornamenting the exterior of other clubs of the day, but the experiment failed to afford satisfaction, either to themselves or to others. The building had a barrack-like aspect, uninviting in the extreme, and although elegant within, it was destitute of the great advantage – the view of the teeming street enjoyed by the smaller edifice. It has consequentially been abandoned for the present edifice.'

In its much more suitable premises at 70 Pall Mall, the Guards Club had as a highly convenient neighbour on its western side the London Joint Stock Bank with, between 1879 and 1889, a most accommodating manager, Mr Gurney Barclay. Later, in 1901, the Club took a lease of the upper part of 69 Pall Mall from their neighbour at an annual rent of £700 together with a payment of

The Guards Club at 70 Pall Mall.

Right: A great clubman when Prince of Wales, the future Edward VII leaves the Guards Club possibly with Lord Rothschild. His fire-fighting companion, Captain Sir Eyre Massey Shaw, watches their late night departure.

£150 in lieu of rates and taxes, and in 1906 a licence was issued by the local authorities to construct living rooms (bedrooms) at 69 Pall Mall.

On the further side of the bank was Marlborough House, then the London home of the Prince and Princess of Wales and the centre of late Victorian society. As its neighbour to the east, the Club had the Oxford and Cambridge Club at numbers 71–76. Further down the street at number 79 was the attractive house where Nell Gwynn had lived, with her gardens adjoining the palace gardens at St James's, with access through a garden door for His Majesty's convenience. However, when the Guards Club came to Pall Mall the moral tone of number 79 had changed; it now housed the Society for the Propagation of the Gospel in Foreign Parts.

Further down the street at numbers 85–87 were military establishments, the headquarters of the Inspector General of Fortifications and the Ordnance Office. Ten years later these offices were combined and became the first home of the War Office, where it stayed until 1912, when the major part of the building was pulled down to make way for the Royal Automobile Club (designed by Mewes and Davies – the same architects who designed 127 Piccadilly).

Accordingly, over a long period of time, the Club must have been highly convenient for serving officers, being only a few yards from the War Office and from St James's Palace with its guardroom, and only a short walk from Wellington Barracks and Horse Guards. It was convenient too for those members who also served as Members of Parliament, particularly those with country constituencies; in a directory of 1865 as many as ten MPs listed the Guards Club as their London address.

Years later, Club members who had been junior officers at the time of the move to the new building remembered the ordeal of entering the Club: as they walked up the staircase and their heads slowly cleared the first floor landing, they came under the concerted scrutiny of the senior members gathered there. In these hallowed halls an ensign would not dare to stand in front of the fireplace, and it was compulsory to wear evening dress for dinner. Moreover, as late as 1911, as Ralph Nevill reported in his book *London Clubs*, 'Few clubs allowed visitors, but took care to extend only a cold welcome to them. As a matter of fact, they were usually treated like the members' dogs – they might be left in the hall under proper restraint, but access to any other part of the house, except, perhaps, some cheerless apartment kept as a strangers' dining room, was forbidden. Of late years, however, all this has been changed except

in a very few clubs, such as the Guards, which positively forbids any strangers to enter its doors.'

However, the Great War saw changes both in spirit and mode of life. The Club accumulated large funds and masses of new members, and 70 Pall Mall became quite inadequate. In 1919 the members authorised the Trustees to sell the house, and to buy and convert numbers 41 and 43 Brook Street into a new home for the Club. There was a short interregnum in 1919 during which members were accommodated at the Travellers Club, a Pall Mall neighbour, and when that was no longer possible after November, they were entertained at the Junior Carlton. At this time also the

HM King Edward VII, Colonel in Chief Royal Horse Guards, 1910.

Right: St James's Palace, c 1815.

Colonel Jeffreys commanded the 2nd Grenadiers in France in the First World War. He was a formidable and terrifying man, who imposed very high standards of discipline.

On one occasion several officers were in a dug-out in the front line. There was a bottle of port on the table, which was forbidden in the front line. A sergeant appeared at the entrance and yelled, 'Commanding officer coming, sir'. Quick as a flash, a candle was put into the neck of the bottle of port. The Colonel entered, took one look and left. All present heaved a sigh of relief. Later on, one of the officers who had been in the dug-out was on leave and lunching in the old Guards Club. After lunch he met Colonel Jeffreys, who offered him a glass of port. After he had taken his first sip the Colonel said, 'Does it taste alright?' The officer replied that it tasted fine. 'Doesn't taste of candle grease, eh?'

MICHAEL SPRINGMAN

Marlborough Club extended hospitality to members of the Guards Club who were on duty on King's Guard. The Club finally moved to its new home in Brook Street on 25 March 1920.

The houses in Brook Street were early Georgian and retained many original features, including several eighteenth-century fireplaces and a fine staircase with turned balusters and curved tread ends. The new clubhouse had a history of over 100 years as a hotel, with many distinguished occupants (although Claridge's, its neighbour in Brook Street, was perhaps a little more famous). Originally run for about ten years by a former wine merchant, Ralph Patterson, the hotel's name was changed in 1859 to Lillyman's

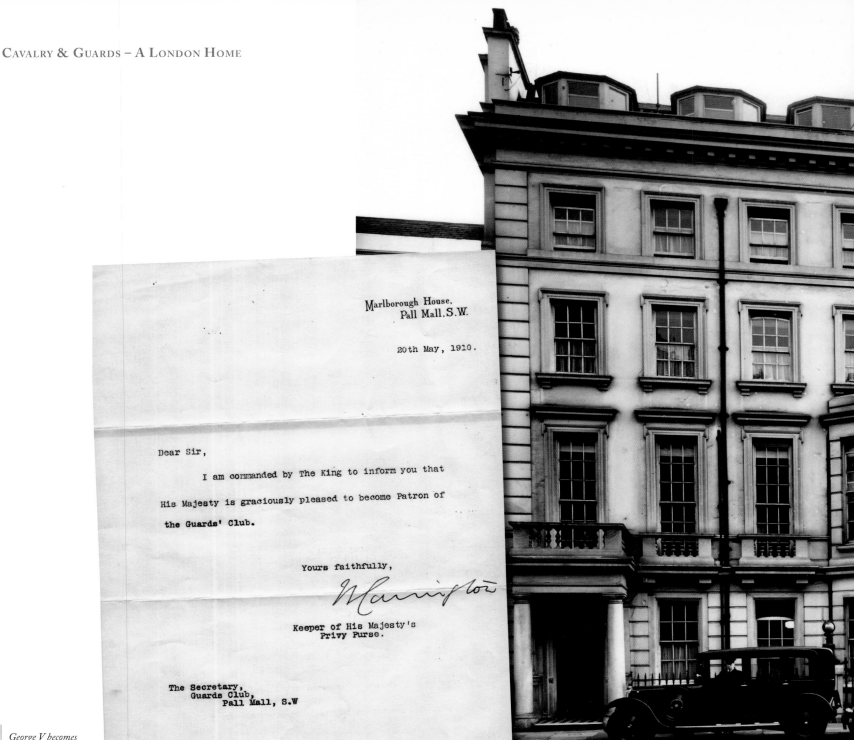

Marlborough House,
Pall Mall. S.W.

20th May, 1910.

Dear Sir,

I am commanded by The King to inform you that His Majesty is graciously pleased to become Patron of the Guards' Club.

Yours faithfully,

Harrington

Keeper of His Majesty's
Privy Purse.

The Secretary,
Guards Club,
Pall Mall, S.W

George V becomes Patron of the Club.

The Guards Club in Brook Street.

Hotel, and in 1879 to Buckland's Hotel, the name it held when purchased by the Guards Club in 1919.

The purchase price was £60,000 and the accounts for 1920 show an additional amount of £10,476 paid to the hotel for furniture and fittings (with further small amounts expended on the purchase of engravings, plate, china, glass and linen from the former hotel's stock). A contract was placed with Trollope's for £26,700 to renovate the buildings, but much to the committee's consternation – and with much debate as to who had given the required authority – the final works came in at around £57,000! However, for the first time, formal recognition was given to the needs of members or the demands of their women – it is not quite certain which – and

a ladies' annexe was opened in 1921. A system of 'vouchers for ladies' was introduced and the 1921 accounts recorded that 500 had been applied for in the amount of £1 1s each. Encouraged by this early success, the committee increased the charge to £3 3s from July 1922.

From 1919 officers of the Household Cavalry were also admitted as members of the Club, and the minutes of a July 1919 committee meeting note that 'The Household Cavalry having been admitted members of the Club and having been granted all the privileges of the same, officers who joined the 1st or 2nd Life Guards and Royal Horse Guards before 4 August 1914 shall be absolved from the payment of any entrance fee on election but shall be liable for the annual subscription for the current and subsequent years on the same conditions as present members of the Club'.

In 1919 the committee appointed Sir John Craggs as financial advisor, and he was able to report in September that year that 'the finances of the Club seem to be in a good state, and further that the loan of £35,000 received from the Royal Insurance Company (for the works) was a good move'. In the event, and due to the extended works at Brook Street, a debenture issue was found necessary to raise additional funds from the members.

Buoyed by the increased membership after the Great War (membership numbers were 1,195 in 1921), the Guards Club enjoyed a period of purposeful activity in the 1920s, not only in daily Club activities but externally also, with Club tents at Royal Ascot, the Eton v Harrow match at Lord's and the Sandown meeting. The effects of the war continued to be felt in other ways too. In February 1921, the Secretary was instructed to write to Major B Levett regarding 'the 500 bottles of German wine which have deteriorated in the cellars… and to exchange the wine for something of decent quality'.

Inventories dating from 1910.

MATTERS OF DRESS IN 1924

Letter from the Chairman, General Sir Ivor Maxse, to the GOC, London District:

I know you have the interests of this Club at heart and therefore write on the following point. Certain instructions have, in the past, been issued about officers' dress at the Club and these instructions have had a bad effect on quite a number of young officers. They gave up using the Club and joined inferior establishments where 'militarism', as they called it, does not prevail. I think they misunderstood these instructions, and thought they were not allowed ever to dine in anything but evening clothes.

On being made Chairman and discovering the above, I took steps to make it known that the committee and not the military authorities are running the Club and make the rules which govern it. I am sure you will agree with this principle, as did your predecessor, but I now hear that quite recently in a certain case fresh instructions had been given to officers and they have been told that they must dress for dinner here, and again the younger ones go elsewhere to dine when they are returning to Aldershot, Windsor, Warley or elsewhere.

In these days I think it is desirable even more than formerly not to 'militarise' this Club, and I hope you will support me, and the committee, in resisting 'interference'.

The GOC, Lord Ruthven, replied:

I entirely agree with your letter of 9 November. My idea of the Guards Club is that it should be a home for younger officers, and they should therefore be able to go to it in any old clothes they liked. I remember, as a boy and living in barracks, many times not going to the Club in the evening simply because I knew I had to put on a white tie and a tail coat. It was not so much I objected to dining in that costume, but I disliked sitting in it in the Club the whole evening after dinner. It meant therefore that in those days one only dined at the Club when one was going to a theatre or an entertainment of some sort afterwards.

I am sorry that this old controversy has been started again and am sending a letter to Lieutenant Colonels to impress on their officers the view I have given you. I am very much afraid that harm has already been done as the subaltern is a shy bird, and it will be a long time before he will return to his nest.

A gift from Queen Mary (1921).

Left: General Sir Joseph Yorke, 1st Life Guard, 1789–92 (property of the Guards Club).

Members also asked for squash courts, and the committee was able to lease ground adjoining the Club from the Grosvenor Estate where two squash court were erected. Such was the success of this facility that in 1928 HRH The Prince of Wales gave a Challenge Cup 'to be competed for by regiments of Household Cavalry and battalions of the Brigade of Guards'.

However, as the 1930s progressed and membership began to wane, the profits slowly turned to deficits and by 1939, on the eve of another war, the committee reported that the number of meals served was 10 per cent down compared to the previous year and there was 'a further decline in the demand for bedrooms'. Finances were not helped in April 1940 when the Club was required to expend a sum of £723 14s 1d on air raid precautions.

At the AGM of 9 July 1941 it was noted that the payment for which the Club was liable under the War Damage Act was £1,100. It was also noted that 'since the last Annual Meeting we are constantly finding it necessary to increase wages and in spite of this a very great difficulty is being experienced in obtaining any staff at all, particularly efficient staff whether men or women. This situation has resulted in a considerably greater strain for many of the staff, arising from longer hours and greater difficulties in supervising the various departments. To obtain many classes of provisions, both rationed and unrationed, and household equipment eg linen, china and glass, as well as dry stores, is a formidable problem not easily overcome.'

At the same meeting a change to 'Rule 8' regarding subscriptions was made, with the proposal that 'Officers holding temporary commissions and not already members of the Club may become temporary members for the duration of the war at an annual subscription of £6'. This once again meant a steady influx of new members.

Earlier in June of that year, 'with a view to protecting the Club's property in so far as may be possible from the results of enemy action', the Club's many paintings and pictures were despatched to a number of safe havens in the country where members undertook their care and storage. These were the homes of Lt Colonel the Lord Glanusk at Brecknock, the Viscount Vesci at Bridgnorth, Sir Charles Venables-Llewellyn at Newbridge-on-Wye and Lt Colonel Windsor Clive at Oakley Park, Ludlow. However, the latter home was requisitioned by the Air Ministry in 1942 and the Secretary had to arrange for the pictures to be transferred to Lord Plymouth's house at Redditch. Here the Club's precious possessions were to reside until the end of the war.

However, the burden of the mortgages taken out for the works was already becoming apparent and the finances were not aided when in 1922 the recently appointed Secretary misappropriated approximately £3,800 – an enormous sum in those days. Having recovered only £1,861 the committee had to write off the rest against the capital account.

At an EGM held in November 1923 to discuss the Club's finances, members pledged £6,796 10s 7d in donations to assist the failing finances. When presenting the 1924 accounts, the Chairman was able to report that the debt had been written off and 'Members may now consider that their Club has emerged from its financial difficulty. The result has been achieved through the determination of everybody concerned to reduce expenditure and to increase income, and because the Club fulfils a real want and has been more used by its members.'

There followed profitable years, and in early 1926 the Club leased some upper rooms at 39 Brook Street, the main part of which later, in 1943, became the showrooms of decorators Sibyl Colefax and John Fowler, after the landlords had turned down proposals for further development. This extra accommodation was to provide seven bedrooms for members and 'contained behind them a most charming courtyard with a fine tree and a goldfish pond and fountain'. In keeping with the times, too, a 'sensational' step was taken by opening a bar on the members' side – a revolutionary move that was greeted with considerable alarm by several of the older members who threatened to resign in horror.

By January 1942 the Club was able to report that the membership had increased to 1,339 and the accounts for that year noted that there had been an increase in the profits from the sale of wines and spirits etc 'due in large measure to the considerably increased rate of consumption of these beverages'. However, by 1944 the Secretary feared that 'at the present rate of consumption the Club's stocks of port and brandy will be exhausted within the year'. He was instructed to introduce a system of rationing 'among the main features of which would be that vintage port could no longer be served at luncheon and at dinner in small glasses only'.

On 14 September 1944, and having survived the blitz, disaster nearly struck the clubhouse. A lighted cigarette, dropped on a sofa in the ladies' drawing room, caused a fire which damaged the carpet, destroyed several items of furniture and did some peripheral harm to walls and ceilings. It could have been worse; and although the Club suffered no further damage during the war, it was noted in the 1945 accounts that a sum of £2,000 had been expended on repairing damage 'caused in the main by the extension of Claridge's Hotel, and increased by a V2 bomb falling nearby in April 1944 – no part of which is recoverable through War Damage Compensation'.

Many members from this period recall enjoying a clubhouse with great charm and many amenities, with its billiards room, squash court and separate, but inclusive, ladies' side. Yet notwithstanding the sentiment Brook Street engendered, the members decided in 1946 to implement their pre-war decision – made on the grounds that the building was too small, too old and likely to fall down – to sell the lease of 41–43 Brook Street and move to another site. The sale was completed in March 1946 and realised £71,230. A Guards Club member wrote later, with a touch of sadness, that all the improvements made by the Bath Club, who took over the premises in July 1946, 'serve to make the building meet the needs of their several thousand members and make envious those who have left'. He needn't really have felt so bad: the Bath Club, having had its share of difficulties, finally closed its doors in 1981.

FIELD MARSHAL LORD CAVAN 1865–1946

Frederick Lambart, son of the 9th Earl of Cavan, was born in Hertfordshire in 1865. He was educated at Eton and the RMC, and commissioned into the Grenadier Guards in 1885. He was ADC to the Governor General of Canada from 1891–2, married his first wife, Lady Hester Joan Byng, in 1893 and succeeded his father as the 10th Earl in 1900. He saw action with the Grenadiers in South Africa from 1900 to 1902 and commanded the 1st Battalion from 1908 to 1912. He was briefly the Master of the Hertfordshire Hunt before being recalled from retirement in 1914 and appointed to command 4th Guards Brigade.

He took over the Guards Division in 1915 and 14th Corps in 1916. He was created a Knight of the Order of St Patrick in the same year. His corps was in action at the Somme and in the Ypres salient in 1917. However, in November 1917 Haig selected Cavan, as the best of his corps commanders, to take divisions to northern Italy to reinforce the Italian army in the aftermath of its reverse at Caporetto. Cavan, whose staff in Italy included the Prince of Wales, came under the command of General Plumer, but on the latter's return to the Western Front, Cavan became GOC of the 10th Italian Army. He was made a GCMG in 1919.

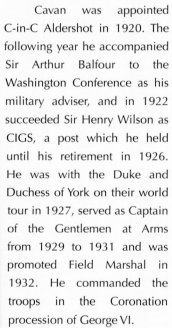

Cavan was appointed C-in-C Aldershot in 1920. The following year he accompanied Sir Arthur Balfour to the Washington Conference as his military adviser, and in 1922 succeeded Sir Henry Wilson as CIGS, a post which he held until his retirement in 1926. He was with the Duke and Duchess of York on their world tour in 1927, served as Captain of the Gentlemen at Arms from 1929 to 1931 and was promoted Field Marshal in 1932. He commanded the troops in the Coronation procession of George VI.

Lord Cavan was one of the last of the Irish representative peers to sit in the House of Lords. Despite having been married twice, he had no male heirs, and on his death in 1946 the title passed to his younger brother.

CHRISTMAS GREETINGS
and
ALL GOOD WISHES
for
THE NEW YEAR

GUARDS CLUB,
16, Charles Street,
W. I.

*Guards Club
Christmas card.*

The members now chose to purchase a ninety-nine year lease of a Georgian mansion at 16 Charles Street, together with the bomb-damaged remains of the two Victorian houses next door at numbers 14 and 15. Number 16 had at the turn of the twentieth century been bought and restored by William McEwan (of the brewery family of that name) and had passed through inheritance to his daughter Mrs Ronald Greville, the great society hostess and good friend of HM Queen Elizabeth. The amount paid for the lease was £30,000 (with the additional property of 11 Hays Mews included in the sale), and the hope was that the Club, with its swollen wartime membership and profits, would be able to rebuild these ruins. This was, sadly, never to prove a viable proposition. More pressingly, as the only immediately habitable rooms were in number 16, with a few in number 15, and the rest of the buildings quite inadequate for immediate needs, the Club also spent £22,000 in February 1946 on the leases of numbers 47 and 48 Charles Street, which it designated the ladies' annexe. It thus started, as it were, to run two Clubs, one for the gentlemen members and one for the ladies.

The end of the war brought further challenges, not least what to do with the former Club Secretary, Lt Commander B R Brasier-Creagh, who had been called up in 1939. The Reinstatement in Civil Employment Act 1944 required the Club to offer him his old job back, but after negotiation and a grant of £750 he graciously waived his right to return. Membership had, as expected, increased and on 1 January 1946 stood at 1,699. There was also a long waiting list for membership of the ladies' annexe; in 1948 there were 808 lady members.

An ambitious scheme to proceed with the required works to the properties was drawn up in June 1946, and a licence signed with the landlords, Samuel Estates Limited, for the works to take place; but at the AGM of 1950 the Chairman had to report that 'repeated applications to rebuild 14 and 15 have met with refusals (the Ministry of Works being required to issue a licence for the works to be undertaken)'. Moreover, shortly after purchasing the buildings, the Club discovered that there was a lot of dry rot, and further expense was incurred in eradicating the problem.

Club life, however, continued throughout this period of financial worry, always with an eye to the future; there were many discussions with other clubs about possible mergers, the first of which was with the Guards Boat Club in 1946. By 1948 the Chairman was required to tell the members that there was a deficit of £4,049 and a reduction in membership of over 100. The consequent shortfall in revenues and increase in costs, partly caused by the statutory increases in the scales of wages for the catering trade, led to some gloomy predictions for future trading, and the committee made the decision to close the Club on Sundays.

In the autumn of 1948 a Commission of Enquiry was set up under the chairmanship of Sir Edward Warner (who had done much to rehabilitate the finances of the Club after the Great War) to undertake an examination of the financial position and management of the Club 'to see where the remedy lay'. Their eventual recommendations included 'the substitution of a smaller management committee and the employment of a catering consultant to review where and how savings could be made in the catering operation'. In 1950 the annual accounts showed a further downturn and the resignation of 170 members, with the overall picture a deficit of some £4,000. Further economies had to be made; one of them was the tent at the Eton v Harrow match, and it was resolved for 1951 that the Guards Club would accept the hospitality of the Cavalry Club tent – surely a sign of things to come.

As a club, the premises in Charles Street have no real history, but elderly club servants recall the occasion when Brigadier Mills-Roberts, who was serving in the Commandos under Lord Lovat, booked room 10, came back late and happy, then stripped and got into bed with Colonel Edgar Brassey of the Blues in room 11. There was also Captain Bruce Wentworth, who on a busy Friday afternoon called for a taxi to take him to Victoria. Unfortunately, his luggage was placed in another taxi. When the second taxi driver asked 'Where is my customer?' the mistake was discovered, and he was instructed to go off and find him. In the meantime, Captain Wentworth returned, looking for his luggage. This happened no fewer than three times and the situation became wilder and wilder. Finally both taxi driver and Captain Wentworth were told to stay where they were and a rapprochement was effected. Another senior club servant recalls the hair-raising occasion when he was on night duty in the hall. It was 3am and everything was peaceful. Then he heard movements above, then more creaks. 'My blood froze,' he recalls. 'I went up the first flight of stairs and lay there. Then I saw a figure all in white coming down. I thought it was a ghost, but it turned out to be Colonel C E Wild in his nightshirt coming down to look for a book in the library.'

CHARLES GRAVES, *LEATHER ARMCHAIRS*

The following year the committee recommended the closing of 47 and 48 Charles Street, the ladies' annexe, at an early date in order to avoid increasing the deficit; £3,000 of the 1950 deficit had been attributable to the costs incurred in running it. The separate building for ladies some hundred yards from the main clubhouse had proved very expensive, involving as it did the upkeep of two kitchens and two bodies of staff. So now, following some years of uneconomic work and declining use, the premises were closed in December 1951 and eventually sold to save further losses in 1953; the sale of the leases was itself compromised by the 'shortness of the lease, the age of the houses and their bad state of repair'. Improvisations were made at number 16 and rather cramped room found for the ladies.

FIELD MARSHAL LORD GORT 1886–1946

John Standish Surtees Prendergast Vereker was the elder son of the 5th Viscount Gort in the Irish peerage, his mother being the daughter of Robert Surtees, the creator of 'Jorrocks'. He succeeded to the title in 1902 while still at Harrow. From Sandhurst, where he acquired the nickname of Fatboy despite his fanatical dedication to physical fitness, he was commissioned in 1905 into the Grenadier Guards. Here his obsession with military matters caused some dismay, and on one occasion he was thrown into the Basingstoke Canal by his fellow officers as a punishment for taking life too seriously. One of the few military qualities which he did not possess in abundance was marksmanship: on a shooting trip in Canada with another Grenadier officer, he fired at what he took to be a moose but, to his horror, killed their Indian guide. In 1911 he married his second cousin, Corinna Vereker, and his only son, Sandy, was born the following year.

Gort went to France in 1914 as ADC to General Monro, commanding the Second Division and later I Corps. In 1915 he became Brigade Major of the 4th Guards Brigade, and in 1916 a GSO2 on Sir Douglas Haig's staff. He was given command of the 4th Battalion Grenadier Guards in April 1917, and swiftly added another DSO to the one he had previously been awarded as a staff officer. His total disregard for enemy fire, despite being twice wounded, was an inspiration to his men, and in September 1918 he was awarded a second bar to the DSO. Two weeks later he won an exceptionally well-deserved Victoria Cross for the capture of Prémy Ridge where, despite a severed artery in his left arm, he led the assault on the first enemy trench before collapsing from loss of blood.

Between 1919 and 1937 Gort rose from substantive Major to Major General, although it was not until 1930 that he again commanded a battalion, and he chafed at the slowness of promotion caused by high-ranking officers who clung to their posts when clearly past their best. He retained his obsessive interest in his profession and almost excessive concern with detail. His marriage had been dissolved in 1925; as one of his superiors remarked, 'He is a very fine soldier and extremely able, but is in a class by himself and works himself to death. It may be the result of his domestic troubles, but if he was like this before I can quite imagine his wife leaving him.' His favourite recreations were skiing, sailing and, from 1932, flying. He bought a Moth aeroplane which he flew in all weathers, on the principle that if one just flew on, something recognisable was bound to turn up sooner or later.

Early in 1937, Gort accepted the invitation of Leslie Hore-Belisha, the recently appointed successor to Duff Cooper as Secretary of State for War, to become his Military Secretary. By the end of that year he had replaced Sir Cyril Deverell as CIGS, the youngest officer ever to hold this appointment, and one in which he and Hore Belisha had to battle for the next two years for increased funding for the army against a government determined to spend the absolute minimum possible on defence. On the outbreak of war Gort was given command of the British Expeditionary Force in preference to Generals Dill and Ironside.

Although as C-in-C BEF Gort was criticised once again for his excessive concern for minor detail, his leadership was unquestionable. During the winter of 1939–40, while the French army stagnated in its Maginot Line defences, Gort maintained the morale and fitness of the army by arduous training and hard work in constructing defences. When the German onslaught was

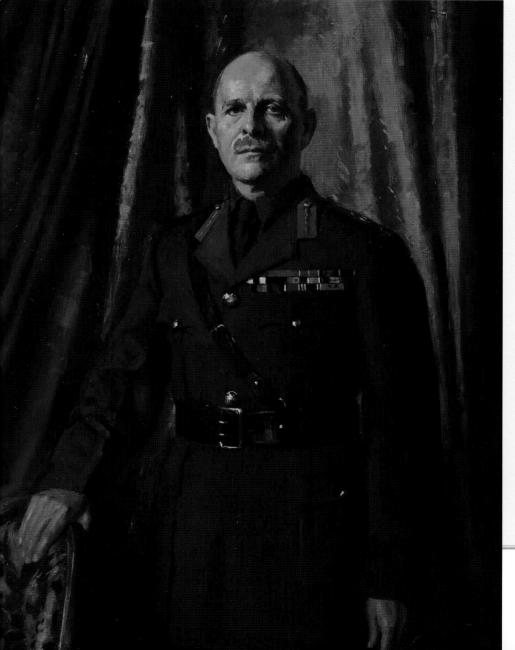

unleashed in May 1940 Gort, beset by collapsing allies and the lack of any realistic orders, eventually took, virtually on his own initiative, the series of decisions which are now generally agreed to have saved the BEF and thus prevented a premature end to the war.

Despite this, Gort was not given another command until April 1941, when he was appointed Governor of Gibraltar. Here his main achievements were a massive extension of the tunnel system originally built during the siege of 1780, and the enlargement of the existing airfield (despite the indifference of the Air Ministry), using the excavated rock from the tunnels to reclaim land from the sea. It is particularly to his credit that he achieved such cordial relations with the local Spanish commanders that the extension, and greatly increased usage, of the airfield caused no friction.

From Gibraltar the following year Gort was posted to Malta, vital as a base from which to attack German convoys carrying supplies for Rommel's forces in north Africa. In May 1942 the island had been under bombardment for two months and was not expected to hold out for more than six weeks. Gort, with his resourcefulness and ability to coordinate, was the ideal choice as Governor. He promptly devised a new method for the rapid refuelling of Spitfires to prevent them being immediately destroyed on the ground, as had previously been the case. He coordinated air defence assets to protect incoming shipping long enough for it to be unloaded, and introduced a universal system of free meals for a population on the verge of starvation. He was badly burned on one occasion while trying to pull cans of petrol from a burning stack, but refused proper medical attention. By December 1942 the siege of Malta was effectively over, and Gort's contribution was rewarded by a Field Marshal's baton and a Sword of Honour from the people of Malta.

His final appointment, in October 1944, was High Commissioner in Palestine, where once again his approach-ability and good sense made some headway with the opposing factions. He frequently walked around Jerusalem unarmed and unescorted, commenting laconically, 'They daren't shoot me; they will get something much worse'. Unfortunately, by mid-1945 he was seriously ill with undiagnosed cancer; in November he was forced to relinquish office and died four months later. He had been created a Viscount of the United Kingdom, and although, as his son had predeceased him, this title became extinct with his death, his Irish title passed to his younger brother.

PAINTINGS

In November 1947 members of the Club were invited to contribute towards the cost of painting portraits of Field Marshal Lord Alexander and the late Field Marshal Lord Gort; the artist was to be Henry Carr. Lord Alexander was reported as not overwhelmed when he was first confronted by his portrait, which was exhibited at the Royal Academy in 1948: 'I don't suppose anyone stops to look at that old b….!' was his comment.

Other Club paintings were proving contentious. In a letter dated 7 December 1947 a member wrote, 'I refer to the picture at present hanging in the dining room of the Club. I do not wish to discuss the artistic demerits of this picture: and no doubt its value is considerable. But I have found a general agreement among a number of members that the painting is a definite blot upon the dining room wall, and that, to put the matter quite frankly, it is so ugly as to be offensive, and so offensive as to be an actual impediment to

digestion… and I would suggest that the walls are again, as previously, decorated with the relatively pleasing portraits of senior defunct Guardsmen.' The painting referred to was the Snyder, a magnificent still life (pictured left) loaned by the National Trust and James Lees-Milne via the heirs of the late Mrs Ronald Greville, from the house's original contents. The picture remained at the Club until as late as 1968, when it was eventually transferred to Trerice Manor.

A more popular picture was also the subject of correspondence at this time. H M Bateman wrote in June 1949 asking to borrow his drawing *The Guardsman who dropped it* (above) for a forthcoming exhibition of humorous art at the Royal Society of Arts. There was some consternation at this request, as the drawing had been sent to the country during the war and the Club was now unable to locate it. It was eventually found, though unframed, and lent as requested. It was later hung on the wall to the downstairs lavatory, and it is on record that General Sir George ('Ma') Jeffreys remarked, without a smile, 'Most unguardsmanlike' when he first caught sight of it.

Dining room, Guards Club, Charles Street.

Portrait of Lieutenant Colonel John Arabin, by Alfred Morris (property of the Guards Club).

Overleaf: Detail of Hougoumont Farm, 1815, *by Ernest Crofts.*

I recall a dormitory where one could 'doss down' for as little as ten shillings a night; if one was based outside London it was a godsend to be able to have a couple of hours' sleep before heading back to base for first parade. We drank far more in those days than people do today and therefore the need to try and sober up was essential; of course there were no breathalysers then. Although one could book a bed in the dormitory, there were occasions when one turned up to find somebody else occupying it which could lead to undiplomatic exchanges in the early hours.

MAJOR GENERAL D M NAYLOR

By 1954 the position had improved slightly, and the Chairman was able to report that, as a result of all the economies effected, the year showed a small profit, which in 1955 even increased slightly. However, by 1956 there was again a deficit – not surprisingly perhaps, since the Chairman noted in his report at the AGM in 1957 that 'we are probably the only service club in London which has not put up its subscription since the war'. But such was the antipathy towards raising the subscription that a Special General Meeting called in October 1957 only managed to win a vote to do so by the narrowest of margins after very heated debate.

Rather typically, the Club had failed to make a profit on the sale of 47 and 48 Charles Street. It then found itself in yet another awkward position. In the light of inflated building costs and the diminution of its available funds, it became clear that the possibility of ever being able to finance the rebuilding of 14 and 15 Charles

Street was remote. Then, to add to the horror, it was discovered that the Club was not free to sell the adjoining buildings in order to make money out of the inflated property values then current. An examination of the terms of the leases showed that there was a covenant imposed on the Club to rebuild the houses as a club – and that no other use was permitted! The Club just had not the money to do this, nor could any other club be found willing to buy the ruins. So by 1959 it became necessary to undertake delicate negotiations with the landlords, which were concluded by 'surrendering' the leases of these two houses for nothing, plus having to pay an increased rental at number 16 and having the term of the lease halved. It was deemed the best bargain that could be made in the circumstances – and it left the Club with just one building, 16 Charles Street, which was too small for its mixed membership. The Guards Club entered the 1960s both wiser and poorer.

Further controversy was incited by deliberations on the future of the Club. A letter written by Captain Ian Weston-Smith, dated 16 March 1960 and addressed to the outgoing Chairman, noted that 'beyond any shadow of doubt, final insolvency is galloping upon us'. It was suggested that the Guards Club should move to a smaller and more efficient building. Then in October 1960, in order to gauge the feelings of the wider membership, a 'referendum to members' was sent out, setting out the various options considered to be available to the Club at the time.

An EGM was called on 3 November 1960 to discuss subscriptions. The issue under discussion was whether the serving officers should be subsidised by the retired officers; as always there were arguments on both sides. A senior member, speaking ▶ 37

FIELD MARSHAL EARL ALEXANDER OF TUNIS 1891–1969

Harold Rupert Leofric George Alexander was the third son of the Earl of Caledon, who died when Alexander was six. He not only enjoyed country sports but also carving, both in wood and stone, and above all painting; one of his earliest ambitions was to become President of the Royal Academy. He was educated at Harrow where he excelled at a wide range of sports, being best remembered for nearly saving the match against Eton at Lord's in 1910.

At Sandhurst his only misdemeanour was apparently failing to put a comma at the end of each line when addressing an envelope, for which he was placed on restrictions. He joined the Irish Guards three years before the outbreak of the Great War, which he spent entirely in France, except when on courses or recovering from wounds. He was awarded the MC in 1915 and the DSO in 1916. In October 1917 he was commanding the 2nd Battalion and in March 1918 took over the 4th Guards Brigade as an acting Brigadier General. He held no staff appointments and despised senior officers who were never to be seen near the front line.

In 1919 he took command of a brigade-sized force of Baltic Germans and led it to victory in a campaign which drove the Red Army out of Latvia, for which he was awarded the Order of St Anne. He commanded the Irish Guards from 1922 in Constantinople and Gibraltar, before attending Staff College in 1926. By the 1930s he and Claude Auchinleck, of the Indian Army, were widely tipped to become the outstanding commanders in any future war. The two officers commanded adjacent brigades on the North West Frontier in 1934; Alexander, being an exceptional linguist in addition to his other talents, was quick to learn Urdu as well as mastering the techniques of mountain warfare. Benefiting from his Great War experience, he was conspicuous for his presence with his leading troops in the Loc Agra and Mohmand campaigns, and he became a CSI in 1936. The following year he was promoted Major General and in 1939 he took the 1st Division to France as part of I Corps. At Dunkirk the Commander-in-Chief, Lord Gort, placed Alexander in command with orders to evacuate all possible British and French troops. Characteristically, Alexander was on the last boat to leave. Later that year, as a Lieutenant General, he took over I Corps, where he introduced a new system of highly realistic Battle Schools.

In February 1942 Alexander was despatched to take command in Burma and attempted against impossible odds to hold Rangoon, where he was fortunate to escape capture, before withdrawing the army into India. Despite this reverse, he was promoted on his return to take command of the 1st Army, which was to invade North Africa as part of a force under Eisenhower. Before this could take place, Churchill decided to replace Auchinleck in Egypt, and Alexander was appointed C-in-C Middle East, with Montgomery (formerly one of his divisional commanders in I Corps and now GOC 8th Army) as his subordinate. Early in 1943, with the arrival of the 1st Army in North Africa, Alexander took command of both armies as C-in-C 18th Army Group. In this appointment he

again displayed his abilities as a strategist, diplomat and inspirer of morale: at the battle of Kasserine in February he was to be seen personally siting gun-positions.

From North Africa Alexander went to Sicily as C-in-C 15th Army Group, and then to Italy, with the task of eliminating Italy from the war and thereafter of containing as many German divisions as possible. To do this he was obliged to maintain the offensive against superior numbers, which, with the assistance of Harding, his Chief of Staff, he did with considerable success, although his part in the decision to bomb the monastery of Monte Cassino remains a source of controversy. For the remainder of the war, Alexander's forces continued to advance, forcing the Germans to commit eight more divisions to Italy after the Allied capture of Rome, and despite having to release seven of his own divisions for the campaign in France.

He was made a KG and Viscount in 1946, and appointed Colonel of the Irish Guards, a post which he held until his death. From then until 1952 he was Governor General of Canada, for which he received his earldom, before returning at Churchill's request to become Minister of Defence until his resignation in 1954. He was awarded the OM in 1959 and died in 1969, his funeral taking place in St George's Chapel, Windsor.

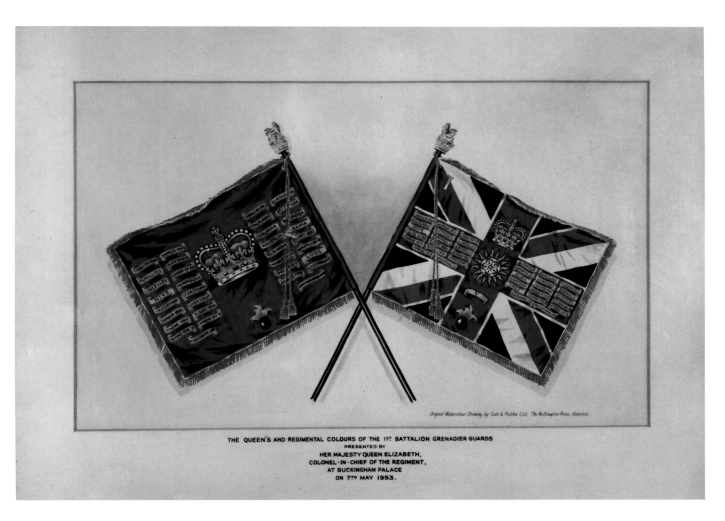

The Queen's and Regimental Colours of the 1st Battalion Grenadier Guards.

against the motion, said 'When I joined the regiment I had to pay the full subscription out of 7s 6d a day. When you go round the London barracks nowadays you see large motorcars, and if they can run around in them I don't see why I should pay their subscriptions' (laughter and applause). It was also reported that the Regimental Colonels of the Household Brigade were of the opinion 'that the time might be arriving when compulsory membership for serving officers should cease.'

The EGM covered a range of other issues, including catering, but as one member commented, 'I think, sir and gentlemen, that it must be alarming to the majority of members to realise in 1960 that this is the first time the committee have admitted that there is no budgetary control of this Club', concluding with the perhaps obvious point, 'No club, no business, no board of directors can function without accurate cost control today'.

There was some hope on the horizon in that a break of lease was possible in 1963, and the Chairman brought matters to a conclusion by stating, 'If we are not going to make a success in the next two years then we have got to give up'. A further policy decision was to increase the facilities available to members for giving private luncheon and dinner parties, with the committee making the valid observation that 'before the war many members had homes

in Mayfair and in the area, and the Club was often treated as a refuge away from the entertaining that went on at their homes'. Now things were different and 'members are looking to the Club as a place for entertainment rather than a refuge from entertainment. There is also today a greater emphasis upon members who are in business having obligations to give parties and to entertain.'

In 1961 the committee launched a special Club Premium Bond Scheme aimed at the 1,400 members and 600 lady members of the Club, with 'a purpose to seek a restoration of the Club to an acceptable standard of decoration, a readjustment to present day demands and the raising of the catering services to a proper state of hygiene and efficiency'. That same year the Chairman's report stated, 'It is possible for a club in the West End to run without incurring losses, and other clubs have, in fact, been running economically. Your committee realise that it is not possible to command success for their efforts, but they are doing their level best and believe that the infusion of capital monies and the completion of the major organisational work, which should be towards the end of this year, may reveal a basis upon which the Club could run on an even keel.'

Even with these good intentions the Club ran at a deficit for the year, although towards the end of the year the committee was able to report that they were getting onto the hoped-for 'even keel'. And in 1962 the Chairman could report that 'the standards prevailing in the Club only a year ago, and the steady losses incurred for so many years, made it impossible for the strong measures applied by the committee to take effect until the last months of the year'. During 1962 the creation of the position of catering manager and the employment of an experienced accounts assistant were intended to help. It was noted that in the pre-war years catering profit had amounted to a little more than a tenth of the subscription income; now things were different. 'Your committee are very pleased to report that under the able management of Mr Quick there has been a complete change around in catering financial results.'

Yet despite the lack of better financial news, morale among the members remained buoyant and at the end of 1962 the first Christmas Ball was a great success. But at the Annual General Meeting in 1966 it was decided to launch a further Premium Bond Scheme to 'help the Club over the difficult times ahead': £5 bonds were offered, with a chance to win a prize every six months.

Change was certainly on the cards. As early as March 1953 one of the options being considered was 'amalgamation with another club, either at 16 Charles Street or elsewhere'. It is clear from a letter the Chairman wrote to a member in advance of the EGM held on 24 July 1968 to discuss the way ahead that he had explored that option: 'I have approached the Cavalry Club but the Chairman has written to say they are not interested in amalgamating with us'. The National Liberal Club in Whitehall Place had also been approached (although this idea was quickly dropped), as was the Lansdowne Club, a much nearer neighbour in Berkeley Square.

The committee now raised the subscription from £30 to £40 which brought a raft of resignations as well as numerous suggestions. As one member wrote, 'Although I know from experience that, when clubs are in difficulties, members without enough background knowledge of the situation tend to put forward bright ideas about how the Club should be run', he nevertheless had a suggestion. 'Up to 1939 it was possible for amateurs to run a London club without losing money. Since then, it has become increasingly difficult. The membership of the Guards Club cannot hope to produce committees of men who have both enough knowledge of the technical side of catering and time to spare to do the work… and the people best qualified to provide these facilities are the big hotel and catering firms.' He then suggested that an outside catering firm should be employed. In fact, the catering company Searcy's had already been approached by the committee and had turned the option down.

TWO RUSSIAN SHELLS
SHELLED   KILLING
AND THE SANDBAG
***BATTERY* AT THE BATTLE OF INKERMAN**
AFTERWARDS SIR HENRY KEPPEL DCB OM
SENT UP A PARTY OF BLUEJACKETS WHO BROUGHT
THEM ON BOARD HMS *RODNEY* AND
SO HOME TO ENGLAND

The above is the result of a rubbing of the brass plate that accompanied the two Russian cannon balls that had found a home in the Guards Club after the Battle of Inkerman. When the cannon balls were being repainted in 1950, the Secretary wrote to General Sir George Jeffries about the gaps in the inscription, in the hope that he could help them ascertain the missing words.

In reply Sir George wrote from the House of Commons, 'I am very interested to hear that the two old Russian projectiles are being repainted and I hope it means that they are going to be set up again outside the door. As regards the inscription, I am afraid, although I think I read it when I first joined, that I have not looked at it for many years and I do not know a bit what the missing words were except one. There is no doubt that at the beginning of line five (*sic*) the word 'Battery' should be inserted. As you know the Sandbag Battery was a very famous point around which the struggle of the Battle of Inkerman ebbed and flowed, and this battery was defended throughout the day by the Guards Brigade.'

There followed an exchange recorded in the minutes of the 1954 AGM. Member (name not recorded): 'I suggest the two black balls of the Guards Club be reinstated in front of the Guards Club. In the premises in Brook Street they were there and many cab drivers in London always referred to the Guards Club as the "Black Balls Club".' Chairman: 'It is a good idea, but you must remember the railings at Brook Street were different. They were pillars. The only pillars we have here are Cleopatra's Needles, and if you put them on top of those, I should not like to think what the cabbies would call them.'

Complaints at the July 1968 EGM ranged over a number of topics, with some objecting to the wage bill – 'ridiculous at £800 per week for seventy staff' – and another member noting that the food was 'filthy… which is hardly surprising as I understand the chef is paid £20 per week. There can be few perks from the trade, and this sum cannot be expected to attract a cook of the correct calibre.'

The Cavalry Club were also considering their options and, despite having rebuffed the Guards Club's Chairman's approach about a merger, only a year later, in 1969, made an offer to the Guards Club that 800 of their members should join the Cavalry Club. The committee decided to ratify this suggestion, and in a postal vote 500 of the 700 who replied voted in favour.

Right: Russian cannon ball restored to its former glory.

FIELD MARSHAL LORD HARDING 1896–1989

John Allan Francis Harding was born in South Petherton, the son of a solicitor's clerk, and educated at Ilminster Grammar School, where his headmaster inspired him by his example of hard work and instilled a habit of logical thinking through many hours of translating Ovid. He became a clerk in the Post Office, and joined the Territorial Army to supplement his pay, being commissioned into the Finsbury Rifles battalion of the London Regiment in May 1914. His battalion was posted to Gallipoli, and Harding was wounded after only five days in action. He continued to serve in the Middle East throughout the war, being given a regular commission in the Somerset Light Infantry and becoming a machine-gun specialist. He was an acting Major at twenty-one as a divisional MG officer and won an MC in 1917. The following year he was the MG officer in XXI Corps, and as a member of Allenby's force learned in particular the art of strategic deception.

He spent the next nine years in India, initially with the MG Corps and then with his own regiment, before going to Staff College in 1928. In May 1933 he became BM of 13th Infantry Brigade, which formed part of an international force supervising the Saarland plebiscite, which he found a useful introduction to diplomacy. In July 1939 he took command of the 1st Battalion Somerset Light Infantry in India, and was mentioned in despatches for operations on the North West Frontier.

The following year he was in Egypt, where he was responsible for the planning of Operation Compass, General O'Connor's highly successful offensive in the Western Desert, which resulted in the capture of 125,000 Italian prisoners of war and for which Harding received the CBE. After the capture of O'Connor, Harding took charge and held the town of Tobruk, for which he was awarded the DSO, to which he soon afterwards added a bar as BGS to General Godwin-Austen. Promoted Major General in 1942, he commanded the 7th Armoured Division at Alamein, and early the following year was severely wounded by a shell burst which put him out of action for ten months. In November he was promoted again and briefly commanded VIII Corps before becoming Chief of Staff to Alexander in 18th Army Group, a long and successful partnership for which Harding received the KCB and which lasted until he was given command of XIII Corps in Italy. The speed with which his corps pursued the retreating Germans across the River Po brought the Allies to Trieste on 2 May 1945, precipitating a confrontation with the Yugoslavs who eventually conceded the city, which Harding ruled as its Governor until 1947, when he became GOC Southern Command.

In 1949, as General and C-in-C Far East, Harding saw the start of the Emergency in Malaya, and it was he who laid the foundations of the system whereby the Chinese Communist insurrection was finally suppressed twelve years later. He returned to Europe to become a GCB and C-in-C BAOR at a time when NATO command structures were being established and SHAPE was formed under General Eisenhower. Harding was CIGS from 1952 to 1955, receiving his baton in November 1953. In 1955, with reluctance, he accepted the governorship of Cyprus, where he established a good relationship with Archbishop Makarios and succeeded in reducing the terrorist leader, Colonel Grivas, to relative impotence, before handing over to Sir Hugh Foot in 1957.

He was raised to the peerage as Lord Harding of Petherton in 1958, and was Colonel of the Somerset Light Infantry (later SCLI), the Life Guards and 6th Gurkha Rifles. He died in 1989. The author of one of his obituaries described 'his skill in forming relationships, lucidity of intellectual apprehension and strength of reasoning that enabled him to grasp the essence of any problem. Those who served with him were exhilarated by the speed and certainty with which he arrived at the right solution.'

Smoking room, Guards Club, Charles Street.

However, under Club rules, the postal vote had no bearing on the decision of the AGM, and that year 200 members attended and, in a remarkable show of solidarity (or sheer bloody-mindedness, depending on the viewpoint), defeated the motion to join the Cavalry Club by twelve votes. This was all the more surprising given that the accounts for 1969 showed a considerable deficit; though to be fair to the supporters of the cause that the Guards Club should remain independent and stay at Charles Street, the figures improved in 1970 and 1971.

In 1972 the Club's auditors urged the committee to raise the subscription, which had been unchanged since 1969, to a more realistic level. The Chairman, Captain Peter Railing, also reported that the usage of the Club, particularly of the dining room and bars, 'still leaves much to be desired'. So in 1974, in a last ditch attempt to stem the losses, subscriptions were raised from £40 to £60. Unsurprisingly, the result was a slew of resignations – 193 by the year end, with a further 228 membership subscriptions still outstanding at that date.

There were no options left. At the Annual General Meeting on 22 July 1975, the members voted to proceed with talks on merger with the Cavalry Club and, at the subsequent EGM held on 15 October, agreed on the merger 'by a large majority'. It was also unanimously resolved that, in the event of a final loss to the Club, the members as at that date (numbering 650) would take over the loss from the Trustees who until then had been legally responsible.

Obviously not everyone was happy with the amalgamation. Major S V Gilbart-Denham (later Lt Colonel Sir Seymour Gilbart-Denham, Crown Equerry), then with the Life Guards in Detmold, wrote on 24 July 1975 that, 'in view of the amalgamation of the Guards Club and the Cavalry Club, it would be appreciated if the table lighter in the shape of a Life Guard helmet could be returned to us'. It duly was. If only the return of the building to its owners had been as easy!

The Club's lease from Samuel Estates Ltd (and now BP Pension Fund) ran until 24 June 1984, and was both 'non-assignable and personal', making sub-letting an impossible option. Moreover, there

I have a sneaking feeling that I must be among the very last to have had a direct connection with Geoffrey Price at both Charles Street and 127 Piccadilly. My uncle was Lieutenant Colonel W H Kingsmill DSO MC, who was a stalwart supporter of the Guards Club and was Chairman during the 1950s. I used to have potted shrimps served upstairs on the ladies' side as a boy, a long time before Geoffrey came to Charles Street, but even after joining 127 in 1962 I still accompanied my uncle to Charles Street for lunch and often for supper – he lived in Hertford Street just around the corner. How well I remember a youthful Geoffrey there – and I seem to recall that we had a very good bookies' runner service going in those days long before online betting.

In 1997, having exported myself and family to South Africa, I made a half-term trip to London with my two sons, then aged seven and eleven, basing ourselves at 127. I had hired a motor car, of which the best feature – for the boys – was that the windscreen washers were able to be redirected so long as you were armed with a pin. It did not take long before we were spraying motor cars sharing the same queue as us. This developed into a game of spraying bicyclists and then pedestrians, and we eventually arrived at 127 with no more water in the reservoir. I sent my eldest into the Club to seek water, and soon, as the queue for the bus stop right outside the club reached its apogee, so appeared this magnificent apparition – Geoffrey in full 127 livery armed with a bottle of Veuve Cliquot, apparently the only available water carrier. I do not think I have ever seen people with mouths quite so agape as those who watched what was evidently champagne being poured into our windcreen washer reservoir by a magnificent man dressed in perfect livery. Geoffrey, as ever, was the master of aplomb and after he had wished me well and given me a tip for the 2.30 at Southwell we went our ways – he back to Geoffrey's Bar and we to dousing the pedestrians of Piccadilly.

REGGIE PURBRICK

Dining room, Guards Club, Charles Street.

sale of the building and that not only is the interest limited by the general condition, but also the value is significantly reduced'.

In a last ditch attempt to salvage some funds for the Club, it was agreed with the owners that the building should be marketed on a new seventy-five-year lease and that, should the lease be assigned prior to the break clause in the current lease, 24 June 1977, dilapidations would be waived and the Club would receive a capital payment up to a maximum of £50,000. However, in the event, no buyer could be found, and the Club was therefore in a very weak bargaining position with substantial payments for dilapidations – possibly as much as £100,000 – a real possibility.

With regard to the staff of the Club, all those who wished to do so had an opportunity to move over to the Cavalry and Guards Club, and a number did so (including Fred Lloyd, the part-time hall porter, Geoffrey Price, of the members' bar, and Jeffrey Winter, a valet). Those who did not transfer received redundancy payments and/or payments from the staff benevolent fund and staff pension scheme.

was a specific covenant which required the entire premises to be redecorated during the last three months of the lease. This problem caused much consternation, and as Richard Lay of Debenham, Tewson and Chinnocks, representing the landlords, was to write, 'There is no doubt that the failure of the Club to have complied with the repairing covenant in the lease seriously prejudices the

The Guards Club finally closed its doors at 11pm on Wednesday 29 October 1975, and for the period 30 October to 31 December all Guards Club members became honorary members of the amalgamated Club, 'thus alleviating the responsibility to collect subscription dues for that period'.

In January 1976 all mundane items of a non-regimental nature, such as furniture, linen and cutlery, were sold in a 'sentimental' auction, realising £37,681 before expenses. All other regimental items were given to the amalgamated Club on permanent loan 'for as long as the Club should exist'.

As no buyer had been found as the 24 June 1977 deadline approached, a decision was made to terminate the lease on that date; but the request to waive the dilapidations liability (on the basis that the property could be re-let at much higher rates for the remaining seven years of the lease) was turned down, much to the dismay of the remaining Trustees. However, after a couple of false starts, a buyer was eventually found in December 1977 and, in recognition of the friendly relations that had existed previously between the Club and the landlords, a compromise was reached whereby the Club would be let off the dilapidations 'hook' in return for paying certain maintenance expenses between the date of surrendering the

Cartoon by Giles, 1962; the caption reads, 'Night guard and officers playing pontoon. Colonel of the Welsh Guards has got the book.'

lease in June 1977 and the date of sale in December 1977. Much to everyone's obvious relief, these totalled only £4,000 and the proceeds of the auction covered this amount.

Thus were matters concluded… though not quite.

A small oversight was not corrected until 1977. At a meeting of the sub-committee formed to discuss the amalgamation of the Clubs in August 1975, the question of Her Majesty The Queen's patronage of the Guards Club was tabled. Noting at the time that HRH The Duke of Kent was President of the Cavalry Club, it was decided to discuss the matter at a later date. As Lord Monteagle then explained in a letter dated 12 October 1977 to Major Blewitt, Assistant Keeper of the Privy Purse, 'Unfortunately, through an oversight, the matter was not discussed further. I am now writing therefore to offer our very belated apologies for this lapse in good manners… The Guards Club, of which Her Majesty was Patron… has ceased to be in existence.'

It was to be September 1978 before the four remaining Trustees were able to write to former members with an update. Even at this late date there was still some concern as to what would happen with the buildings in Charles Street. Peter Kearon, writing from the Knight Frank and Rutley offices in Hanover Square to Lord Monteagle, commented, 'Sad to say, nothing seems to have been done with the building since it went into other hands, although I hear rumours that the Arab owners are now thinking of reselling. I wish them joy with this – the market for these enormous and more or less uninhabitable buildings seems to have dried up.'

Finally, at the end of 1984, it was decided to commit the last act and close the former Guards Club account at Lloyds Bank, which had been kept in existence 'in case any outstanding bills or debts should come to light'. In the event nothing had happened. The sum of £2,500 had already been loaned to the combined Club for the repairs and maintenance of former Guards Club property, and now a cheque of £527.53 was drawn up and given to the Secretary on 21 November 1984 with the final proviso that 'it is just possible, though very unlikely, that some of this money may be needed to refund a few former members whose banks still insist on paying standing orders despite having been repeatedly told to cancel them'. □

To the Guards Club, with best wishes, from Giles '62.

My only claim to writing this piece is that, as far as I am aware, I am the only surviving member of the Guards Club committee before the two clubs merged. At the risk of boring you, this will be a somewhat personal account of my memories.

My first recollection of the Club, then housed in Brook Street, was just after I was commissioned in the Irish Guards in November 1945, when I was taken to lunch there on the day I was due to report for duty for the first time. I was somewhat intimidated by being introduced to my future commanding officer – Sir John Reynolds, a well-known Irish Guards character – who was very friendly and welcoming. Not then being stationed in London, I had little cause to use the Club, and that lunch was, as far as I can remember, the only time I went there.

The Club later moved to 16 Charles Street, where it remained until the merger. This was, in my opinion, a lovely, elegant house. However, in spite of its qualities, it was not very practical for use as a club. The front part of the house, overlooking Charles Street, and the back part of the house, overlooking Hays Mews, were joined only on the ground floor, which was extremely inconvenient for house staff working on the top floor of the front part when they wanted to get to the top floor of the back part. Various ideas were discussed for the internal layout, for instance moving the bar, which happened so often that one member suggested that it might be put on wheels! We also wanted to install some new bathrooms, but this idea came to a grinding halt as Westminster Council were, unsurprisingly, not keen on bath water being emptied on to Charles Street. Room 21, overlooking Hays Mews, had a specific problem, in that immediately below the bedroom window was a taxi drivers' all-night lavatory. One's sleep was inevitably punctuated by the pulling of lavatory chains and the sound of rushing water. Harold Macmillan – an ex-Grenadier – used to stay at the Club quite frequently after he left Downing Street, and always asked for room 21 as he said 'It is at the back and also so quiet'. His hearing must have been past its sell-by date! A great friend of ours, after spending a night in that room, left me a note next morning saying, 'If you like the sound of rushing water and cannot afford to go to Niagara Falls, try sleeping in room 21'. We did, and realised what she meant.

The lead up to the merger really began in 1970. A meeting was convened to consider a possible merger with the Cavalry Club and a large number of members attended. One member was heard to remark that, if we could have a similar meeting every month, the bar profit would be so large that we wouldn't need to merge at all. It seemed to me that the general feeling was that we should merge with the Cavalry Club, but a number of members who were very good orators, and also fuelled by nostalgia, emotion and alcohol, made a case for going it alone, saying words to the effect 'that it was disgraceful that the Brigade of Guards couldn't run a club on their own'. This argument just won the vote, and the Chairman and the existing members of the committee resigned, with Peter Railing, an ex-Grenadier, becoming the new Chairman. When picking his committee he asked me if I would like to be one of them, and I agreed. Things went reasonably smoothly until the end of 1974, when the country went through an economic crisis and the stock market hit rock bottom. A lot of members who belonged to other clubs as well had to make financial economies and decided to leave the Guards Club. We then seriously had to reconsider the question of a merger and, although one or two other clubs were mentioned, it became obvious that the Cavalry Club was by far the best option. The first merger meeting took place on 20 August 1975 and I still have a copy of the minutes. Four Cavalrymen and three Guardsmen sat opposite each other, with both Secretaries in attendance, and very amicably discussed a myriad of matters. On only one issue did we have a major disagreement, and that was over lady members. The Guards Club had for years had about 100 lady members in their own right, ie widows, mothers and sisters. An elderly cavalry officer at the meeting thought this was very bad news, and we had to say that if we couldn't bring the ladies with us the deal would have to be off. It was eventually agreed that they should come, and I personally think this was the right decision. The merger took place on 1 January 1976; on that day Peter Railing said to me, 'I have*

Guards cartoon.

Lord Monteagle dancing with Mrs Mayfield.

organisations were jealous of the Brigade of Guards, I was somewhat apprehensive; but to my relief, the interviewer was very friendly and it passed off all right.

By far the biggest problem was the question of what should be done with our lease, and this entailed complicated negotiations with the landlord's agent. A buyer was eventually found for the premises in December 1977 by Algy Asprey, whose firm did a lot of business with rich foreigners. We were therefore let off the hook of having to pay considerable dilapidation costs; I had had visions of having to write to the 650 members asking them to ante up something in the region of £200 each, and probably losing a lot of friends in the process.

The members of staff who wished to transfer were able to do so and those that did not received payments from the staff benevolent fund and staff pension scheme. Jack Savage, who had been Secretary for a number of years, retired just after the merger and Arthur Bell, ex-Irish Guards, came at about the same time to help with all the liquidation problems and did an immense amount of hard work.

Rather surprisingly, the building remained empty for many years, but eventually became offices. In 2007 I was walking past and saw one of the employees having a cigarette outside the front door. I explained my connection with the building, and she took me round on a conducted tour. The inside had been considerably altered and it had lost all its previous ambience and elegance, but it brought back many happy memories.

I would not like to finish without saying a word about General Jackie d'Avigdor-Goldsmid, who become Chairman of the merged Club. The Guardsmen who joined were a very much smaller proportion of the new Club than the Cavalrymen, but General Jackie went out of his way to see that we were in no way treated like second-class citizens. He insisted that his deputy should be a Guardsman, and very kindly asked me to take this on. However, because he lived very close by in London and was in the Club frequently and took a tremendous interest in everything, I had practically nothing to do. He also insisted that a Guardsman should become Chairman after he retired. When this happened it proved quite difficult to find a Guardsman replacement. I was asked to approach General Sir Digby Raeburn, a very old friend, to see if he would be interested. I thought it prudent to sound out his wife before approaching him. She jumped at the idea, saying 'I married him for better for worse, but not for lunch', and he duly became Chairman.

been Chairman for the past five years and have had enough. You must now take over.' As the Guards Club was still a legal entity I was then in the somewhat unusual position of being Chairman of a club with no members.

There were many problems to be sorted out, and these took much longer than expected. One of them was the rule, made some years before, which made the Trustees – General Sir George Burns, General Sir Rodney Moore and Captain Algy Asprey – responsible for any shortfall in the Club's finances. They were not wildly enthusiastic about this arrangement, and the rule was altered to offload the liability on to the membership. Another issue was how to dispose of the Guards Club's furniture and chattels. It was agreed that the merged Club would take over any furniture and pictures that they needed, and that Phillips would then auction those items not required. This was an emotional and nostalgic occasion, particularly for the older members. It raised £37,681, considerably more than expected. One of the items in the sale was a bundle of about a dozen dish cloths tied up with string. There was a deathly hush, with no bidders coming forward. Eventually someone bid ten shillings, and when the auctioneer asked for his name someone from the back of the room shouted 'Rothschild'. As a souvenir, I bought a set of blue leather menu holders with gold lettering and the brigade crest. Included in the list of items on the menus were 'smoked salmon, ten shillings, fillet steak, seventeen shillings and Club port, three shillings and ninepence'. I was interviewed on the six o'clock news that evening about the sale in particular and the merger in general. Not being used to fast bowling from the media, and knowing that some

LORD MONTEAGLE

Ladies and Lady Members

One of the most vexing issues in clubland has always been that of lady members. Undoubtedly set up originally as establishments for gentlemen, London clubs have wrestled with this problem for over a century and still to this day the matter can cause grievous splits in committees and membership. Obviously one solution has been the setting up of separate clubs specifically for ladies – the Ladies Lyceum Club next door at 128 Piccadilly was one such club – but increasingly clubs felt that accommodation for ladies within their own premises would not only bring increased use (and consequently revenues), but would also make the club more universally appealing. Some clubs were able to adapt their premises and successfully provide a separate side for ladies (such as Boodle's), but others have had to struggle with separate rooms, times of use and other partial solutions. The army, having always been very family orientated, was inevitably in the forefront of finding ways of accommodating ladies within the service clubs, and although neither the Guards nor the Cavalry Clubs have a straightforward history in this area, the accommodation for ladies has always been a primary concern.

As early as the 1901 Cavalry Club committee minutes, it was noted that 'Members cannot introduce ladies who are not dining with them into the Club on Sunday evenings when the band plays, between the hours of 8 and 11pm'. But conversely, ladies who were dining were most welcome.

When the Cavalry Club reopened in 1909, a separate ladies' entrance was created, giving direct access via the lift to the drawing room and dining room on the second floor, and thereafter ladies were not permitted to use the main entrance or staircase; though an exception later to this rule, certainly since 1967, was that ladies were allowed to use the main entrance for parties following the annual Cavalry Memorial Parade. So strong was the belief that ladies should only be permitted on the second floor that when the Club was considering a memorial to the dead after the Great War, it was decided that a drawing of the chosen design should be obtained to allow the ladies to view it without fear that they might descend the stairs to see the real thing.

Suggestions regarding the acceptance of ladies were commonplace, such as that in 1922 when Lieutenant Colonel the Hon D M

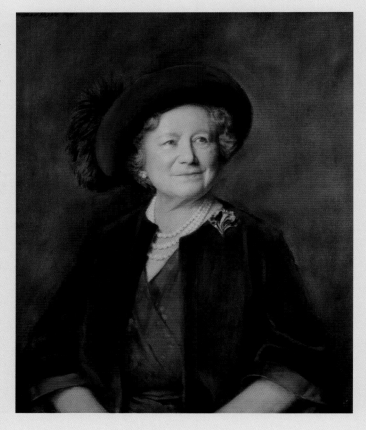

HM Queen Elizabeth The Queen Mother, Patron of the ladies' side, by Norman Hepple.

P Carleton proposed 'that the wives of members of the Cavalry Club residing in England or of members serving abroad in the British, Indian and Egyptian armies, or in our overseas possessions, shall be qualified to become temporary honorary members'. The Secretary wrote in response, 'At present our accommodation in the ladies' department is very often not sufficient to meet the demands on it, and I think it would cause considerable inconvenience to our regular clients to find the place crowded out by the wives of members not present themselves'. In the end the matter was not brought forward to committee.

So for more than fifty years ladies were welcome in the Cavalry Club, but only as guests and certainly not unaccompanied. The Guards Club, of course, had already provided separate accommodation for ladies when they moved to Charles Street in the post-war years, and this was proving to be most successful.

3rd NOV 1953

LADIES DINING ROOM
SET LUNCHEON 6/-

SERVICE CHARGE MEMBERS 6d GUESTS 1/6

Grape Fruit   Crême Garbure
Consommé

Turbot Grilleé Mtre d' Hotel
Spaghetti Napolitaine
Omelette aux Jambon
Goulash a' l' Hongroise
Rognons Saute Turbigo
Roast Leg of Lamb & Mint Sce

Boulaugere, Baked Jacket or Boiled Potatoes
Cabbage & Cauliflower

Baked Apple Dumpling   Meringue Chantilly
Strawberry, Chocolate, Vanilla, Coffee Ices, or Cream Rice
Stewed Apricots or Prunes or Figs or Apple Tart,

Menu, 1953.

Spurred on by the need for further change, the Cavalry Club committee decided in 1968 that the wives and daughters of members should, for a trial period of six months, be allowed to use the ladies' drawing rooms unaccompanied between the hours of 3pm and 6.30pm. During this period they would be permitted to have tea and purchase drinks, but not to entertain guests or use the dining room. They had to leave the Club or be joined by a member at 6.30pm. Such was the success of this initiative that at a 1969 EGM a member asked whether full lady members could be considered. This suggestion was turned down by the committee. But the seeds of change had been planted, and in 1971 double bedrooms were introduced for the first time on the fourth floor and were immediately successful. (When these were redecorated in the early 1990s the first one was refurbished by a lady interior decorator – Lady Henrietta Spencer-Churchill.) Further, by 1971, ladies could lunch or dine alone without a member (but were not allowed the privilege of inviting guests). Progress had indeed been made.

Second floor, 127 Piccadilly, 1909.

When I was due to be married in 1956, I was serving with my regiment, the 8th Hussars, in Germany, so my future wife, Elizabeth, had the task of organising the wedding reception at the Cavalry Club. In those days ladies were tolerated, but only just: they were not allowed in the Club except through their own entrance and direct to their floor, they were not allowed onto the ground and first floors and there was no question of double rooms in the Club. After an exchange of letters and a telephone call to the Secretary, it was agreed that she could go round to the Club to see the function room in the ladies' side. At the briefing by the steward, my fiancée was instructed that on her arrival from the church, she had to go up to the reception in the lift at the ladies' entrance. There was, however, one concession, but only because the wedding was to take place at the weekend: on the day of her marriage she would be allowed to go down the main staircase as she left with her husband.

A few years later, in October 1968, my wife and I were giving lunch to my brother in the Club. Halfway through the meal, my wife excused herself and went to the ladies' cloakroom. Unbeknownst to my brother and me, the attendant in the cloakroom decided that my wife needed a doctor, who was duly summoned. After a quick diagnosis, during which the Secretary apparently paced about outside, the doctor explained that Mrs O'Rorke had pregnancy problems, to which the Secretary retorted, 'She can't have it here!' Only then was I told that there was a problem.

Later again, in spring 1982, I was having dinner in the Club with my wife and her sister-in-law, whose husband, Rear Admiral Sandy Woodward, was in the south Atlantic leading the Task Force sent to recapture the Falkland Islands. During the main course, the head steward came up to me and said that he had just heard that HMS Sheffield had been sunk by an Argentinian missile. Not only was this the first Royal Navy casualty of the battle, but my brother-in-law had been the ship's first captain when it was commissioned just before the Queen's Silver Jubilee in 1977. Needless to say gloom descended on all the diners, and we had to leave shortly afterwards as my sister-in-law was so upset.

LIEUTENANT COLONEL BRIAN O'RORKE

Waterloo Ball, 2008.

suggestions still rankled. In the first year, a request for ladies to be permitted on the terrace (which, it was noted, the Guards Club had allowed) was thought by the membership to be the 'thin edge of the wedge' and was voted down in committee by twelve votes to one.

By the mid-1980s however, and after pressure from the younger members, it was decided that ladies should indeed be able to use the main staircase, and by 1993 the committee itself proposed that Geoffrey's Bar, the old television room and the Club garden should be open to ladies after 5.30pm each evening – thereby effectively removing the requirement that ladies should remain only on the second floor. To accommodate this move, a practical solution was required to one problem, and in 1994 a ladies' cloakroom was opened on the ground floor by the wife of the Chairman, Mrs Mariette Hall.

In the same year, 1994, the Club rules were changed to allow applications from any potential lady member proposed by two 'full gentleman members' ie not restricted to relations of officers from qualifying regiments, and the committee considered whether they might not invite one or more ladies to join the committee. This did not in fact happen until 2005.

However, under the chairmanship of Colonel Tom Hall, the first Ladies Advisory Group meeting took place on 4 April 1995 with the brief of 'discussing the development of the ladies' floor, the facilities provided for lady members and how best to encourage lady members to join the Club', and letters were sent by the Chairman to all ladies inviting them to join the group. In the end, about twenty ladies joined, and the group held several successful meetings and also established a *Ladies Broadsheet* to tell lady members about new initiatives (although this lasted only one issue before it was incorporated into the *127 Gazette*). Attempts were also made to establish a lady members' club table, but this initiative was less successful.

Inevitably, having started with a flurry of suggestions, the group began to concentrate more on the social side of the Club's life and by November 1995 had mutated into an events committee, with Mrs Anne Curran nominated as Chairman. It was to last only a couple more years before petering out altogether, and the idea of ladies contributing to Club life lay dormant for several years. It was revived under the chairmanship of Colin Methven with a new ladies committee set up under the chairmanship of Mrs Sandra Nelson. Since 2005 this group has met on a monthly basis and assisted in the revival of an active Club social programme, which includes a ladies luncheon, theatre visits, club outings, bridge afternoons and major events such as the Waterloo Ball.

However, at the time of the amalgamation in 1976, the disparity between the two Clubs concerning provision for ladies was still great enough to cause much comment and discussion, both at committee level and among the general membership. Inevitably, to accommodate the union, the new Club was required to adopt many of the practices enjoyed previously by the Guards Club, but some

LINES BY A LADY (1968)

(the daughter of one member and the wife of another)

For a period of trial,
Ladies may three hours beguile
In the ladies' drawing room,
Waiting for the hour of doom.
They may ask for cups of tea,
So the hour be after three;
They may wash, if they be dirty,
So the hour be not six-thirty.

Only members' lawful spouses
(Dwelling in the members' houses)
Or their girls in wedlock born
Shall these noble halls adorn.
Lo! The shining spoon and knife
Wait the grip of hungry wife;
Lo! The flask of barley water
Waits the sip of thirsty daughter.
Thus these modern Cinderellas
Faithfully attend their fellas.

Here a girl with anxious gaze
Scans the clock in deep amaze –
Flits a thought beneath her frown,
'Daddy's Jag has broken down!'
There a slender nervous wife
Feigns to study Country Life,
'John has missed the train again'
echoes the urbane refrain.

Majors' wives are very brave –
Rarely tear their hair and rave.
Generals' daughters seldom blub
When obliged to quit the Club.
Now the fateful hour doth chime;
Waiters wail 'Tis time! Tis time!'
Many a matron, many a maid,
All whose sponsors are delayed
Softly to the groaning lift
As a cloud of petals drift.

All accept their fearful fate,
Whose protectors came too late.
They must stand on Piccadilly
Feeling pretty fairly silly!

A gentleman member adds –
Might they not await their blokes
Hiding in the ladies' cloaks?

Cavalry Club ladies'
drawing room, 1909
(below) and 2008 (right).

THE CAVALRY CLUB
1890 to 1975

'It still remains remarkable that a Cavalry Club had not been formed at least a century ago when it was said that the role of the cavalry was to lend tone to an otherwise vulgar brawl.'

CHARLES GRAVES, *LEATHER ARMCHAIRS*

By the last quarter of the nineteenth century, London clubs were prospering as never before and the number of clubs was reaching its zenith. The formation of each new one was a response to the demands of a particular group of enthusiasts or like-minded individuals, and many new clubs founded during this period were break-away groups from already well established bodies, or were formed by those who had simply tired of being on an endless waiting list.

Although several military clubs had been in existence for many years by this time, the concept of a club specifically for cavalry officers was a new one and, if contemporary records are to be believed, an idea which did not originally have the backing of the first President of the Club, HRH The Duke of Cambridge, 'who disliked the idea of confining its advantages to one branch of the service' (though how he squared this notion with his support of the Guards Club, one finds difficult to comprehend).

Thus it was that the first committee meeting of the Cavalry Club was held at 15 Chapel Street, Belgrave Square, on 8 April

Minutes of the first committee meeting of the Cavalry Club, held at 15 Chapel Street, Belgrave Square, on April 8 1890. Present were:

Maj Gen Sir Baker Russell
Maj Gen Dickson
Maj the Hon J Napier
Maj the Hon M Stapleton
Col Philippe MacKenzie

Also present Capt H A Weatherall

The above gentlemen attended the first committee meeting of the Cavalry Club and, at the request of Sir Baker Russell, joined the committee and were elected original members. The following gentlemen were invited and consented to join the committee and were elected original members:

Col H Abadie, late 9th Lancers
Gen Sir Sam Browne, Indian Army, 2nd Punjab Cavalry
Capt The Earl of Dudley, Worcestershire Yeo
Col G Fitzgeorge, AWC
Col Allan Maclean, Royal Dragoons
Col H McCalmont, 4th DG
Col the Hon O Montagu RHG
Lt Col J Poynter, Bucks Yeo
Maj C Swaine, 11th Hussars
Col E Wood
Col F Wardrop, 12th Lancers

Letters were read from Col Fitzgeorge and Capt Gore notifying that HRH The Duke of Cambridge and HSH Prince Edward of Saxe Weimar would accept the posts of President and Vice President of the Club.

The proposed circular to be issued to officers inviting them to join the Club was approved.

The name of the Club was to be the Cavalry Club.

Officers serving in the Royal Horse Artillery were eligible to become honorary members on the payment of the year's annual subscription.

The site was to be left to the approval of Lt Gen Dickson and Col Philippe MacKenzie; Col Poynter also joined this sub-committee.

After some discussion, it was agreed that the proposal by Maj Stapleton, seconded by Col P MacKenzie, should be carried, which provided for all candidates to be balloted on joining the Cavalry Club.

In response to Col A Maclean, who wrote that he hoped bedrooms would be provided in the permanent house of the Cavalry Club and that this would be stated in the circular, it was agreed that this should be stated and that a limited number of bedrooms would be provided at a later date.

The reading of the proposed rules of the Club was postponed to allow Mr Tyrrell Lewis, solicitor to the Club, to revise the same.

Signed   W Redston Warner
Secretary

PUNCH, OR THE LONDON CHARIVARI.—AUGUST 26, 1908.

A SKELETON ARMY; OR, THE CHARGE OF THE VERY LIGHT BRIGADE.

Mr. HALDANE (*at the Cavalry Manœuvres*). "YOU SEE THOSE THREE MEN? WELL, THEY'RE PRETENDING TO BE ONE HUNDRED. ISN'T THAT IMAGINATIVE?"
Mr. PUNCH. "REALISTIC, YOU MEAN. THAT'S ABOUT WHAT IT WILL COME TO WITH US IN REAL WARFARE."

Cartoon from Punch, *26 August 1908.*

Previous pages: Charge of the lancers at Omdurman *by Allan Stuart, 1899.*

Opposite: HRH The Duke of Cambridge, first President of the Cavalry Club, 1890–1904.

1890 under the chairmanship of two of the Club's early supporters and instigators – Major General Sir Baker Russell and Major General Dickson. As the minutes for this meeting show, the small gathering laid the primary foundations for the Cavalry Club, and were fortunate in having present at the meeting Captain H A Weatherall (20th Hussars) who offered as a clubhouse his premises at 127 Piccadilly.

Six initial committee meetings were held at the Chapel Street address and at the third meeting, on 28 May 1890, it was resolved to hold these meetings weekly on every Monday; this practice continued until the late 1930s, although the attendance at each one for many years involved only two or four individuals. The first meeting held at the clubhouse, 127 Piccadilly, was therefore the

seventh committee meeting. It took place on Thursday 3 July 1890, and it was after this date that the members were able to use the facilities in this splendid, though much smaller, house.

Initially a proprietary club, it was not until a year later, in October 1891, that a notice of an Extraordinary General Meeting went out to the members to be held in the clubhouse on Saturday 28 November at 3pm, 'at which your attendance is earnestly requested' to discuss the scheme for constituting it as a members' Club, and authorising the committee to formulate an agreement for purchase from the proprietor. Proposals included a debenture issue with a fixed rate of 4 per cent (and 1 per cent bonus when the profits of the Club would permit) to assist in the purchase of the building from the owner.

While the Club prospered in these early days, with both a good demand for membership and a busy clubhouse, the negotiations for the purchase of the freehold were both slow and prolonged. It was not until 6 April 1893 that Captain Weatherall granted to the Trustees of the Club a lease of the premises for seventy-four and a quarter years at a rental of £5,000 per year, together with an

GENERAL SIR SAM BROWNE 1824–1901

Born in 1824, the son of a medical officer in the East India Company's army, Sam Browne was educated in England before returning to India in 1840 to join the 46th Bengal Native Infantry. He fought at Rannagar in 1848 and served throughout the Punjab campaign of 1848-9 before becoming a Captain in 1855.

When the 2nd Punjab Cavalry was raised in 1849, Browne transferred to the new regiment and in 1851 became Adjutant. In 1858, now in command, he was involved in operations against the mutineers around Lucknow, and the story of how he lost his arm was told to Lord Roberts by Sir Dighton Probyn as follows:

'During the mutiny an officer of the Punjab Cavalry had told Sam Browne that he had taken to wearing chains on his shoulders as a means of warding off sword cuts; he had strongly advised Sam Browne to do the same, and gave the latter two curb-chains which he insisted on him having sewn on his coat. Some time later the officer was killed, and a day or two after his death, when Sam Browne and his friends were talking together, one man said that at the sale of the officer's effects he had bought some saddlery, and that it was a curious thing that neither of the bridles he had bought had curb-chains on them. "I know where they are," said Sam Browne, who went to his tent, took off the two curb-chains and gave them to the purchaser of the bridles. Some time afterwards, in the hand-to-hand fighting in which Sam Browne gained his Victoria Cross, he received two sword cuts, one on the knee, from which he nearly bled to death, and the other on the left shoulder which cut off his arm.'

The Sam Browne belt was of course devised to enable him to carry his sword and other equipment more conveniently with one arm, and his regiment was named after him.

By 1870, Browne was a Major General and was involved with the Prince of Wales's tour of India in that year. He became a KCSI in 1875 and Lieutenant General in 1877, being appointed Military Member to the Governor General's Council the following year. In this capacity he was actively concerned with the preparations for the Second Afghan War, about which he had serious misgivings. He took command of the 1st Division of the Peshawar Field Force, with orders to force a passage of the Khyber Pass. Despite inadequate logistic support he reached and occupied Jellalabad in December 1878, but could make no further progress, due to the threat to his lines of communication. This was the end of his active service, since his age debarred him from a field command in the second phase of the war. He was made a KCB in 1879 and GCB in 1891. He died in 1901.

FRANK WILSON after REGINALD CLEAVER.

MILITARY EDUCATION 1892

GENERAL. "MR DE BRIDOON, WHAT IS THE GENERAL USE OF CAVALRY IN MODERN WARFARE?"

MR DE BRIDOON. "WELL, I SUPPOSE TO GIVE TONE TO WHAT WOULD OTHERWISE BE A MERE VULGAR BRAWL."

Military Education,
*Frank Wilson after
Reginald Cleaver.*

establish their title to the furniture; they were fortunate that the previous assignment was upheld.

Sun Life (the insurance company) now held the mortgage and were therefore deemed to be the legal landlord; and following negotiations they responded with a reduction in rent to £ 2,750 for the first year rising to £3,000 in year three (with the maximum rent never to exceed £4,000). This offer was ratified by the Club at an EGM on 8 March 1894. By this time the Club's social life was also well under way, with a fiftieth anniversary Balaclava dinner confirmed in the ladies' dining room on 25 October that year.

Much of the early debate in committee was about the detail of the rules, and there was much experimentation with the best approach. For example, the initial decision to close the Club at 1am, after which time entrance would not be permitted, was extended by popular demand to 2am some months later. Committee minutes also record as 'experimental' the decision to arrange for a military band to play in the Club from 9pm to 11.30pm on Sundays, commencing on 28 October 1894. And on 20 May 1895 an early indication of the start of a long tradition, continuing to this day, of decorating the Club for significant royal occasions was the instruction given to the Secretary to put up 'the same illumination as usual on the occasion of Her Majesty's birthday'.

Not all decisions required of these early committees were momentous. The minutes of the meeting on 15 July 1895 record that 'a box left in the Club, and supposed to be the property of a kitchenmaid named Standbrook who left the Club on 12 June without an address, was opened in the presence of the committee, fastened up again and placed in the store room'. History, it is sad to relate, does not reveal what it contained.

As early as 1896, such was the growth both of membership numbers – by January 1900 the total was 1,101 – and Club use that the committee began to consider the possibility of acquiring the lease of the adjoining properties, 125 and 126 Piccadilly. At the same time, there was a great deal of debate and concern about the likelihood that a new underground railway would be built under Piccadilly (see page 116). ▶ 63

assignment of furniture and effects, the cost of which was between six and seven thousand pounds.

It was not a moment too soon. The following August, Captain Weatherall was declared bankrupt and his Trustee both disputed the lease arrangements and claimed back the furniture. The Club Trustees were therefore required to undertake legal proceedings to

FIELD MARSHAL EARL HAIG 1861–1928

Douglas Haig was born in 1861, the son of John Haig of Fife, a younger branch of the Haigs of Bemersyde, Berwick. He was educated at Clifton, Brasenose College, Oxford, and Sandhurst, whence he passed out as the Senior Under Officer of his company and top of the Order of Merit, and was commissioned into the 7th Hussars in 1885. He became Adjutant in 1888 and Captain in 1891. He spent much of his leave in France and Germany, studying languages, and in 1896 passed into the Staff College, where he was a contemporary of Allenby, having initially been rejected on the grounds of colour-blindness. The following year he was selected to join Kitchener's Sudan campaign, and was employed with the Egyptian cavalry in the advance to Omdurman.

On his return, he became Brigade Major of the 1st Cavalry Brigade at Aldershot, under General (later Field Marshal) French. The brigade was ordered to South Africa in 1899, and Haig was largely responsible for the planning of the battle of Elandslaagte, one of the few major British successes in the first months of the Boer War. With French, he escaped from Ladysmith by the last train, and was present at Colesberg, where French's brigade did well to hold a superior force of Boers in check.

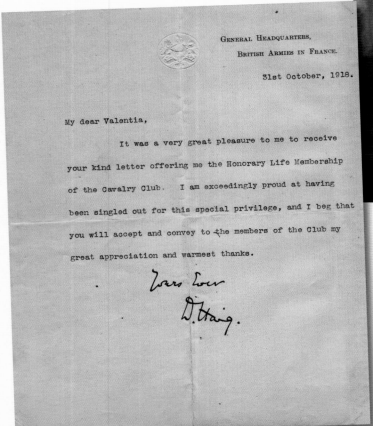

During the guerrilla phase of the war, Haig commanded a column until the end of hostilities in early 1902, being awarded the CB and appointed ADC to King Edward VII and also briefly to the command of the 17th Lancers, from which he was promoted the following year to become Kitchener's Inspector General of Cavalry in India. In 1904 he became a Major General and in 1905 married the Hon Dorothy Vivian, a descendant of one of Wellington's leading cavalry commanders. In 1909 he returned to India as Chief of Staff to Sir O'Moore Creagh, the Commander-in-Chief, where he was largely responsible for completing the planning, begun by

Earl Haig by James Bell Anderson RSA after Sir James Guthrie.

Field Marshal Earl Haig on parade.

the early breakthrough by the Tank Corps at Cambrai was due in part to the loss of five divisions which had been sent to assist the Italians after a major reverse at Caporetto. By late 1917 the transfer of massive numbers of German troops from the Eastern Front forced Haig to extend the British line still further to the south, leaving it dangerously exposed to the German offensive in March 1918. It was Haig, however, who was the first of the Allied commanders to realise that the initial British successes in August 1918 might signal the final collapse of the Germans and the possibility of victory by the end of the year, and accordingly committed all his resources to the massive offensive by which this victory was finally achieved three months later.

After his return from the Rhineland in 1919, Haig devoted himself tirelessly to the welfare of disabled ex-soldiers, and the establishment of the British Legion in 1921 was one of his most lasting achievements. He was created Earl Haig in 1919 and died in 1928.

Kitchener, whereby the Indian Army was prepared to take part in the forthcoming Great War.

Haig was promoted Lieutenant General in 1910 and received his knighthood in 1913.

On the outbreak of war the following August he went to France as GOC I Army Corps. His corps was relatively lightly involved in the retreat from Mons, but played a major part in the first battle of Ypres, and when Field Marshal French was recalled after the failures at Loos in 1915, Haig succeeded him as Commander-in-Chief.

His achievements in that appointment have been the subject of controversy which persists to this day, but it should be borne in mind that many of the actions for which he has been criticised were forced on him by the needs of his allies. The Somme offensive was prolonged by the need to divert German forces from Verdun. The campaign of 1917 which culminated at Passchendaele was undertaken under pressure from Marshal Pétain to give the French army time to recover from the mutinies which followed Nivelle's unsuccessful offensive in Champagne. The failure to exploit

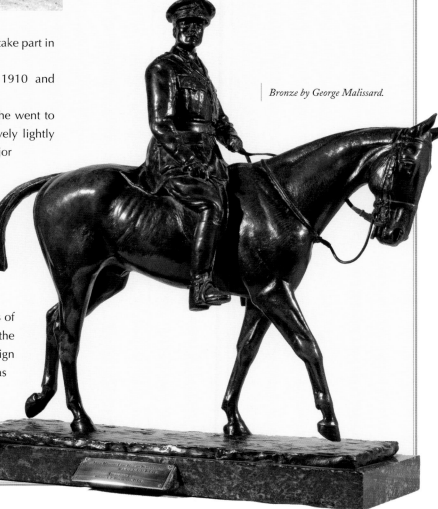

Bronze by George Malissard.

59

FIELD MARSHAL LORD BYNG 1862–1935

The Hon Julian Byng was born at Wrotham Park in Hertfordshire in 1862, a younger son of the second Earl of Strafford. His family was related to the Admiral Byng who was shot in 1757 for his failure to relieve Minorca, or, as Voltaire put it, 'pour encourager les autres'. Despite the title, the family was not particularly affluent, and although Byng was educated at Eton, rather than proceeding to Sandhurst he was commissioned into the 2nd Middlesex Militia. However, his father was a friend of the Prince of Wales, who arranged for him to transfer to the 10th Hussars, of which the Prince was of course the Colonel, and in 1883 Byng joined the regiment at Lucknow. The 10th were a notoriously expensive regiment, and Byng was obliged to supplement his income by training polo ponies.

Later in the following year the 10th Hussars left India en route for Britain, but were diverted to the Sudan to join the Suakin expedition. Byng took part in the battle of El Teb, and had his horse killed under him at Tamai. He was appointed Adjutant of the 10th in 1886 and promoted Captain three years later. In 1892 he commanded the pallbearers at the funeral of Prince Albert Victor, the elder son of the Prince of Wales, who had also served in the 10th Hussars.

Byng was promoted Major in 1897 and arrived in South Africa at the outbreak of the Boer War as Provost Marshal. However, he was immediately ordered to raise and command the South African Light Horse. In the guerrilla phase of the war he, like Haig and Allenby, became a column commander, being rewarded for his work with the MVO 4th Class, promotion to brevet Colonel and command of the 10th Hussars, now once again in India. He was married in the same year to Marie Evelyn Morton. In 1904 he broke his arm so badly in a polo accident that it was feared that he would have to leave the army. He recovered, however, and was appointed to command the new Cavalry School at Netheravon, and shortly afterwards the 2nd Cavalry Brigade, being awarded the CB in 1906.

In 1912 he became Commander British Troops Egypt, returning to Europe as GOC 3rd Cavalry Division in time to take part in the first battle of Ypres. In 1915 he briefly replaced Allenby in command of the Cavalry Corps before being sent to Gallipoli, where he successfully conducted the withdrawal from Suvla Bay.

Byng returned to France in 1916 and took command of the Canadian Corps, whose legendary feat of the capture of Vimy Ridge in 1917 set the seal on his reputation. Shortly afterwards he took over the 3rd Army from Allenby when the latter was posted to the Middle East. Later the same year, Byng was responsible for the first major tank battle at Cambrai, where initial success was quickly followed by a well organised German counter-attack which recovered almost all the ground gained in the first phase. In the German offensive of March/April 1918, the 3rd Army successfully resisted enemy assaults on Arras and Vimy, and later played a prominent part in the Allied advance which ultimately ended the war.

Byng retired from the army and was created Baron Byng of Vimy and Thorpe-le-Soken in 1919. In 1921 he was appointed Governor General of Canada where, in addition to being conspicuously energetic and popular, he is now remembered largely for the 'King-Byng' episode, a dispute with the Canadian Prime Minister which eventually created a precedent for the modern constitutional status of Governors General. He returned from Canada in 1926 and was raised in the peerage to a Viscount. He served as Commissioner of the Metropolitan Police from 1928 to 1931, when he handed over to Lord Trenchard, the founder of the RAF, and in 1932 was promoted Field Marshal. He was Colonel of the 10th Hussars from 1924 until his death in 1935, when in the absence of an heir his title became extinct.

FIELD MARSHAL SIR WILLIAM ROBERTSON 1860–1933

William Robertson was the eldest son of Thomas Robertson, a villager of Welbourne in Lincolnshire, and was educated at a private school. In 1877 he enlisted in the 16th Lancers. Although he was 'crimed' three times (once for allowing a deserter to escape, once for letting a horse break loose and once because a member of a party under his command was drunk and unhorsed), he nevertheless reached the rank of Troop Sergeant Major in 1885, and with the regiment's encouragement began to study for a commission. Two years later he passed the necessary examinations and joined the 3rd Dragoon Guards in India as a 2nd Lieutenant. Although his fellow officers treated him with civility, he found it difficult to manage in a very expensive regiment, and began to study for language qualifications to supplement his pay. He discovered an extraordinary gift for languages, and qualified in Persian, Pushtu, Punjabi, Urdu, Hindi and Gurkhali. His regimental duty ended in 1892 when he was posted to the Intelligence Department in Simla, specialising in the North West Frontier and Russian activities in particular. He explored routes into India from the Pamirs and his reports were highly commended. In 1894 he joined the Chitral Relief expedition, was severely wounded and awarded the DSO. He was married in the same year to Mildred Palin, the daughter of an Indian Army Lieutenant General.

Robertson was the first officer commissioned from the ranks to qualify for the Staff College, and on graduation was posted to the Colonial Section at the War Office. He served briefly in South Africa during the Boer War, becoming a brevet Lieutenant Colonel shortly after returning to the War Office. By 1903 he caught up with most officers of his own age when he was promoted Colonel, and received the CB in 1905. After serving as Brigadier GS to General Smith-Dorien at Aldershot, Robertson became a Major General and Commandant of the Staff College, where he showed 'an uncanny knack of spotting at once the weak points of a plan'. He made the course more practical, and devised exercises which replicated the strain on a staff in times of crisis. He twice accompanied King George V on visits to army manoeuvres, and was awarded the KCVO.

As Director of Military Training in 1913, Robertson foresaw a German assault through Belgium, in exactly the spot where the British army was most likely to be deployed, and planned exercises to study the conduct of a long retreat. In August 1914 he became QMG at GHQ in France, and was successful in keeping the BEF supplied during the retreat from Mons. Early the following year he replaced Sir Archibald Murray as CGS at GHQ, and strongly opposed the Gallipoli campaign as a dangerous diversion of forces. He is of course best remembered at this time for advising General Smith-Dorien of his impending dismissal by Field Marshal French with the immortal words "'Orace, you're for 'ome'.

Robertson was appointed CIGS early the following year and promoted General soon afterwards. His tenure of office became more difficult after December 1916, when Lloyd-George replaced Asquith as Prime Minister, and friction occurred throughout 1917 over objectives, methods and political control of the army. Robertson finally resigned in February 1918 over Lloyd-George's plans for an Allied General Reserve on the Western Front controlled by a committee, and was replaced by Sir Henry Wilson. He took over Eastern Command and in June became C-in-C Home Forces and later C-in-C of the Army of Occupation. He was promoted Field Marshal in 1920 and granted a baronetcy, in which he was succeeded by his son Brian, also a General.

Robertson was Colonel of the Royal Scots Greys, the 3rd Dragoon Guards and the Blues. He died in 1933.

Walsingham House
Piccadilly
20 November 1891

Sir Baker Russell
& the committee of the Cavalry Club

Gentlemen,
I beg to forward the following explanation asked for by the house committee with reference to the lady, whom I introduced to the Club as Mrs Greville, and whom I understand the committee to state is not what she represents herself to be, and as what I have always regarded her, viz the wife of Mr George Greville.

I was introduced to the lady in question at a ball in South Kensington in aid of some hospital charity. I subsequently met her at a ball at the Metropole Hotel, in aid of the Home for Rest for Horses at which, as per attached list, ten members of this Club were stewards, and of those ten, three are at present on the committee.

At her invitation, I called on her and met at her house ladies, both married and single, of undeniable reputation, and whose names I am willing to give. Neither by her manner or otherwise did she give me reason for a moment to doubt that she was what she represented herself to be, and what I understood from others was the case, viz the wife of a Mr Greville, at present in China, and whom she was unable to join on account of her children's health. On the strength of this, I asked her on two occasions at least during the spring and summer to dinner at the Club. On one of these she chaperoned a young lady, at whose house in the country I have been asked to stay, and on another a member of the Club dined with me. I also brought her twice into the Club tent at Ascot. I introduced her to the Colonel of the regiment to which I am attached and his wife, and she was asked to and went to their house, and they proposed to call upon her. I know also that she was invited and went to lunch at one of the leading clubs in London on the occasion of the Emperor of Germany's visit to the Guildhall, by a man of position and standing who would have been the last person to compromise himself in such a way.

I can most truthfully assure the committee that the Secretary's letter of 12 October was the first intimation of any sort that I had that Mrs Greville was not what she represented herself to be and I was intensely surprised at receiving it. I was away in the north of Scotland at the time, and as there was no direct charge made against her, could then offer no further explanation than to give her address and the name of her husband. I presented myself to the house committee on the day of my return to London.

I beg most respectfully to submit that, if it was a generally known fact that there was anything wrong about the lady during all this time it ought to have transpired, as I introduced her to the Club on several occasions when numerous members and their friends were present, and to the Club tent at Ascot, where were men representing most sections of the upper classes in London. I did this in a most open way and courted no concealment. I am at the present moment quite unable to prove whether she is married or not. If the committee knows that she is not, or knows anything against her reputation, I trust that they will believe me, on my honour as a gentleman, that I have all along been in complete ignorance of it, and most sincerely regret having introduced any person into the Club whom I ought not to. I have the wellbeing of the Club as much at heart as anyone, and wish to be the last person to injure its reputation. I have my own reputation as a gentleman and an officer of the army to think of, and consider that I should soil both by wilfully introducing an improper person to my friends, my Club or my military superiors: and I appeal to you, sir, and to the committee, to say whether in face of the facts I have stated and of the solemn declaration of my innocence of the mistake I may have been making, you believe I have been guilty of knowingly introducing an improper person to the Club.

I have the honour to be etc…

VALENTINE

On 1 March 1898, the Club's solicitors wrote as follows to the Secretary:

Dear Sargeaunt,

I return the Valentine. In view of the difficulty of proving from whom it comes and the uncertainty of what might result (beyond expense) from placing the matter in the hands of a detective I think the Club had better do nothing. I doubt very much if such a scurrilous production would make any unfavourable impression on the mind of any decent person reading it.

Valentines Day 1898.

However, before any consideration could be given to expansion of the premises the lease of number 127 was still a cause for concern, and in December 1899 an EGM was held to consider the purchase of the lease. In 1900 this was done, with the lease for a term of sixty-seven years of the Club premises purchased from Sun Life Assurance Office for the amount of £38,000. The Club later went on to acquire the leases of 125 (in 1904 for the sum of £800) and 126 (in 1903 for £2,250).

The minutes of the committee meetings of this era record both the effect on the Club of external events and more mundane matters. On 21 May 1900, the Chairman announced that he had sent a telegram to Colonel Baden Powell on behalf of the Club congratulating him on his successful defence of Mafeking. But when in 1901 the committee decided to open the Club for luncheon on the

Relieving Officer. Sorry to see so many tradesmen seeking relief. Who is to blame for so much distress?

Applicants crying altogether. We trusted the Cavalry Club and they have not paid us.

Relieving Officer. But surely they can be made to pay their debts. Who are the Trustees and Committee?

Poor Applicants. Hand Officer book of rules and names of Committee.

Relieving Officer. Have you sued any of these men?

Poor Applicants. Yes but they trade upon their position, and the law as to clubs as it at present stands protects them, (*viz.*) several of them want a club, one of their fraternity is chosen (the one with least character and money) a committee is formed of the biggest among them, they order everything of the best to be supplied, the one running the Club keeps in the back-ground, the Committee always most prominent, at last pay day comes, the Committee drop behind, and say we are not responsible, the law allows us thus to deceive, we are not running the Club. The man that they say is responsible we find has turned bankrupt, the Committee then comes to the front once more, takes possession of the Club and all the furniture without the payment of one farthing (tip how to get a cheap club,) but we want bread.

Relieving Officer. I am not here to give advice on law, but the sooner clubs are under the same law as hotels, the better; such schemers should be punished but surely some of the names I see here are honorable men.

Applicants. Hand up their motto in Secretary's writing:

If tradesmen err to our interest don't correct their Books –

Relieving Officer. I am surprised! Grants an order at once to admit A. C. cook, C. D. steward, E. F. fishmonger, S. H. chimney sweep, J. N. butcher, L. M. baker to receive indoor relief.

St. Valentine Day, 1898.

Club menu, 1902.

Overleaf: The Royal Horse Artillery stables, *by Geoffrey Douglas, 1888.*

day of Queen Victoria's funeral and to charge £1 for each member and guest attending, one member was not happy. He accused the committee of a 'repulsive and loathsome resolution', writing 'Surely, sir, you will agree with me, when I say that the funeral of Her Late Majesty was not an occasion to select for a club – and more particularly a service club – to give a picnic to its members and any guests they may elect to introduce'. The outcry in defence of the committee was such that an EGM had to be called on 26 February, at which the member was called upon to resign because of the language used in his letters and his attack on the committee.

In 1902, Lieutenant General Sir John French was given honorary life membership of the Club in recognition of his role as General Officer Commanding the Cavalry Division in South Africa. It was also suggested that a dinner be held in his honour in the Club under the Presidency of HRH The Duke of Cambridge. The following year a letter was received from Major General Baden-Powell suggesting that 'Our cavalry, when you include Imperial Yeomanry, RHA , Colonial Mounted Troops etc, has increased so enormously during the past five years that it has come to be a most important branch of our army…'. ▶ 67

FIELD MARSHAL SIR JOHN FRENCH, EARL OF YPRES 1852–1925

John Denton Pinkstone French was born in 1852, the only son of Commander John French RN. He was educated at the Portsmouth Naval Academy and HMS *Britannia*, and appointed a midshipman in 1868, but left the Navy two years later to join the Suffolk Artillery Militia. He transferred to the 8th Hussars in 1874 and to the 19th Hussars a few weeks later. He was a successful regimental officer and sportsman, being promoted Captain in 1880 and Major in 1883. The following year he went to Egypt to command the 19th Hussar detachment in Wolseley's expedition to relieve General Gordon in Khartoum, and joined Sir Herbert Stewart's column. Before this force reached their objective, news came that Gordon was dead and a withdrawal began in which French displayed considerable skill in command of the rearguard, and fought at Abu Klea. For his services he was promoted, and took command of the 19th Hussars in India from 1888 to 1893.

After some years under Sir Redvers Buller at the War Office, French took command of the 1st Cavalry Brigade at Aldershot as a temporary Major General. In 1899 the brigade arrived in Natal and French took command of Sir George White's cavalry. At Elandslaagte he had his first experience of commanding all arms in the field, and achieved the only British success in 1899, a victory which has been attributed in part to the brilliant staff work of his Brigade Major, Douglas Haig. French and Haig escaped from Ladysmith by the last train to leave and returned to the Cape, where his mounted troops cleared most of the colony of Boer insurgents before the arrival of Lord Roberts in January 1900. Under Roberts, French led his cavalry with great panache to clear the way to Kimberley, which he relieved in February. His force took some 4,000 Boer prisoners at Pardeberg, and French then made another spectacularly successful advance to Bloemfontein, the capital of the Orange Free State. His exploits up to this point led the author of *Celebrities of the Army*, published in 1900, to refer to him as a 'heaven-born general', but he had little opportunity to repeat them as GOC Cape Colony in the guerrilla phase of the war. He was described by one of the surrendering Boer commandos as 'a squat, bad-tempered man, though he did his best to be civil'. French was promoted Lieutenant General and made KCMG in 1902, and appointed to the Aldershot command.

In 1907, he was promoted General and made a GCVO, and after some years as Inspector General of Forces he was appointed CIGS in 1912 at a time when preparations for a major European war were in full swing. However, the episode for which French's tenure of office is best remembered was the so-called Curragh incident: in early 1914, French had endorsed a pledge by the Secretary of State for War that Irish officers would not be required to take up arms against their fellow-Ulstermen to coerce them to join a united Ireland. When the Cabinet repudiated this pledge, French sent in his resignation. This was withdrawn after further negotiations, but the incident divided the officer corps and left considerable ill-will.

On the outbreak of the long-expected war, French, now in his sixties, was appointed Commander-in-Chief of the British Expeditionary Force, and arrived in France with four divisions of infantry and one of cavalry. On 21 August he met General Lanrezac, who commanded the French 5th Army, and a mutual antipathy was quickly established. Asked for his opinion on the enemy's intentions, Lanrezac replied that he imagined the Germans merely planned to come down to the river to go fishing. After this unpromising start it was not altogether surprising that French refused to allow Haig's I Corps to assist Lanrezac at Guise when the German offensive began.

French's handling of the retreat to Mons and subsequent advance to the Aisne has received considerable criticism. His two corps became separated, and he continued to retreat despite the success of II Corps under Smith-Dorien, which halted the German advance at Le Cateau, and it was necessary for Kitchener, the Secretary of State for War, to visit France in person to persuade French to halt his withdrawal. His handling of the BEF in late 1914 and throughout 1915 produced no significant victories, and his dismissal of Smith-Dorien in May of that year was seen as an act of personal pique. After failures at Aubers Ridge, Festubert, Givenchy and Loos, French finally resigned his command in December and was succeeded by Haig. He was created Viscount French of Ypres in January 1916 and appointed C-in-C Home Forces, one of his first actions being to despatch two divisions to Ireland in April to suppress the Easter Rising in Dublin. In May 1918 he became Lord Lieutenant of Ireland, in the hope that he might be able to introduce conscription there. This proved a forlorn hope, and an attempt to recruit volunteers was almost equally unsuccessful in a country descending into a cycle of outrage and reprisals. French himself was nearly killed in December 1919, when a convoy in which he was travelling came under attack from bombers. He finally resigned in April 1921 as the Earl of Ypres, and retired in 1923 to Deal Castle, where he died in May 1925.

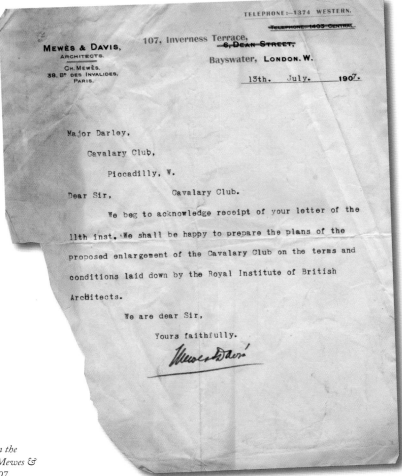

Letter from the architects Mewes & Davis, 1907.

Various bills from the refurbishments, 1908–9.

The Club continued to grow. By the middle of 1903 the membership stood at 1,338, and the decision was taken to limit the numbers to 1,300 and to accept no new applications for membership until the existing numbers were whittled down to that limit, a process that took the following fifteen months. It was not until 1906 that the number was increased to 1,400.

In April 1907 the committee decided to take numbers 125 and 126 Piccadilly into the Club upon the agreement of terms, and the enlarged premises were granted a new lease by the Sutton Estate for £3,000 per annum for a term of eighty years. Included in the covenants was a clause to 'well and sufficiently repair and keep the premises in repair', including painting 'with two coats of best oil paint and in a workmanlike manner' the inside every seven years and the outside every three and a half years. However, the enlarged premises of 125, 126 and 127 Piccadilly did not in itself now constitute a workable and acceptable clubhouse, and the committee began negotiations immediately to undertake the extensive works that would be required to provide a suitably grand home for the growing membership.

One of the leading firms of architects of the time was Mewes & Davis, who had already proved themselves masters of the grand Edwardian scheme and had provided plans and works for a significant number of landmark buildings in the West End. ▶ 72

He went on to suggest that, while extending the premises as proposed in the near future, the committee should allow a room for professional purposes to serve as a cavalry museum, library and a meeting place for discussions. And in May 1904, the day-to-day convenience of the members was addressed when an extra page boy was employed to help fill the gap caused by the move of the local post office away from Down Street to Queen Street; at the same time a charge of 3d for the porterage of telegrams was introduced.

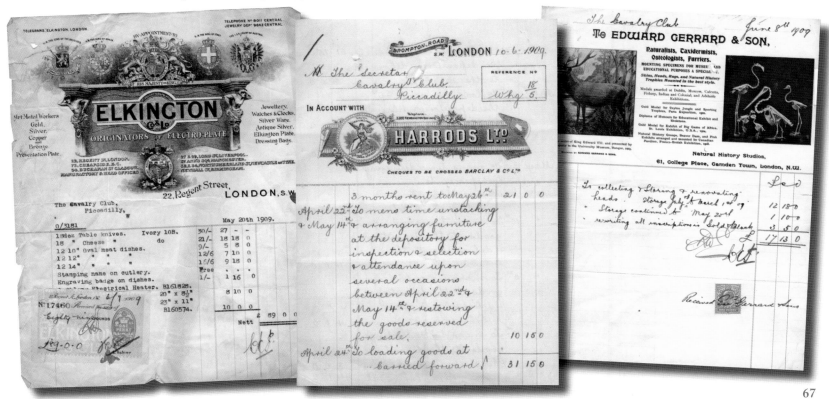

FIELD MARSHAL LORD BIRDWOOD 1865–1951

Born at Kirkee, India, the son of an official of the Indian Civil Service, William Riddell Birdwood was educated at Clifton College and RMC Sandhurst before being commissioned into the Royal Scots Fusiliers in 1883. Two years later he transferred to the 12th Lancers, and in 1887 to the 11th Bengal Lancers (Probyn's Horse). In 1893 he was seconded to the Viceroy's Bodyguard as Adjutant.

He served on Kitchener's staff during the South African War, first as DAAG and later as Kitchener's Military Secretary. He was promoted Major General in 1911 and became Secretary to the Indian Army Department the following year. His reputation grew in these years, and shortly before the outbreak of the Great War Lord Roberts paid him a signal, if indirect, compliment when he described Field Marshal French in a note to Kitchener as 'the only man except Birdwood whom I would trust to use a body of cavalry with dash and intelligence'.

In 1914 Birdwood was appointed to command the Australian and New Zealand troops (later known as the ANZAC) in Egypt. Being content, as a rule, to accept Australian and New Zealand soldiers as he found them, rather than attempting to impose British standards of discipline, he quickly established a better rapport with Antipodean troops than many of his contemporaries.

In March 1915 Birdwood advised Kitchener that the Royal Navy alone could not achieve success in the Dardanelles, and when his division was deployed to Gallipoli he expected to take command of all British ground forces. He was, however, disappointed in this aspiration when he was superseded by Sir Ian Hamilton. Birdwood's contempt for danger and his frequent presence in forward positions made him one of the more popular senior officers, and on one occasion he narrowly escaped being very seriously wounded. He was alone among the corps commanders to oppose the evacuation of Gallipoli, and he eventually replaced Hamilton as GOC Mediterranean Expeditionary Force.

From the Mediterranean, Birdwood was posted to France, and in September 1916 was appointed to command the Australian Imperial Forces as part of the 5th Army. As a corps commander he incurred some criticism for unsuccessful operations at Fromelles and Pozières, and it was felt that he should have been more resolute in resisting unreasonable demands from Gough, his army commander, and indeed from Haig himself. However, in 1917 his corps was transferred to the 2nd Army, under the more amenable Plumer, who also had experience of Australian troops and was much liked by them.

Plumer's handling of the Messines battle did much to restore the confidence of Birdwood's men in British generalship.

After the third battle of Ypres all five Australian divisions in France were placed under Birdwood's command, giving him one of the largest corps in the army. During the German offensive of March/April 1918, this corps held the Somme front from 4 April for several critical weeks, and at the end of May, when Gough was relieved of his command, Birdwood took over the 5th Army. His force played a relatively minor part in the final Allied offensive.

In 1919 he was created Baron Birdwood of Anzac and Totnes, and the following year toured Australia, where he was given a rapturous welcome. He was appointed GOC Northern Army in India, being promoted Commander-in-Chief, India, with the rank of Field Marshal, in 1925. Retiring from the active list in 1930, he hoped to become Governor General of Australia, but was disappointed in this aspiration by a decision of the Australian government that Governors General should in future be Australians. On his death in 1951 he was succeeded by his son as the 2nd Baron.

Overleaf: A very gallant gentleman, Capt LEG Oates at the South Pole, 1912, *by John Charles Dollman, 1913.*

CAPTAIN OATES 1880–1912

Lawrence Edward Grace Oates was born in 1880, the son of a noted big game hunter. After two years at Eton he was educated privately, and joined the 3rd West York Militia in 1898. He transferred to the regular army in 1900, and was commissioned into the 6th Inniskilling Dragoons; he joined them in South Africa, where he was recommended, unsuccessfully, for the Victoria Cross. In March 1901 he was severely wounded and sent home, but he recovered in time to return to South Africa before the end of the year. After the war he served in Ireland and Egypt, becoming Adjutant in 1906. His recreations were hunting, steeplechasing and sailing. In 1910 he applied to join Captain Scott's expedition to Antarctica, and was put in charge of the nineteen ponies. The expedition sailed in June 1910 and established a base on Ross Island in January 1911. Most of that year was spent in establishing depots and, despite his dedication, several of Oates' ponies were lost before the expedition set off for the South Pole in November. At Beardmore Glacier the remaining ponies were slaughtered and the sledges man-hauled thereafter. The five-man expedition reached the Pole on 18 January 1912, only to find that the Norwegian explorer Amundsen had beaten them to it by thirty-four days. The return journey began the same day. The first death, that of Petty Officer Evans, occurred a month later. By 16 March, Oates' feet were severely frost-bitten and he asked to be left behind. The request was refused, but the following morning, his thirty-second birthday, Oates walked out into the blizzard in his socks, as his boots were too painful to put on. His sacrifice should have enabled

the remaining three men to reach the supplies at One Ton Depot, thirty miles further on, but in the event the appalling weather delayed them and they died on or about 29 March. Their bodies were recovered later but that of Oates has never been found.

Portrait of Rathore Rajput Risaldar of the Poona Horse (17th Queen Victoria's Own Cavalry), by Lance Harry Mosse Cattermole, c 1930.

THE INDIAN CAVALRY

The history of the Indian cavalry is long and complex. The recruitment of Indian cavalrymen under the command of British officers by the Honourable East India Company began in the last quarter of the eighteenth century, and by 1805 there were some sixteen regular and eight irregular cavalry regiments in the Bengal and Madras presidencies. Over the next fifty years further regiments were raised in the Bombay presidency, Hyderabad, the Punjab and Central India. A number of these, including all the regular cavalry regiments in Bengal, were disbanded as a result of the Mutiny in 1857, and the remainder were reorganised with a much smaller establishment of British officers, normally some eight or nine in each regiment. In 1903 all the Indian cavalry regiments (apart from the Guides) were renumbered into a single sequence from 1 to 39, with the 24th for some reason omitted.

Although the Indian cavalry was seldom employed outside India during the nineteenth century, some Bengal regiments took part in the Second Opium War in China in 1860. They were not involved in the Boer War but played a major part in both World Wars, and Lord Birdwood, a former officer of the 11th Lancers (Probyn's Horse), subsequently became a Field Marshal.

Apart from their military and equestrian prowess, the most notable feature of the Indian cavalry regiments was their spectacular uniform, particularly that of the British officers, who in most units before 1914 wore both a European-style full dress tunic with white tropical helmet, and native-style uniform with lungi (turban), khurta (a knee-length tunic) and cummerbund. Although the majority of regiments wore dark blue uniform, others had scarlet, green, drab and French grey, while the 1st Bengal Lancers (Skinner's Horse) were famously dressed in yellow.

After the Great War the Indian cavalry suffered an even more drastic programme of amalgamations than their British counterparts, with their total number reduced to twenty-one. A few regiments were selected for Indianisation, but mechanisation had barely begun before the Second World War. On Partition in 1947, thirteen cavalry regiments remained in India while the other eight went to Pakistan. All these regiments still retain their pre-1947 titles, and although many additional armoured regiments have been raised, these are also designated as cavalry.

The new Royal Automobile Club in Pall Mall, the Ritz Hotel further along Piccadilly and a building at the end of the Strand (later to become the fashionable No 1 Aldwych hotel) were all Mewes & Davis projects. A contract was drawn up with this partnership dated 27 November 1907 for the decoration of the principal rooms at a total cost of £3,685.

However, this cost did not include all the new furniture and fittings that would be required, and many invoices exist from the time for these necessities, such as that for bedroom furniture from Maple & Co including five hair mattresses at 32s 6d each, and from Harvey Nichols for an inlaid parquet lino for the ladies' cloakroom in the amount of £5 14s 8d. Substantial work also took place to

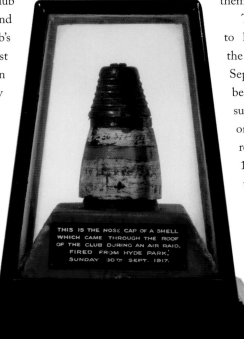

provide the most up-to-date kitchens, and again a variety of items were ordered, such as an ice tank for fish from Richard Crittal & Co of Wardour Street in the amount of £15 12s and an ice safe in the larder for £69 10s.

Buoyed by the prospect of enlarged premises, the committee decided at the beginning of 1908 that 100 new members would be elected from a waiting list of 178. The Club then closed on 26 July 1908 for the works to take place and members were accommodated at the Wellington and United Services Clubs until the reopening on 24 May 1909. With an enlarged clubhouse it was now possible to consider long-term residents, and as well as accommodating the Club Secretary, two leases were issued in 1909 – one to Colonel John Rutherford for no 1 suite and one to Captain John Orr-Ewing for no 2 suite on the third floor, both for a term of two years. 'Meals will be served in the said suite of rooms but in the case of luncheons and dinners at an extra charge of one shilling per head. The tenant may if he wishes employ his private servants, for whom, however, no board or accommodation can be provided in the Club.' Long-term tenancies continued for many years.

The Club records of the Edwardian period reflect that halcyon era for society in general before the storm clouds of war began to loom. In 1911 the Secretary was instructed to invite all the colonial officers attending the coronation of King George V to be honorary members of the Club during their stay in the mother country. And in 1912, a letter was written to the Club's landlord, Sir Richard Sutton Bt of the 1st Life Guards, sending congratulations on attaining his majority and offering honorary life membership of the Club.

All was not, however, invariably well. Following the committee meeting of 6 May 1912, a special meeting was convened to examine the case for the suspension of a member. This was not necessarily unusual, but on this occasion the misdemeanour related to the statement of a page boy, Thomas King, which began, 'It was about last Thursday week night about 6pm, when I took Mr R up in the lift to the third floor. While I was taking him up, he squeezed my behind and when he left the lift

Remnant of a shell that hit the Club in 1917.

he hit me in the private parts with his umbrella and then went to his bedroom.' Later in the same testimony, Thomas recalled Mr R saying 'You're a duck' and becoming even more familiar with him in his bedroom. The committee were initially inclined to doubt the page boy's story, but when he was backed up by other page boys who gave evidence that similar things had happened to them, Mr R was promptly asked to resign.

The onset of war in 1914 was inevitably to hit the Club hard. Eleven members of the staff enlisted during the first week of September, and members still serving quickly became embroiled. The decision to limit the subscription of members serving abroad to only one guinea was bound to affect the Club's revenue, but in presenting the accounts for 1914 the Chairman was pleased to be able to report that, not only had a small surplus been achieved (£951 3s 5d), but that 'as regards the future, the committee have the pleasure to announce that the generous and almost unanimous response of the members serving abroad to their appeal for increased subscription has rendered the continuance of the Club for this year an assured fact. An approximate estimate of the numbers of members

serving aboard with the Expeditionary Force, and so liable for a subscription of one guinea only, was 1,040; of this number, 974 voluntarily paid the extra nine guineas and the committee wish to convey to these members their grateful thanks for their public-spirited action in this crisis.'

At least one member, however, found himself in financial difficulties, as a letter received on 13 October 1914 records: 'In three weeks' time I hope to be off to the front and am writing again to say how sorry I am that there should have been an oversight about my cheque. I can quite assure you that it was not intentional but all owing to the war and the dividends not being paid… Having been a member for the last ten years I look forward to a favourable reply before leaving the country.' The Secretary replied that 'a special

meeting of the committee has been summoned to consider your application for reinstatement'. What happened? Who knows?

Despite the looming war, members could still find themselves concerned about Club manners and morals. A letter of 19 September 1914 raised the issue of drunkenness: 'Dear Darley, I am sorry to say that an unpleasant incident has occurred at the Club in your absence. Deasy and I turned up yesterday and signed cheques and Pardoe reported to us that it had been brought to his notice by the hall porter and other servants that (Major) B had been in the club lately several times the worse for liquor. We went to the smoking room and found him asleep with a drink beside him and discovered that it was his fourth that morning. He remained asleep at any rate till 2.30pm…'.   ▶ 78

THE EMPTY SADDLE

'Let those who come after see to it that their name be not forgotten'

Without doubt, the most significant bronze in the Club is that commissioned from Captain Herbert Haseltine in 1923 to honour those members of the Club who had died during the Great War.

Although the war had ended in 1918, the idea of providing such a memorial did not surface until committee meetings in 1922 when it was decided that a memorial should be placed in the Club to honour the war dead. A sub-committee was set up to review various design suggestions, and the committee meeting on 14 November 1922 recorded that, after inspecting the design, they considered the estimated cost (£700) to be excessive and that the proposed expenditure should be limited to about £500. With a view to raising this sum they decided to appeal to the members for subscriptions of 10s each, and no more than £1 per head. The sub-committee were requested in the meantime to procure other designs.

By early 1923 correspondence between the chosen artist, Captain Herbert Haseltine, and the Club Secretary was both lengthy and antagonistic. The artist found difficulty with allowing the committee to comment upon a sketch or model prior to commissioning the work: 'If you have no confidence in my ability to carry out this work it would be much wiser for you to give the commission to a firm who would execute your order mechanically. Such a statue would undoubtedly satisfy the majority – who, as a rule, is (sic) bereft of any sort of artistic appreciation'; and the committee were equally unprepared to countenance a work that was incorrect in detail. They eventually, however, allowed the artist to proceed as he saw fit, but insisted on providing a saddle and bridle (via his agents, Knoedler of Old Bond Street), to ensure that the details were accurate, since a photograph was deemed inadequate.

It was not until December 1923 that the committee were able to note that 'the design for the proposed Club war memorial submitted by Mr Haseltine as regards the statuette (for the price of £250) and by Sir Edwin Lutyens as regards the plinth (for the sum of £231) was approved. A pictorial representation of the proposed memorial was to be prepared for circulation to the members with a request for subscriptions not to exceed £1.'

In the event – and due to the artist travelling between his Paris studio, a sick mother in Rome and New York (causing the Secretary much agitation and concern) – the statue was not finished and made available until the AGM of June 1924.

The base by Lutyens carries the following inscription: 'In Memory of the Two Hundred and Seventy Two Members of the Cavalry Club who fell in the Great War – 1914–1918', with the later addition: 'In memory of the One Hundred and Fifty Seven Members of the Club who fell in the 1939–1945 War'.

Mr J Betlem was commissioned to compose the original Roll of Honour, and today there are three books contained within the marble base in the place designed for that purpose by Lutyens:

Book One – those who died at Ashanti, Benin, Sudan, South Africa and at the South Pole, 1897 to 1912
Book Two – those who died in the Great War, 1914–1918
Book Three – those who died in the Second World War, 1939–1945

Following completion of the main work, Herbert Haseltine offered 'the provision of smaller models for the price of £50', although the Secretary's reply says 'I am afraid that the price of £50 will considerably limit the number of customers'.

In 1995, and following the deaths of other Club members on active service throughout the world, the committee decided to commission a further book, and committee member Major Robin Wilson devoted much time to identifying members of the Club who had been killed in action since the end of the Second World War. This fourth book, made possible by financial contributions from regiments, is now located in a glass case in front of the *Empty Saddle*, proudly bearing the names of Club members killed in more recent campaigns – Northern Ireland, Iraq and Afghanistan, among others.

CAVALRY MEMORIAL

About the time of the disbandments and amalgamations following the Great War, cavalry regiments for the first time formed The Combined Cavalry Association and made a decision to erect a memorial to those members of their regiments who had given their lives in the war. On 21 May 1924 the memorial was unveiled by Field Marshal Lord Ypres at Stanhope Gate, Hyde Park (near the Dorchester Hotel in Park Lane). In 1962 it was moved to its present position, adjacent to the Serpentine, to make way for the road improvement and enlargement scheme in Park Lane. The epitaph on the memorial has been amended twice, firstly to include comrades who died in the Second World War and then to add those who have died on active service since.

The Club has always exercised a proprietorial interest in the memorial, although not in its maintenance or upkeep. In 1961 Lord Barnby presented the Club with a painting by Mr G Hayman showing the memorial in its original position at Stanhope Gate; the Chairman in accepting this gift said that 'it would be cherished by all members of the Club as a permanent record of the original siting of the memorial'.

The statue portrays Saint George, the patron saint of cavalry, having just broken his lance in the dragon, giving the coup-de-grace with his sword, raising it high in token of victory. At the rear is a bronze panel inscribed with the titles of every cavalry regiment of the empire which took part in the Great War. Between the columns of titles appear four Field Marshals' batons, recording the fact that the cavalry arm gained four such honours during the war.

The Combined Cavalry Old Comrades Association came into being also about 1924, and originally appeared to be a social affair concerned with organising dances in the Royal Horticultural Halls for up to 1,500 cavalrymen and their ladies. Today the association has taken on a more formal approach, with three representatives from each regular cavalry regiment, the Indian Cavalry and five regiments of yeomanry forming the committee.

This committee organises the annual parade (pictured left and opposite), which normally takes place on the second Sunday of May. The memorial service that follows differs only slightly in format from that used in 1924, although on the day of dedication a trumpeter from the Royal Horse Guards (the Blues) placed the first wreath, followed by HRH The Prince of Wales. Following the parade and service, luncheon at the Club has always been a popular choice, and in recent years the QDG, Scots DG, Light Dragoons and QRL have all held regimental luncheons in the private rooms, with many more officers, wives, children and friends using the Club on this very special day.

The war years saw mixed fortunes at the Club. There were no Club tents at race meetings or at Lord's during those years, and by 1917 minutes recorded cost-cutting decisions such as 'until further notice Wednesday in each week should be observed as a meatless day' and 'it was decided to discontinue the supply of cream in the Club until further notice'. In that same year, the finances saw 'the decrease of £1,544 8s 4d in receipts, which might at first sight strike one as serious, but which is entirely accounted for by the passing of the Special War Rule that candidates serving in the forces shall pay no entrance fee on election'. Yet in 1916 the figures were such that the committee could invest the sum of £8,600 in 5 per cent exchequer bonds, which were then converted into the new 5 per cent war loan; this was to be used in 1921 for the building of the annexe.

There were also, of course, many deaths among members; the total number killed in the Great War, as was to be later recorded on the memorial, was 272; of these fifty-four were killed in the first four months of the war between September and December 1914.

With the coming of peace in 1918 the Cavalry Club, along with the rest of the country, hoped that 'some of the difficulties with which we are confronted will disappear, but at the same time it must be recognised that conditions of living have been materially

changed, and that consequently the working expenses of the Club will be considerably increased'. Indeed, in June 1920 there was the prospect of a strike by the Coffee Room waiters who had applied for a rise in their wages, and the committee 'saw the two senior waiters of those who had threatened to strike and explained to them that their wages were higher than the maximum in other clubs'.

Financial difficulties loomed, as was made clear in a report which the auditors and Secretary had been asked to prepare in 1920 and which showed a probable annual deficit of £4,200. As a result the committee had to suggest a subscription increase of three guineas per member. However, the presence at Ascot (which showed a loss of £230) and Lord's (a small profit) resumed, and it was not long before these events regained the full support of members and began once again to show healthy profits.

Cavalry Memorial at Stanhope Gate.

"*Found a feller in the Pioneer Corps or something, actually goin' up the steps of the Cavalry club!*"

A timeless enquiry!

Cartoon (above) by Fenwick.

The Club now began to think about additions and improvements, and on 31 March 1920 signed a contract with Mullen & Lumsden of South Norwood for 'reconstructing and extending sundry domestic buildings and outbuildings at the rear of the premises, 127 Piccadilly W1, for £11,146 being the estimated cost of the works', the funds coming from the realisation of the sale of the war stock. The work took about a year, and in April 1921 the Chairman

DISCIPLINARY MATTERS IN THE 1920s

Any form of drunken, licentious or inappropriate behaviour required the offending member to come before the committee, explain himself and then probably be asked to resign. This was clearly an automatic response when in 1921 an officer late of the 4th Hussars with an MC was imprisoned for a month because of his cruelty to a seventeen-year-old pony by tying waste to its tail and setting light to it. His statement to an RSPCA officer that he had done it to frighten the pony because it strayed into his mother's garden carried little weight either with the judiciary or with the Club committee: in 1926, attempts to reinstate the membership of this officer were still being rebuffed.

Some explanations were, however, accepted. After the Secretary had written to one member, 'It has been brought to my notice that you were intoxicated in the ladies' room on Wednesday night', his apologetic reply – 'I regret to say it seems futile to attempt to excuse my conduct but I would like to state that I had a horse put me on my head the previous morning and that this, following as it did on a rather severe concussion I received not long before when riding in a steeplechase at Birmingham, had probably upset my mental equilibrium' – was accepted and his membership reinstated.

It is also encouraging to note that occasionally a joke was treated as such, like this response to a rebuke in December 1922: 'I was having coffee in the ladies' drawing room with two friends, a lady and a gentleman. The lady, who is an old friend of my sister's, I have known for many years. She laughingly leant forward, and touching my tie made some facetious remark about the colour. I jokingly replied that if she treated my school colours with disrespect she would immediately incur the penalty of being kissed. Taking up my challenge with a laugh, she immediately caught hold of my tie. I at once leant forward and attempted to keep my word (in which, however, I failed). I admit that the whole episode was foolish and out of place in the Cavalry Club, but I acted on the spur of the moment, forgetting that, although we were old friends, my action might very naturally be misunderstood by an onlooker. I trust that the committee will accept my sincere apologies for my foolish behaviour which I very much regret.' They did.

FIELD MARSHAL HRH THE DUKE OF CONNAUGHT 1850–1942

Prince Arthur, later Duke of Connaught, was the seventh child and third and favourite son of Queen Victoria, and godson of the first Duke of Wellington. He entered the Royal Military Academy, Woolwich, at the age of sixteen, and became a Knight of the Garter the following year. Despite a severe attack of smallpox during his cadetship, he was commissioned in 1868, initially into the Royal Engineers, but transferred in 1869 to the 1st Battalion of the Rifle Brigade, then stationed in Montreal. His first experience of action was against a Fenian incursion from the United States in 1870. On his return to Europe, he visited his eldest sister, the Crown Princess of the newly-unified Germany, where he received the Order of the Black Eagle, the Prussian equivalent of the Garter. In 1874 he transferred briefly to the 7th Hussars, but in 1876 returned to the Rifle Brigade as Commanding Officer of the 1st Battalion, now in Dublin.

He married the German Princess Louise Margaret in 1879, and the following year the couple moved into Bagshot Park, later the headquarters of the RAChD and now the home of the Earl and Countess of Wessex.

The Duke was promoted Major General at the age of thirty, and assumed command of the 3rd Infantry Brigade in Aldershot. In 1882, when hostilities broke out in Egypt, he was appointed to command the 1st Guards Brigade, and in that campaign was conspicuous both for his steadiness in action and his concern for the soldiers under his command. He had a narrow escape when a shell burst between himself and another officer. After the battle of Tel el Kebir, his superior, Sir Garnet (later Lord) Wolseley, reported: '…on all sides I hear praises of the cool courage displayed yesterday, when under an extremely heavy fire, by HRH The Duke of Connaught… He is a first-rate Brigadier General and takes more care of his men and is more active in the discharge of his duties than any of the Generals now with me.' The Duke was awarded the CB for his services, and on his return to Europe received the Pour le Mérite (better known as the Blue Max) from his brother-in-law, Crown Prince Frederick of Germany, and the colonelcy of the Scots Guards. His military service effectively ended in India, where he became Commander-in-Chief of the Bombay Army in 1889. He had hoped, with good reason, to succeed the Duke of Cambridge as Commander-in-Chief of the British Army but, despite this

being also the wish of Queen Victoria, that appointment went first to Lord Wolseley and then to Roberts, before being abolished early in the twentieth century. The Duke's application for a command in South Africa was also refused, although he was appointed Commander-in-Chief in Ireland in 1900.

After the death of Queen Victoria, the Duke's energies were directed to matters of state, a role for which his military reputation and immense popularity made him particularly well suited. He represented his brother, King Edward VII, at the Coronation Durbar in India in 1903, and in 1910 opened the Union Parliament in South Africa on behalf of his nephew, George V, another great personal and political success. The following year he became Governor General of Canada, a country whose people he had held in great affection ever since his first posting there as a subaltern of the Rifle Brigade, and held this post until 1916.

The Duke died in 1942, his heir, Prince Arthur of Connaught, having predeceased him in 1938. The title was inherited by his grandson, the Earl of Macduff, but became extinct on his death in 1943.

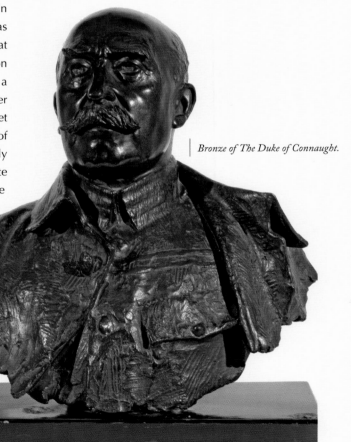

Bronze of The Duke of Connaught.

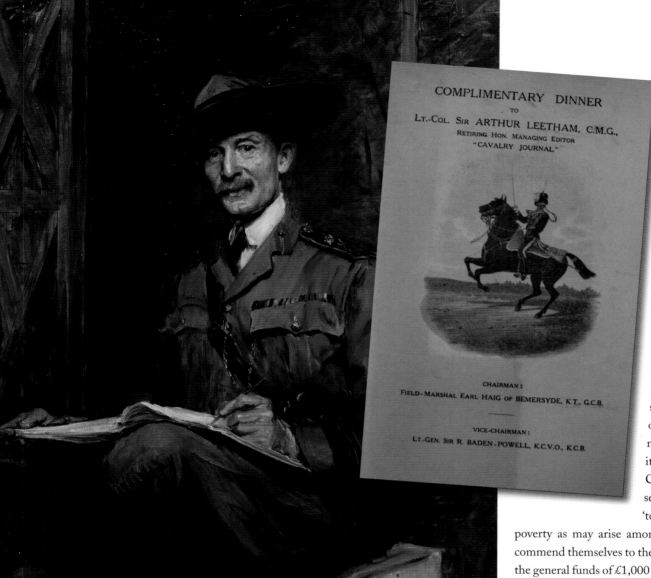

COMPLIMENTARY DINNER
TO
LT.-COL. SIR ARTHUR LEETHAM, C.M.G.,
RETIRING HON. MANAGING EDITOR
"CAVALRY JOURNAL."

CHAIRMAN :
FIELD-MARSHAL EARL HAIG OF BEMERSYDE, K.T., G.C.B.

VICE-CHAIRMAN :
LT.-GEN. SIR R. BADEN-POWELL, K.C.V.O., K.C.B.

Portrait of Sir Robert Baden-Powell by Sir Hubert von Herkomer RA, sold by the Club in 1988.

was able to report the completion of the New Buildings (known as the Annexe or 3 Down Street Mews). But costs had inevitably risen above the initial estimate, and the Club had to seek further funding. In November 1921 the Secretary was successful in persuading three wealthy members to act as guarantors of a loan of £6,000 which was being sought from Cox & Co to cover the shortfall; the three were Colonel G B Winch, Lieutenant Colonel F V Willey and Major D McCalmont. A fourth member, Colonel

The Cavalry Club has no affiliation with any other for the good reason that there is no similar club anywhere else in the world. The Prince of Wales used the Club considerably. On one occasion, shortly before midnight in 1923, several of the maids tried to catch sight of him on his first visit as he sat in the smoking room. Eventually Major Fruity Metcalfe, his constant companion, noticed this and had the bright idea of asking him to walk across the hall so that they could see him. This he did, and for good measure said goodnight to them. They were thrilled.

CHARLES GRAVES, LEATHER ARMCHAIRS

Sir John Rutherford, had also offered a guarantee in the amount of £1,000, but as this was in the form of Boodles Club debentures, which the bank deemed a non-negotiable security, the amount requested by the Club was dropped to £5,000.

During 1926 the Club enjoyed great success, with the figures showing increases in all areas – entrance fees, subscriptions and profits on the provision of wines, spirits and meals – and the membership was noted as having 'reached its highest point in the history of the Club'. The following year the committee set up the Cavalry Club Charitable Fund, 'to afford relief in cases of distress or poverty as may arise among the staff or their dependents which commend themselves to the committee' with an initial transfer from the general funds of £1,000 in trust. The wording, though seemingly applicable at the time, would have repercussions in the 1980s when the Charity Commissioners deemed that payments to ex-members of staff did not fall under the provisions of this objective.

Expansion continued. In 1928 the committee committed the sum of £700 to the capital expenditure necessary to purchase a lease, together with the United Service, Army and Navy, Naval and Military, Guards and RAF Clubs for a ten-acre site for a sports ground. 'It is unnecessary to enlarge on the advantage to the Club staff, and therefore to the Club, of a permanent ground for football, cricket, tennis, running etc. A pavilion is being erected, and it is hoped to open the ground in time for the coming cricket season.' It was noted the following year that the service clubs' sports ground was a success, and that the Cavalry Club were the winners of the Inter-Services Clubs Football and Billiards Challenge Shields and the Schweppes Football Challenge Cup, open to all West End clubs. In 1938, however, the Service Clubs Sport Society was wound up 'due to lack of support from other service clubs' according to a letter from Air Chief Marshal Sir John Steel.

In 1929 the Club was glad to accept a portrait of himself offered by Lieutenant General Sir Robert Baden-Powell, which hung in the building until 1988 when it was sold to raise money for the purchase of the freehold. Meanwhile the financial depression of the later 1920s did not seem to affect the Club's fortunes to any great degree, although there was a considerable falling off in the number of meals served in 1929. However, that year showed a profit, as did the difficult year of 1930, at the end of which the committee were able to report that the original mortgage of £26,000 had been completely paid off, and they were turning their attention to the reduction of the debenture debt, paying off first those debentures 'which have passed to the hands of the executors and representatives of deceased members'. Membership numbers too were holding up and at this time stood at 2,105, with apparently 'no lack in the supply of fresh candidates'. A year later, however, ninety-four members had resigned, and the records note the committee's hope that 'many members who have found it necessary to curtail their expenditure for the moment will rejoin the Club when conditions become more favourable'.

On April 25 1931 the Club lost its longest serving Secretary with the death of Major Henry Read Darley, who had held the post for thirty-three years. The minutes record, 'Not only has the Club lost a most capable and efficient Secretary, who devoted thirty-three of the best years of his life to its service, but every member of the Club has lost a personal friend'. His funeral service, held at Christ Church, Mayfair, was attended by a large number of members and a memorial fund was set up in his name to which members

FIELD MARSHAL VISCOUNT ALLENBY 1861–1936

Edward Henry Hynman Allenby was born in 1861 and educated at Haileybury. Having twice failed the entrance examination for the Indian Civil Service, he was commissioned from Sandhurst into the Inniskilling Dragoons in 1882. He was described at that time as being strongly built, with a dominating character and a good eye for country. The Inniskillings were stationed in South Africa, and Allenby had his first experience of active service in Bechuanaland and Zululand. He was promoted Captain in 1888, and became Adjutant of the regiment the following year, an appointment which 'induced a certain grimness of disposition'. In 1896 he won a competitive vacancy to the Staff College, an extremely rare achievement for a cavalry officer, and while there was chosen as Master of the Drag Hounds in preference to a better horseman in the person of the future Field Marshal Douglas Haig. In later years there was friction between the two men, though whether the matter of the drag hounds mastership played any part in it is not known.

Allenby rejoined the Inniskilling Dragoons at the start of the Boer War, and served successfully under French at Colesburg and in the relief of Kimberley. In the second phase of the war he commanded a flying column of two regiments of cavalry supported by artillery and an infantry battalion. The column was notably efficient and sustained no reverses and few casualties, and Allenby received the CB. From 1902 to 1905 he commanded the 5th Royal Irish Lancers before taking over the 4th Cavalry Brigade. He was promoted Major General and appointed Inspector General of Cavalry in 1909, by which date his uncertain temper was becoming increasingly evident. As Inspector General he must be given some credit for the intensive training in marksmanship which was to pay huge dividends in later years.

In 1914 he joined the BEF as GOC of the Cavalry Division, and proved cool and resolute in charge of the rearguard during the retreat from Mons, though he was felt by some to have been over-cautious in the subsequent advance to the Aisne. The Cavalry Division was shortly afterwards split into two and placed under a corps headquarters, with Allenby again in command. The corps' first dismounted action was at the first battle of Ypres, where their high standard of marksmanship was notable. Allenby took over V Corps in the second battle of Ypres, and was appointed to command the 3rd Army in October 1915. His greatest success was at the battle of Arras in April 1917, where elements of the 3rd Army achieved an advance of three and a half miles, the longest since the beginning of trench warfare. Unfortunately, the gap created by this breakthrough was never widened sufficiently to allow the Cavalry Corps to pass through, and German counter-attacks eventually restored their line.

In view of his uneasy relationship with Haig, Allenby was probably pleased to be given command of the Egyptian Expeditionary Force, comprising seven infantry and three mounted divisions, in Palestine. His forceful manner inspired confidence and he rapidly became popular with the Australian troops. His plan of attack was based on an appreciation prepared by his Chief of Staff, Major General (later Field Marshal) Chetwode, and was based on the capture of Beersheba, followed by an enveloping movement by the mounted divisions to cut off the bulk of the Turkish army. A breakthrough was achieved at Gaza and Allenby drove the enemy northwards beyond Jaffa, capturing Jerusalem intact on 9 December 1917, having inflicted 28,000 Turkish casualties.

The next phase of operations was delayed by the requirement to send two of his divisions back to France to counter the German offensive in March 1918, and it was not until September that he was able to undertake major operations again. In the meantime, he used a force of Arabs under Colonel T E Lawrence to keep the enemy in check around Der'a.

The final assault, which was to be the last campaign of cavalry in strategic mass, began on 19 September. Damascus was taken on 1 October and Aleppo some three weeks later. When an armistice was finally signed on 30 October, Allenby's forces had taken 75,000 prisoners and 360 guns at a cost of 5,600 casualties. The 5th Cavalry Division had marched 550 miles in thirty-eight days, for the loss of 21 per cent of its horses, reflecting unusually high standards of horsemastership.

In March 1919 Allenby was appointed to a Special Commission for Egypt, then in the throes of a Nationalist revolt. He believed that Egypt must be granted sovereign status, and this was achieved in 1922. In the meantime he had been promoted Field Marshal, created a Viscount and appointed Colonel of the 1st Life Guards. He resigned from the Special Commission in July 1925 and thereafter, apart from assuming the Presidency of the British National Cadet Association in 1930, he dedicated himself to fishing and bird-watching. His only son had been killed in action in 1917, and on his death in 1936 his title passed to a nephew.

VISCOUNT VALENTIA 1843–1927

Arthur Annesley, whose magnificent portrait dominates the upper part of the main staircase at the Club, succeeded his grandfather as the 11th Viscount in 1863. He served with the 10th Hussars from 1864 until 1872, when he transferred to the Queen's Own Oxfordshire Hussars as a Captain, becoming the commanding officer in 1894 and Colonel of the Regiment in 1904. Presumably because his title was an Irish one, it did not debar him from membership of the House of Commons, and he represented Oxford from 1895 until he was created Baron Annesley of Bletchington in the English peerage in 1917. He also served as Comptroller of HM's Household from 1898 until 1905. Neither of these appointments prevented him from military service in South Africa during the Boer War, in which he was mentioned in despatches. He was a Lord in Waiting from 1915 until 1924, being made a KCVO in the previous year. He died in 1927 and was succeeded as 12th Viscount by his younger son, who appears in the Army List as being attached as a militia officer to the Royal Dragoons. The portrait shows the 11th Viscount in Levée Dress uniform of the Oxfordshire Hussars.

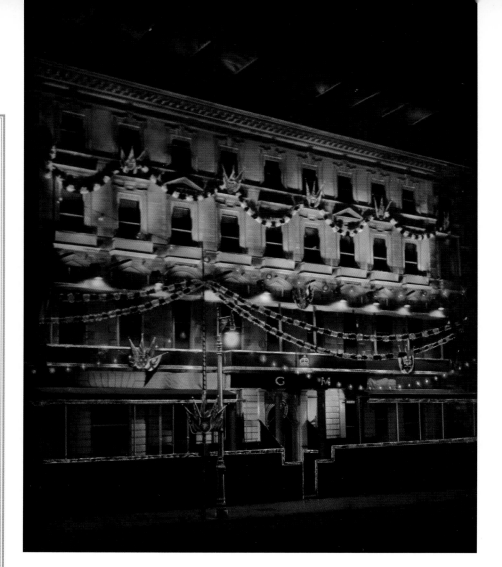

subscribed £1,325. A portion of this sum was paid out in cash, and the balance invested in an annuity in favour of his widow.

That times were becoming increasingly hard and the future worrying is perhaps reflected in a letter sent by the Chairman in April 1932 to all the commanding officers of cavalry regiments, urging them to encourage young officers to join: 'I am sending herewith a list of officers of your regiment who are not members of the Club. At the present time it is particularly desirable that we should get as many of the new entry as possible. If you can use your influence to this effect it will be doing the Club a service.' This letter did not find favour with Colonel D C Boles, who pointed out that he had previously asked the committee to look favourably upon accepting every officer joining the Household Cavalry, but under special terms which the committee had declined.

Even during the financially troubled 1930s, however, there clearly were funds available to effect improvements to the premises and the amenities offered. In 1934 the committee were pleased to announce that they had 'decided to proceed with the installation of hot and cold running water in the Club bedrooms', work which was completed by September of that year along with improvements to the kitchens which were 'electrified and fitted with gas, in place of coal'. Works to the ladies' dining and drawing rooms and the external painting of the building were undertaken in 1937, possibly in anticipation of the coronation of King George VI; the Club

The Club decorated for King George V's Silver Jubilee, 1935.

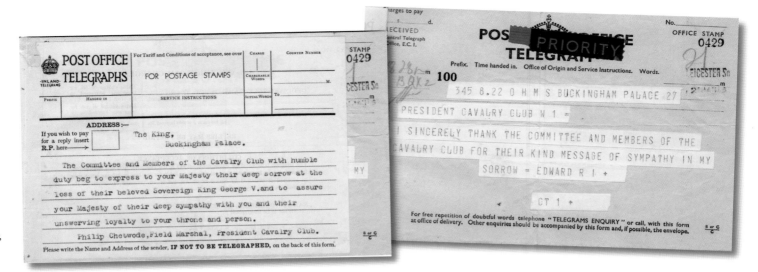

The King,
Buckingham Palace.

The Committee and Members of the Cavalry Club with humble duty beg to express to your Majesty their deep sorrow at the loss of their beloved Sovereign King George V. and to assure your Majesty of their deep sympathy with you and their unswerving loyalty to your throne and person.

Philip Chetwode, Field Marshal, President Cavalry Club.

PRESIDENT CAVALRY CLUB W 1 =

I SINCERELY THANK THE COMMITTEE AND MEMBERS OF THE CAVALRY CLUB FOR THEIR KIND MESSAGE OF SYMPATHY IN MY SORROW = EDWARD R I +

The death of a King, 1936.

had celebrated King George V's Silver Jubilee in 1935 by providing stands and decorations for the occasion and offering 'a bonus of three days' wages to each member of staff', which was increased to four days at the subsequent committee meeting due to the success of the day. However, by 1938 the committee decided to postpone indefinitely the roofing over of the terrace outside the smoking room; and as tensions grew during 1939, the committee felt bound to point out to the chef – Monsieur Metivier, who worked at the Club for thirty years and was there until his death in 1949 – that 'there has been a big drop in the number of meals served'. The chef had received an annual bonus of £40 throughout the 1930s, and the bonus was approved for 1939 too, although some members attributed the reduction in meals served not so much to the uncertain times but to a falling-off in quality.

As war became increasingly inevitable during 1939, a sub-committee on air raid precautions was established, which called for shelter for fifty members in the barber's shop, fifty women in the women's staff room and shelter for male staff in the carpenter's shop. While the committee 'did not consider there is any necessity to enlarge the membership of the Club at present', they nevertheless suggested the closure of the ladies' dining room and the 'entertaining of ladies at the east end of the members' Coffee Room'. In fact the whole of the ladies' floor was closed by 1940; and prices inevitably went up – 'a surcharge of a penny in the shilling to be added to every breakfast, luncheon and dinner'. The recruitment and retention of staff would prove an additional difficulty; while rebuking a member for his behaviour in the dining room in December 1939, the committee were minded to accept his apology but the Secretary was directed to tell him that they 'take a very serious view of such conduct especially at a time like the present when the difficulties of staffing a Club are greatly increased'.

The committee decided that officers of the Household Cavalry Reserve Regiment at Knightsbridge should be offered temporary membership while serving at Hyde Park barracks during the war for a mess subscription of 10s per head per month. At the same meeting it was decided to postpone 'the question

of the Royal Armoured Corps being eligible for the Club'; but it was also agreed that members might introduce to the Club men in uniform who were not commissioned, with the proviso that the member was to be responsible for the guest. One of the temporary members during the war was Captain the Viscount Valentia, late Royal Dragoons and son of the late Club Chairman.

Right: The non-member, *cartoon by HZ.*

85

When the Chairman presented the accounts for 1939 in April 1940, he was able to report that 'the surplus amounted to £392 5s 0d. This surplus is small, as compared with previous years, but not smaller than was to be anticipated in view of the unsettled conditions prevailing throughout the year culminating in the outbreak of war in September. It will be noted that air raid precautions entailed an expenditure of £595; there is also an item of £926 for loss in provisions. This loss was entirely due to the sudden rise in prices of all commodities and services following the outbreak of hostilities.'

I still have a letter written to my father, Major M E B Portal, by a manager at Lloyds Bank dated 4 February 1944. In it he is reminded that 'your account at the moment shows a credit balance of only 2s whilst your subscription to the Cavalry Club of £2 2s 0d awaits payment. We shall be glad, therefore, if you will kindly arrange for sufficient funds to be sent to us to enable us to make that payment.' My grandfather has added a handwritten note at the foot of the letter: 'Has been POW in Japanese hands since Feb 1942'. I don't know whether my grandfather paid the subscription but think it likely that he did.

My father, who was commissioned into the 17th Lancers in 1920, transferred later into the Coldstream Guards and came safely back from Changi Prison in 1945, still with three pots of jam that he had somehow managed to hoard all through the war and his imprisonment by the Japanese. He'd always saved them for when things got really bad, but somehow they never got eaten. My mother and I were very glad of them when he got home – despite being pre-war, they were still very good and a luxury amidst all the rationing.

He also brought home the radio which he'd secreted from his captors while in Changi, and which would deliver very welcome news of the war which he would then spread around the camp. The Japanese knew there was a radio somewhere, and mounted regular searches to find it which caused him a lot of anxiety, but they never did. I kept it for several years, but eventually handed it over to the Imperial War Museum.

My grandfather, who commanded the 17th Lancers in 1904, had been commissioned into the regiment in the late 1880s before the foundation of the Cavalry Club, and so was not a member, having joined the 'In and Out' and saw no reason to change. My father, however, was a member of both the Cavalry Club and the Guards Club all his life; he would regularly remark, when it was time to pay his subscriptions, that he really ought to cancel one or the other, but he never did so. He died in 1971, before the merger. I myself have been a member for over fifty years, both during and after my service in the 17th/21st Lancers.

SIMON PORTAL

He was also pleased to note that 'it will be of interest to members to know that 1 July 1940 is the fiftieth anniversary of the opening of the Club'. On 1 January 1940 there were still forty-one original members on the roll – and five remained in 1951, when they were given honorary life membership.

The provision for members sleeping at the Club during air raids became an issue in 1940, and it was decided that camp beds with mattresses and two blankets each should be provided 'to be erected as room permits in the air raid shelter'. The camp beds would

HM King George VI, as Colonel of the 11th Hussars, by Simon Elwes.

general committee to carry out the duties that would have fallen to the Secretary. One of these, Colonel J J Richardson, was to be the resident member occupying the Secretary's rooms in the Club. However, he died in April and thereafter Lord Huntingfield, a Trustee of the Club, became honorary Secretary for a year until the role was taken over in 1944 by Major W Guy Horne.

The loyalty of the Club staff during these challenging years was much appreciated. In 1942 a war bonus equivalent to 10 per cent of their wages was granted to all members of staff, and in 1943 the annual report mentioned the committee's gratitude for their 'loyalty and devotion to duty during four years without any real holiday'.

Regular bulletins of members killed in action were issued, augmented by lists of those who were being held as prisoners of war and those reported missing. In total, 157 members of the Cavalry Club lost their lives during the Second World War; their names are inscribed in the memorial book.

As the war ended so the committee were able to report that the membership had reached 2,272 as a good number of temporary members converted to permanent membership, and in 1947 the Club tents returned to Ascot and to Lord's for the Eton v Harrow match.

The end of the war also saw the start of discussion about the role of the Secretary and the type of person needed to fill it. In 1945 a sub-committee, convened 'to recommend to the committee the procedure for securing a new Secretary', concluded that there were two types of Secretary obtainable:

A) The type as hitherto, viz a gentleman, either a member or eligible as an honorary member, who in normal cases will be without the detailed knowledge of a trained hotel manager, though there are suitable individuals with that knowledge who may apply.

B) The professional hotel manager type who would not be suitable to be an honorary member or, if he were, would command such a salary as the Club could not afford.

And 'if the type B Secretary were appointed, it would be necessary to have a house committee to whom members could lodge their complaints'.

In 1947 a questionnaire was sent to members asking whether Royal Tank Regiment officers should be accepted as members of the Club; the proposal was defeated by 836 to 160, and at the same time it was decided to limit the membership of the Club to 2,300.

cost a shilling a night in addition to the charge for a bedroom, and they would not be available to members who had not also booked a bedroom.

The Prime Minister, Winston Churchill, accepted honorary membership of the Club in December 1941, and the following year the Duke of Gloucester was invited to become Club President following the death of the Duke of Connaught. But there was a blow in January 1942 when the Secretary, Captain P G Davidson, died. He had served the Club admirably as Secretary for ten years, and the decision was taken not to replace him directly since war conditions would inevitably have shut out many suitable applicants. Instead, the committee appointed a sub-committee of three members of the

It would also be necessary to raise subscriptions. As the Chairman noted in his report, the increased expenditure caused to a great extent by the forty-eight hour week and the minimum wages provisions of the Catering Wages Act, linked with increases in National Insurance, rates and taxes, made it necessary to generate more revenue if the standards of the Club were to be maintained.

However, it was pointed out that 'members of the Cavalry Club probably do not realise that the rate of annual subscriptions has only been raised three guineas in the last forty-eight years'. In 1900 it stood at ten guineas and it was now a mere thirteen guineas.

The immediate post-war years were difficult ones for the Club, and with the exception of 1949 when a small profit of £778 was made, there were deficits from 1947 until 1954. There was also a need for change in governance. In 1948 Field Marshal Chetwode had been Chairman for twenty-four years; indeed in 1935, the committee minutes had

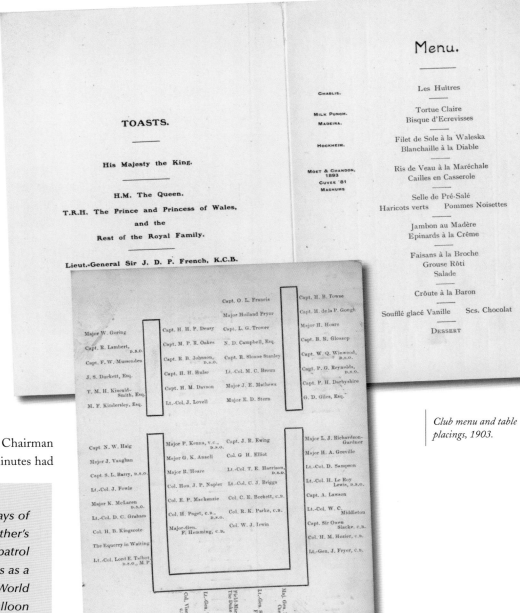

Club menu and table placings, 1903.

recorded a vote of thanks to Brigadier General CEG Norton who, as Vice Chairman of the Club, had chaired most of the meetings since 1929 during Chetwode's absence in India where he was Commander-in-Chief. Now this sensitive issue had to be faced, and an amendment to Rule 35 was sought which aimed to limit the term of office for a Chairman to three years, with the possibility of a further three year extension.

The Club increasingly had to address the challenges being thrown at it in the new post-war world. In 1950 it was resolved that National Service officers would be eligible for membership; and in 1952 a number of members made an urgent request that the Club should appoint a professional secretary and manager. ▶ 92

As a subaltern in the 15th Hussars in the early days of the First World War, Major W Guy Horne (my mother's cousin) had the misfortune to be surprised by a patrol of Uhlans behind a haystack and spent five years as a prisoner of war. In the early days of the Second World War he joined the RAF and took command of a Balloon Barrage Squadron in south-west London. He described flying a barrage balloon as being very like playing a salmon; the 'line' had to be kept taut however much vertical movement varying winds might impart, and so it was bad luck for him when one of his balloons broke free and towed its cable over roofs and telephone lines, and worst of all, electric cables, all the way down into his own village in west Sussex. Major Horne took over as Club Secretary in 1944 and ran the Club for nine years. It was a difficult time – but he found staff and food and kept morale high. After the death of his first wife in the 1950s, he married a French lady and lived on the Riviera until his death in 1974.

P M LUTTMAN-JOHNSON

FIELD MARSHAL LORD CHETWODE 1869–1950

Philip Walhouse Chetwode was born in 1869, the eldest son of Sir George Chetwode, the 6th Baronet. He was educated at Eton, where he was in the Field and also had his Oppidan Wall colours, and from there joined a militia battalion of the Oxfordshire Light Infantry. He transferred in 1889 to the 19th Hussars, then under the command of Colonel French, later Field Marshal the Earl of Ypres. The regiment was in India, and Chetwode saw active service on the Chin Hills expedition and in Burma in 1892–3.

In 1899 he married Hester Stapleton-Cotton, a great-granddaughter of the 1st Viscount Combermere, one of Wellington's most successful cavalry commanders in the Peninsula. He inherited the baronetcy in 1905.

During the Boer War Chetwode served with Sir George White during the siege of Ladysmith, and was awarded the DSO. After the war, the fact that he was not a Staff College graduate prevented him from accepting General French's invitation to join his staff on his appointment to the Aldershot command, although he later became French's assistant Military Secretary before commanding the 19th Hussars from 1908 until 1912.

In March 1914, he was offered the command of the 3rd Cavalry Brigade in Dublin in place of Brigadier General Hubert Gough, who had resigned his commission during the Curragh incident. Although the matter was resolved and Gough resumed his post, the fact that Chetwode had agreed to replace him led to some lasting ill-will. In 1914 Chetwode was in command of the 5th Cavalry Brigade, which did well to check the German advance at Cérizy, and when the Cavalry Corps was formed under Allenby, Chetwode took over the 2nd Cavalry Division. He was made a CB in 1915.

In December 1916 he was posted to the Egyptian Expeditionary Force under Sir Archibald Murray, and showed his remarkable ability in planning bold manoeuvres, although the execution of these plans was sometimes compromised by his concern over water supplies for the horses. When Allenby took over from Murray in mid-1917, Chetwode was appointed GOC XX Corps and was responsible for planning the campaign which opened the way for the capture of Jerusalem in December of that year, for which he received the KCB.

After the war, despite his lack of formal staff training, Chetwode filled some important posts in the War Office, including Deputy CIGS, before being appointed to the Aldershot command. Here, although he was somewhat sceptical of the value of the tank, his emphasis on the importance of manoeuvre in warfare encouraged younger men to envisage lightning strikes by armoured forces.

Lord Chetwode receives the ceremonial key to the Tower of London, as its new Constable, in May 1943.

Left: Lady Chetwode, after Durin Markovich.

In 1928, Chetwode returned to India as CGS and later Commander-in-Chief. He faced many difficulties, with conflicting demands for the modernisation and indianisation of the Indian Army and the need for economy. He addressed these problems in his customary style, described as 'gripping his audiences with shrewd and incisive comment, delivered in a racy Newmarket twang'. His imaginative plans were not, as they sometimes were in war, jeopardised by occasional hesitation, and his achievements included the formation of an Indian Air Force and an Indian equivalent of Sandhurst. He was awarded the GCB in 1929 and promoted Field Marshal in 1933. Further honours followed, including the OM in 1936 and the colonelcies of the Greys, the 15/19th Hussars and the 8th Light Cavalry.

During the Second World War he was instrumental in setting up a joint organisation of the Red Cross and the Order of St John, becoming Chairman of its executive committee. He was also Constable of the Tower of London and the father-in-law of John Betjeman, who married his daughter, Penelope, in 1933. He became the 1st Baron Chetwode in 1945 and died in 1950.

1st February. 1950.

The Rt.Hon.Harold Wilson,OBE.
President,
Committee of Privy Council for Trade.
Board of Trade,
Millbank,S.W.1.

Dear Minister,
      I acknowledge receipt of your personal letter of the 26th January,asking that the Club should offer to set aside a certain number of bedrooms in the Club for the use of American and Canadian visitors during the coming season.

      Whereas I am sure we are all eager to offer hospitality to visitors from America and Canada, Countries which have been extremely kind to us in our difficulties and to thereby bring dollars into our depleted coffers,you will appreciate that,although our rules allow us to introduce prominent people into the Club as temporary Honorary Members,your request raises an issue which I would have to place before my Committee and it is possible that a Meeting of the Members of the Club would be needed before sanction could be given.

      It would help in the meantime if you could see your way to inform me how other Clubs,such as ourselves,have responded to your request,and if you could give me the names of any of the visitors you would like us to entertain. It might also be of interest to you to know that we already have reciprocating arrangements with several of the prominent Clubs in America.

      Yours sincerely,

(signed)   CHETWODE,
              F.M.

I had just come down from Cambridge in July 1950, having left the KDG nearly three years previously, when I was recalled to the army off the RARO to go to Korea. After a week or two, I managed to get sent to the 8th Hussars who were taking double strength officers to the Far East including regulars and reservists from nearly every cavalry regiment. Being an armoured car officer, I was posted to the 8th's Recce Troop.

I was on embarkation leave when I met my former commanding officer, now Brigadier AG17, in the hall of the Club. He asked me what I was doing and I told him I was going to Korea. His reply was, 'Whatever for?' I said that I had been so ordered, and he bowled me over by saying, 'But you don't have to go if you don't want to. All you have to do is tell your commanding officer, who has been told not to take any civilian officers unless they have specifically volunteered to go.' This was an aspect of the army I had not met before, but as I was in the process of landing my first job I quickly informed the CO, and after eight weeks back in the army I became a civilian again.

The 8th Hussars Recce Troop was captured en masse by the Chinese. In the course of time all the men came back. The three officers were never seen again. It is for this reason that I have always had perhaps an exaggerated affection for the Club and have tried to serve it for many years. (Needless to say, I very quickly removed myself from the RARO to join the AER of the KDG!)

ROBIN KERNICK, COMMITTEE MEMBER 1980–2004

After the Second World War, Brigadier George Todd, late Colonel of the Royal Scots Greys, used to lie in wait near the front door of the Cavalry Club watching to see if any members of the regiment came in for lunch without wearing a bowler hat. He was a charming man and an old friend of mine – but a great stickler for dress.

THE 2ND EARL HAIG

the Club would close after lunch on Saturdays to save staff costs. The accounts for that year also recorded the worrying statistic that for the first time ever receipts from subscriptions did not cover the total salaries and wages bill; before the Second World War a third of subscription income had remained after those costs had been met. Clearly income was not keeping up with expenditure and rising costs. But the raising of subscriptions was always a contentious issue, and when it came up again in 1963 – and it was pointed out that there had been no increase for eleven years and that the Club had the lowest subscription rate of any club in London – thirty-three members resigned in protest. The matter continued to rumble on throughout the 1960s, with the committee promising in 1966 that they would avoid a subscription increase for as long as possible, and maintaining this promise in 1968 although it was once again noted that 'our subscription rates are the lowest of any comparable club in London'. Membership, however, was buoyant: in 1961 there were 2,514 members of whom 1,061 were under thirty-four years of age.

The Coffee Room, 1970s.

Expert consultants were called in to look at expenditure, and concluded that the staff had already been cut down to a minimum and the profits on liquor could be improved by running the bars on purely commercial lines.

The need for a professional secretary was finally resolved in 1953 when the outgoing Chairman was able to tell members that the committee had selected from a large number of applicants a man of considerable experience and high reputation who would be responsible for the internal management of the Club; and 'it is expected that economies will be introduced which may reverse the current £2,000 annual deficit'. He was spot on; and 1954 saw an increase in membership of almost 200, to 2,211.

Professional management allowed the Cavalry Club to continue to offer its usual services during the remainder of the 1950s, but by 1960 further economies had to be made and it was decided that

EXTRACTS FROM THE LAST INDIAN *BY MAJOR NARINDAR SAROOP,*
CLUB MEMBER SINCE 1954

In Down Street lived Sir Henry Craik who had been Governor of the Punjab when my grandfather was a minister, and who kindly invited me for a drink one evening, to be followed by dinner at the nearby Cavalry Club. Craikie, as he was popularly known, had lost none of the elegance which I had admired as a boy in Lahore and Simla. Always fastidiously dressed, he sported a monocle and a grey homburg hat. Although no longer ensconced in the splendours of the Governor's residences in the Punjab, he lived extremely well, with a manservant in attendance serving us our pre-dinner drinks. We then adjourned to the Cavalry Club in Piccadilly, my first visit to premises that have given me so much pleasure over the years, and which became my first London club. With characteristic English quirkiness, in the Cavalry Club one lunches and dines in the Coffee Room, where coffee is not served, and you move to the smoking room for that purpose. Our Coffee Room has marvellous views of Green Park, and when we had ordered Sir Henry said he did not wish to ruin my appetite, but did I know what those mounds were in the park? He then informed me that they were the mass graves of the people who had died in the city during the Great Plague, and their bodies had been brought for burial in what was then open country to the west. Over dinner Sir Henry also said that I should have a London club, and I was happy to say that I had just been proposed and seconded for the Cavalry Club. 'Oh well, then it's all very simple,' said my host. 'I am on the committee here, and I shall have it dealt with.' I expressed my gratitude, and then ventured to enquire how he was a member, let alone on the committee, as he had had a distinguished civil service career but had never been a cavalry officer. He chuckled and said, 'My boy, as Governor I was also honorary Colonel of the Punjab Light Horse (an auxiliary unit). After I retired, somebody found this out, and I was elected a member and shortly after that to the committee because they said I had time on my hands.'

The Cavalry Club in those days was an extremely friendly and jolly place. With all the timidity of a new member, I used to run the gauntlet of being eyed up and down by severe looking senior members, some with very military moustaches, others with just one arm or leg or just one eye, and I heard those who had fought in the Boer War reminiscing about Mafeking and Spion Kop. But I soon learnt that they were not glaring at me, they were just curious about the new face. They were also extremely tolerant about the hearty and noisy behaviour of us younger members. One who was not quite so tolerant was Field Marshal Lord Birdwood, formerly Commander-in-Chief of the Indian Army. One particular chum was Peter Martel, son of a distinguished General who had been involved in the invention of the tank in the First World War. Peter and two or three others were particularly boisterous one early evening in the smoking room, where Lord Birdwood was reading the evening paper. As they got more boisterous, he left in a huff muttering about having a word with the Chairman. The young bucks did not take to this kindly, and hatched a plot. After a good dinner, they went to Shepherd's Market and selected the fattest, blowsiest tart they could find, enquiring whether she would go to bed with a Field Marshal for three guineas. The deal was done after she said, 'Young gentlemen, you should know that for three guineas I would go to bed with a camel'. Somehow they managed to sneak her past the night porter, took her to the third floor, gingerly opened the Field Marshal's bedroom door, shoved her inside and fled in different directions. There was hell to pay the next morning. The committee met and Lord Birdwood fulminated until the youngest committee member said, 'But Field Marshal, you must be aware of Club rules which strictly forbid lady guests in members' bedrooms.'

The Club has a large membership of those who can be fairly described as characters. There was one who always said the same thing to the waiter in the smoking room when ordering his drink: 'Tell the porter if my wife calls I'm not here.' There was also the late Lord Dunsany with luxurious growths of hair protruding from his ears, and each time the Club barber tried to trim them he would be stopped with the remark, 'Leave them alone; they keep out the Irish mosquitoes.'

In those days, a three course dinner in the Club was 7s 6d and a four course with a savoury at the end 9s 6d – ie around 38p and 47p in today's currency. A pot of tea with lashings of toast served in a muffin dish would cost 6d. The staff were absolutely marvellous, long-serving and loyal. When the new Hilton Hotel in Park Lane was trying to poach our senior hall porter, their very generous offer was declined with the comment, 'Here I serve aristocrats and gentlemen; at the Hilton it would only be people with money.'

Until the early 1970s, the Club also employed one, if not two, page boys. Whatever their other duties were, they had almost fixed duties in the mornings and evenings. There used to be a chemist not far away at 100 Piccadilly, and the Club members must have provided it with regular business. Each morning a page boy would go there for powders which they made on the premises which were supposed to be a cure for hangovers. Each evening he would make the same trip, but this time to purchase rubber products for those members who harboured lustful aspirations for the night to follow.

As a young subaltern and a member of the Cavalry Club for only three years, I was lucky enough to be successful in the Club ballot for seats to watch the Coronation procession on 2 June 1953. The Club had built scaffolding stands with two or three rows of bench seats between the balustrade and the main facade of the building, with the seats approached through the windows on all three floors.

I had joined my regiment, the 16th/5th Lancers, in the Middle East direct from Sandhurst, so it must have been almost my first time in the Club. I remember being in awe of the senior members, so many of whom had only recently served with distinction in the Second World War.

Outside the Club on the pavement the crowd stood three or four deep, but our seats on the ground floor allowed us a clear view over their heads. Across the road, inside the railings of Green Park, were large stands similar to those now erected on Horse Guards for the Queen's Birthday Parade. There was a loudspeaker system along the processional route over which it was memorably announced that Edmund Hillary and Norgay Tensing had reached the summit of Mount Everest.

It was at about 3.15pm that the procession started to pass the Club. The processional route from Westminster Abbey went down Whitehall, across the south-west corner of Trafalgar Square, along Pall Mall, up St James's Street and then turned left into Piccadilly. From the Club we had the splendid spectacle of the whole procession coming down Piccadilly towards us. Heavy drizzle was falling as it passed us and we felt some sympathy for those standing on the pavement, but no one was going to miss this great occasion.

The procession was led by the Colonial and Commonwealth contingents, then the RAF contingent followed by the army with all the corps and regimental contingents in reverse order of seniority – those at the rear, being most senior, nearest to the sovereign. Each line cavalry regiment was represented by an officer, a warrant officer, a sergeant and five other ranks, and of course this contingent was greeted with loud and vociferous applause from the Club. After the Royal Navy contingent came the carriage procession of colonial rulers. No one will forget Her Majesty the Queen of Tonga in her open

Coronation of HM The Queen, June 1953.

carriage. All the other carriages were closed to protect the occupants from the rain; not so that of the formidable Queen of Tonga, all smiles and clearly enjoying herself enormously. She received huge cheers from the Club and the whole crowd, and there was another one for Sir Winston Churchill, who had returned to office as Prime Minister in 1951, with his mounted escort of the 4th Queen's Own Hussars.

Finally we had the memorable sight of Her Majesty Queen Elizabeth II and the Duke of Edinburgh in the Coronation State Coach passing the Club to the uninhibited cheers and applause of the members, which conveyed in no uncertain terms our affection and respect for her. It was the conclusion of a spectacle that will never be seen again. The number of horse-drawn carriages and mounted officers could never be repeated. How privileged I am to have watched the Coronation procession from the Cavalry Club. And how fortunate I am to be still enjoying membership of the Club fifty-five years later.

BRIGADIER JOHN POWNALL

Queen of Tonga.

The issue of the lease also came up at this period. In 1960 the committee received a letter from the landlord's agents suggesting that the Club might give up its current building in exchange for new premises to be built off Old Park Lane just behind the current site. The answer was no, but it was suggested that the Chairman and Sir Henry Floyd should meet the Sutton Estates for a general discussion on the matter. This meeting went ahead and the Chairman was assured that the landlord would consider an extension of the lease to 2017, bringing the property into line with the lease of the RAF Club next door. The agent also advised the Club that it was too early to consider a lease renewal.

However, the approaching expiry of the lease had its effect on discussions about improvements. When in November 1961 the matter of the modernisation of the Club kitchens was raised, the Secretary reported that 'while the kitchens remain in their present position there is little point in the Club spending a large sum on modernisation as there would not be any saving on staff'. Moreover, the Club had been informed that 'the building will almost certainly be pulled down on the expiry of the lease' in a mere twenty-six years, and the cost of new kitchens would be at least £10,000 and almost certainly more than that. 'Perhaps', a committee member suggested, 'the building could be scheduled as an ancient monument'. One wonders if he had in fact seen the kitchens at that time! And it is salutary to note that the bill when they were eventually overhauled in 1991 was £800,000.

In April 1962, as the Chairman wrote, 'there is no reason to excuse a profit… but I feel it is my duty to warn you how quickly a profit can disappear… Major boiler replacement must be expected in the next twelve months. In fact our old building is beginning to feel its age… Remember that anything we can put by now will be

Years ago, long before I became a member of the Club, I worked at the old Stock Exchange. Several of us used to lunch in a small restaurant called Birch's in the Stock Exchange building, and our favourite waitress was a splendid Irish lady called Biddy. It was the mid-1950s, and the smartest cocktail parties to which I was occasionally asked were often held in the Cavalry Club. There, dishing out the champagne and canapés, was no less a figure than Biddy who had somehow migrated westwards. She always welcomed her Stock Exchange clients effusively as did we her in turn. So the noise level rose accordingly.

JAMES BRUXNER

'I have never had any trouble getting a bed at the Club.'

It was early morning in 1955, we were in a smoke-filled tent halfway up Mount Kenya and the speaker, Henry Huth, was shaving delicately round a noxious-smelling cigar in his mouth. Lt Colonel Henry Huth DSO MC was at the time a Major commanding the East African Armoured Car Squadron, and subsequently went on to command the combined 4th and 8th Hussars as the Queens Royal Irish Hussars.

A couple of years later I mentioned this conversation to a subaltern friend. 'Hah,' he said. 'I have seen Henry getting a bed at the Club.' Apparently my chum was playing billiards one evening when Henry appeared at the door with the porter carrying a camp bed. 'I hope you chaps aren't going to be too long,' says Henry. And, without waiting for an answer, the porter erects the camp bed and slides it under the billiards table, as Henry climbs into his pyjamas. Exit two bemused subalterns!

MAJOR G V GOODEY

of the utmost help when our present lease runs out in 1988.' There was nevertheless still some capacity for improvement and change. Redecoration of the ladies' dining room proved to be a great success in 1967; and in the same year a jackpot machine was installed in the Club to a mixed reaction, though it proved to be very profitable and stayed until 1971.

But the writing was beginning to appear faintly on the wall. In 1968 a sub-committee was set up under the chairmanship of General Jackie d'Avigdor-Goldsmid (a future Club Chairman) to look at 'Future Policy'. Their conclusions were primarily that the membership of the Club needed to be increased by approximately 1,000, having identified additional capacity in all dining and bar areas, and that an immediate approach should be made to the Guards Club with a view to a merger.

They also looked at other membership possibilities, 'and came to the conclusion that opening eligibility for sons of members, the Royal Tank Regiment or the Green Jackets would not achieve the aim. Sons would presumably only cover one generation and they felt that very few members of the RTR would wish to join. Green Jackets, on the other hand, would probably already belong to other London clubs and would probably not feel inclined to change.' In fact, within ten years all these groups would be accommodated as members.

It is clear from the histories of both the Cavalry Club and the Guards Club at this time that the two clubs were dancing tentatively round each other, eyeing each other up with thoughts

of amalgamation but also fiercely keen to retain their individual identities. In July 1968 it was reported in committee that Sir Henry Floyd had been asked by General Deakin, Chairman of the Guards Club, whether the Cavalry Club might consider a merger. After consulting the Cavalry Club Chairman, Sir Henry had informed General Deakin that the Cavalry Club were at the moment 400 members oversubscribed and there was no chance of any interest in such an amalgamation at that time. Yet in November of that same year forty members forced an EGM to discuss the future of the Cavalry Club and more than eighty members turned up to express diverse views; and by the following April, at a further EGM with over 120 members in attendance, a resolution was passed that 'membership of the Club be opened to members of the Guards Club, past and present, but excluding special lady members'.

The Guards Club were, however, reluctant in their turn to consider a merger at this stage, and the first Cavalry Club approach in 1969 met with a rebuff. But at this stage it was noted that, 'We have informed the Guards Club that our option remains open as ratified for a limited period, and nothing that has been done or said has in any way affected the happy relationship and friendship between our two clubs'.

At the same time a postal vote was taken on the resolution that all serving officers of the Royal Armoured Corps be eligible to join the Club; 1,023 members voted in favour, with 175 against. The committee noted that they did not consider that this issue was 'in

As a boy in the late 1950s I was often taken to the Cavalry Club and came to terms with eating spinach, which I learned to enjoy. I would sometimes stay the night at the end of prep school term before catching a plane to Germany. I well remember the picture on an easel at the door to the ladies' dining room, Ladies Bathing *by J E C Mathews (above), showing cavalry officers on a recce viewing the lasses bathing in the nude on the beach below.*

One evening in the 1960s I arranged to meet a friend from Yorkshire, also a member, in the Club. I was running late after being busy casting sculpture at art school, and had no time to change. Seeing various blobs of plaster about my clothing, the hall porter felt duty bound to pursue me to ask if I was a member.

A few years later in 1975, having finished my tour in Northern Ireland, I arranged to meet my mother and stepfather (Ken Hedley, a Club regular) in the Cavalry Club before going on to a wedding the next day. I parked their car, complete with the usual 'coffin' or flower box for cut flowers from their market garden in the back, somewhere in the side streets at the back of the Club and we went in for dinner. As the main course was served, we were all told to move away from the windows as there was a car bomb warning. I asked a policeman about the car, which turned out to be my parents'. He made a quick call and drove me round in the squad car to retrieve it. Relief all round, and when I said I was just back from Northern Ireland the policeman sent the traffic warden packing too.

REVD TODDY HOARE

MAJOR GENERAL SIR JAMES D'AVIGDOR-GOLDSMID 1912–87

Jackie D'Avigdor-Goldsmid, as he was known, was the younger son of the 1st Baronet. He was educated at Harrow and Sandhurst, and joined the 4th/7th Dragoon Guards in 1932. A fellow officer who served with him at this time recalls that D'Avigdor-Goldsmid was the only officer in the regiment to purchase his own full dress uniform at a time when full dress, if needed for the occasional levée, was normally hired from the regimental tailor. He was a keen point-to-pointer, who retained a lifelong interest in racing. By 1940 he was Adjutant of the 4th/7th, and was with the regiment at Dunkirk. On D-Day he landed in France with them as A Squadron leader, and in the subsequent fighting was awarded what was initially understood to be a DSO but later changed to an MC. He was wounded near Brussels in August 1944, and later served on Mountbatten's staff in Burma. He commanded the 4th/7th in Libya from 1950 to 1953, for which he was awarded the OBE, and 20 Armoured Brigade from 1958 to 1961, becoming DRAC the following year, Colonel of the 4th/7th in 1963 and President of the Regular Commissions Board in 1965.

Shortly after his retirement, D'Avigdor-Goldsmid became Conservative MP for Lichfield and Tamworth in the Heath government. He became a CB in 1975 and the following year succeeded his brother as the 3rd Baronet. He played a major part in the negotiations leading to the amalgamation of the Cavalry and Guards Clubs. He was a notable racehorse owner, his greatest success being the 1977 Grand Military, which was won by his Double Bridal, and at his death in 1987 was Chairman of both Tattersalls Committee and the Stable Lads Welfare Trust. He had no heir, and on his death the baronetcy became extinct.

any way conditional upon the matter affecting the Guards Club', and therefore went ahead to give effect to the resolution. A further postal vote about the proposal to offer membership to individual Green Jackets also resulted in an overwhelming yes, and so 'your committee has offered membership to all Green Jacket officers past and present with effect from 1 January 1971'.

Money was found to install an essential new boiler in 1971, as well as a new fire escape. Also in that year, 'I am sure you will all be pleased to know that your committee have decided to provide bedroom accommodation for members and their wives on the fourth floor of the Club. Double rooms have always been a high priority as regards amenities asked for by members, and I am convinced that this will be a popular move. To offset the loss of single rooms, six further small rooms will shortly be opened in the annexe and

six more rooms will be provided in the basement.' These were in place by August 1971, but this new provision meant the loss of the billiards room – though the table reappeared, by popular demand, in the library some years later.

Subscriptions clearly had to go up. In July 1971 a review tried to tackle the problem partly by increasing the rates – by a not insignificant 50 per cent! – but also by reviewing the existing age groups, which had not been altered since 1932. Among other changes, the lowest subscription rate now applied only to those aged under twenty-five, rather than twenty-seven as before, and the rate itself was increased from £9.45 to £15.00. This was only the third rate increase since the war, the others having been imposed in 1953 and 1964. However, the sixty-seven members who had joined more than fifty years before found that their rate was to be

Having recently returned from living for ten years in the USA, I sat myself down at the communal lunch table at the Cavalry Club – only to be regarded with the greatest suspicion by the only other member present. 'My name is Antony Snow and I currently enjoy the great luxury of not having to converse because I no longer know anyone in the Club,' I said, in a rather lame attempt at introducing myself. 'Why do you belong?' 'Because I didn't have to speak to anyone until you arrived.' We are now, needless to say, long-standing friends.

ANTONY SNOW

held at the existing level, a compassionate measure that cost the Club about £700. Members of over sixty years' standing already received honorary membership.

There were ongoing attempts to attract younger members. Trips to Sandhurst to canvass recruits began in 1971, though the initial success rate was low, with only seven cadets joining out of sixty-one who were approached by the Secretary, although many joined immediately on reaching their regiments upon commissioning. Then there were plans in 1973 to convert the library into a bar to attract a younger clientele, but the idea was thrown out at an EGM.

General D'Avigdor-Goldsmid's sub-committee reviewing the workings of the Club and considering its future started its work again in 1974. Its main recommendation at this stage was the establishment of a finance committee, which then included Ian Frazer, a Club member; he is still, more than thirty years later, Chairman of 127 Piccadilly plc, a Trustee of the Club and involved with the committee.

The Annual General Meeting held in June 1975 under the chairmanship of Colonel 'Kate' Savill (who had decided to step down as Chairman after only one year to make way for General D'Avigdor-Goldsmid) was momentous, and saw sixty members turn out for a controversial session.

VIEW FROM THE CHAIR
COLONEL KENNETH 'KATE' SAVILL, CHAIRMAN 1974–5

Early in 1976 the IRA threw bombs into the Army and Navy and Naval and Military Clubs, and also into Brooks's. Several waiters were badly maimed at the latter club, and the Army and Navy Coffee Room suffered from fire. The bomb thrown into the bar at the Naval and Military was quite small, and did very little damage. Within a minute, shots were fired from Green Park across the road in the direction of the hall porter's desk in the Cavalry Club. But the only effect was to set on fire a small car which was parked in the road just below the hall porter's window.

I went to see Commander Huntley, the officer at Scotland Yard who was in charge of anti-terrorist investigations. He advised the installation of a sheet of quarter-inch steel plate behind the hall porter's desk, as this would afford protection against ordinary rifle bullets. This was supplied and fitted by Messrs Locks of Acton Royal. The hall porter at that time was an Irishman called Paddy, who was fairly tall and complained that his head was higher than the top of the steel plate. His friends, however, said 'Not to worry', because there was nothing in his head anyway!

Colonel Savill, whose nickname 'Kate' dated from his schooldays, remained a regular attender of Club events after stepping down from the chairmanship prior to the merger. He lived to a great age, earning the distinction of being the oldest living member of the Club before his death in December 2007 at the age of 101.

LONDON LAUGHS: Cavalry Club

"I don't care if you HAVE been mechanised, you can't leave that there 'ere."

Cartoon by Lee.

implemented the result would be mass resignations from serving officers. This issue had already been flagged up to the Chairman earlier in the year, when a committee member had suggested that the proposed subscription increases for serving officers by some 70 per cent might have a devastating effect on membership. The Chairman pointed out that the Club already had a one-day's pay scheme for subalterns which the committee had proposed to encourage the young to join; and he also assured the meeting that any change would have to satisfy the 80 per cent of the membership who were non-serving. The matter would be put to an EGM in the autumn; but in the event the motion to increase the subscription rates was not agreed.

> When I joined the Cavalry Club in 1960, the smoking room in the afternoon was full of very old members, either asleep or drinking quantities of port. One afternoon I was sitting reading a newspaper near a very aged member who appeared to be sound asleep. He was woken by another old member who entered the room and exclaimed, 'Henry, is that you? They told me you were dead!' Henry opened one eye and said, 'No George, I'm not dead; it's my brother who died.' 'Well, Henry,' came the reply. 'I'm very glad you're not dead, because you are the only man alive who can help me with this question I have to put to you. The regiment has asked me to write a history of our exploits in the First World War and you are the only one who will know the answer to this. Now tell me, did we take the polo ponies to France in 1914?' I cannot now remember the answer, but I think it was yes. One wonders what they did with them, but there we are!
>
> Another smoking room memory: one older member was approached by another who said to him, 'Sorry I'm late, but we've been having trouble in the office with our computer.' The other member replied, 'Computer? Computer? What's a computer? I though it was a fellow who came up from Guildford every day on a train?' 'No,' came the reply. 'That's a commuter. A computer is some newfangled machine they've invented that adds up for you!'
>
> CAPTAIN CHRISTOPHER D NEWTON

Expenditure had risen by some 10 per cent in 1974 while income had risen by only 1.9 per cent; with inflation running at high rates and although there had been a small surplus for the year, the committee had decided that action needed to be taken.

First on the agenda was a substantial increase in subscriptions which would come into effect on 1 January 1976. This caused a number of members to speak on the subject of subscription rates for serving officers. The general opinion was that serving officers up to the rank of Lieutenant Colonel should be allowed to subscribe on the basis of a number of days' pay according to rank; the members who spoke threatened the meeting that if this was not

Secondly, the committee proposed improving the facilities for members' wives by allowing them to use the dining room on the second floor, whether accompanied by a member or not, and being able to entertain guests. Colonel Alexander said that he was in favour of increasing the facilities for ladies within the Club 'since the Club had the best ladies' side of any in London', but saw no reason why they should be asked to pay as they did in other clubs. The response from the chair was that the committee had decided against associate membership for ladies, and the extra facilities were being offered to offset the subscription increase to their husbands.

Other new resolutions passed at this meeting were the final acceptance that the sons of members should be allowed to join the Club, and that members should be allowed to pay their subscription in quarterly instalments. But the nub of the meeting concerned the possibility of a merger with another club. A question from the floor raised again the issue of negotiations with the Guards Club. The Chairman asked the meeting whether they would be prepared to widen the membership of the Club by amalgamation with another club and also if they would agree to the committee pursuing the question of opening the membership to a much wider field of service provided that they were approved by the committee. It was unanimously agreed that the committee should look into all possibilities.

The Club building was also discussed. Major Lycett suggested that the committee should consider the possibility of moving to smaller modern premises, but this did not meet with the approval of the meeting, and Field Marshall Hull (Vice President) said that it was apparent that 80 per cent of the members wished to remain in the present building and to maintain the standards of the Club. There was also some discussion about the question of the lease and its extension.

This Annual General Meeting was to be the last held by the Cavalry Club as an individual entity. Having effectively been given the green light by the membership – and after renewed overtures from the Guards Club, who found themselves in an increasingly untenable position – the two Clubs finally accepted the need to merge, and the committee spent the next six months finalising an amalgamation which was to become effective on 1 January 1976.

The name of the merged Club was to be the Cavalry and Guards Club, a decision that was agreed quite early in the negotiation process. Factors taken into consideration included the cavalry regiments' precedence in the army list, the fact that the merged Club would be using the Cavalry Club premises and the need to avoid

taxis dropping members in Charles Street rather than Piccadilly, or even worse at Cox & Kings. The two Clubs worked both together and separately on the various issues that the merger threw up. It was noted that it would be necessary to keep the staff establishment within financial limits. The existing Guards Club staff numbered over thirty and the merged Club could not take them all, though it was hoped that the amalgamation of the two staffs would result in an improvement in the service provided. On the other hand, the pressure on the staff from the increased membership, in premises that had not been extended, would test them to the full.

*Field Marshal
Sir Richard Hull,
Vice President
1968–89.*

Not all, of course, went smoothly. The Secretary of the Cavalry Club, in a confidential memo to the Chairman in September 1975, wrote, 'Sadly, I fear that we are being led up the garden path by the committee of the Guards Club. This despite the fact that the first overture on a merger came from them. It would seem that we are chasing a diminishing asset.' His concerns apparently arose from the fact that a new approach had been made to the St James's Club (itself to disappear some years later), that young Guards officers were being given special terms to join Buck's and that the Guards Club staff were evidently being told that they would have to work longer hours for less pay.

Despite everything, however, discussions and agreements continued, and in a remarkably short space of time the merger became fact and the Cavalry and Guards Club opened its doors under its new name on 1 January 1976.   □

The Charge *by CE Stewart.*

Club Staff

Over the years, all three Clubs have been fortunate in having a good number of loyal and long-serving staff working for the comfort of the members. Indeed, such was the relationship that many of the staff only 'retired' in their late old age, and many are the stories of Club members resisting any attempts to change or retire certain members of staff. One of the primary reasons, of course, for such lengthy periods of service was that in the latter part of the nineteenth and early twentieth centuries pensions did not exist and 'servants' were unable to manage without their Club stipends. Although both Clubs ensured that retirements were recognised with a monetary gift or offer of support, this was not formalised by the Cavalry Club until as late as 1921, when it set up a charitable fund specifically for the purpose. Even then, the terms of the grant were to provide 'relief in cases of distress' for present staff members (a problem of wording which was to have costly consequences, when in the 1980s the Club was required to

satisfy the Charity Commissioners that it was not misappropriating the funds). Members were still, however, reluctant to let long-service retainers leave and many stayed on well into their seventies and eighties.

Among their number have been a considerable number of 'characters' over the years; here are just a few:

Chelsea Pensioner Price, who was born in 1904, took up his position at the Cavalry Club in 1919 when he was fifteen and remained for two and a half years before enlisting in the Royal Dragoons and departing for India. Interviewed in 1994 for the *127 Gazette*, he still had excellent memories of those early days and told how when he had outgrown the page boy uniform, he was promoted to valet and then into the dining room, where he wore a tailcoat. He had particularly happy memories of the Prince of Wales (later King Edward VIII), who sometimes changed his clothes nine times in one day from uniform to lounge suit to afternoon dress to evening dress. With a salary of 30s a month in 1919, the gratuity from the Prince of Wales of a florin was much welcomed by 'page' as he was fondly known.

C J Everett retired in January 1946 from the position of assistant Secretary of the Cavalry Club after service of nearly fifty-six years and having worked for four Club Secretaries and the sub-committee during the interregnum. In a committee minute dated 27 March it was recorded that 'he was presented by the Chairman (Field Marshal Lord Chetwode), representing the committee, with a silver inkstand, suitably engraved, and a cheque for £1,183 5s 7d, the total amount subscribed by the members of the Club, and was invited to enjoy the freedom of the Club for the remainder of his life'. According to the author Charles Graves, he had been able to recall 'the days when the grandest dinners were given by Colonel Sir H M Hozier, the father of Lady Churchill, and the excitement of the night of George V's wedding day'.

Fred Lloyd went to work in 1921, aged fourteen, at the Guards Club. Following six years' war service with the Welsh Guards, he took up where he left off as a hall porter in 1946. He soldiered on

E R Boote was the head hall porter and retired in 1965 after forty-five years' service with the Cavalry Club. There are many stories about him (see boxes). One recounts how after lunch one day the Secretary went up to him and said, 'Boote, a member has fallen down outside the front door and probably died. Please remove him immediately. It is most inconvenient for the other members trying to get in and out.'

Following Boote's retirement, a member enquired at the AGM whether it would not now be better if members 'placed their bets directly with their own bookmakers or on the Tote and not with the hall porters'. He went on to ask whether the Club paid for all the telephone calls the porters made, and whether the Club was responsible for any debts incurred, and was assured by the Secretary 'that there was a direct telephone line paid for by the bookmakers'.

Webb was one of the better known of the liveried valets employed by the Cavalry Club, both on the bedroom floors and in the members' changing rooms on the lower ground floor. He served in this post for many years before and after the war, and took a

in that capacity, part-time, at 127 Piccadilly, retiring in 1991. His familiar utterances, such as 'I remember your great-grandfather, sir,' are an important if small part of the rich fabric of the Club.

F King worked at the Cavalry Club for forty-nine years as basement valet and billiard marker. In the committee meeting of June 1958, it was reported that Mr King, who was eighty-two years of age, had expressed a desire to retire. The committee agreed that Mr King should receive the normal maximum pension of 50 per cent of his current wages, which would amount to £2 11s 6d per week.

One day, in the gentlemen's cloakroom, I saw a rat run across the floor. I scuttled out and reported it to the head porter, Boote. Boote was always resplendent in full green livery, with lots of gold buttons, a wing collar and, I think, a black tie. He used to sit rather high up behind a boxed-in cabinet and looked at you rather disapprovingly over his glasses. I went up to him and said, 'Boote, I've just seen a rat running across the floor of the gentlemen's cloakroom'. Boote raised his eyes very slowly from the Sporting Life *which he spent most of the day perusing, looked at me very solemnly and said, 'Have you, sir? Most members see two', and immediately looked down to his racing selection. I slunk away, realising I had not impressed him.*

CAPTAIN CHRISTOPHER D NEWTON

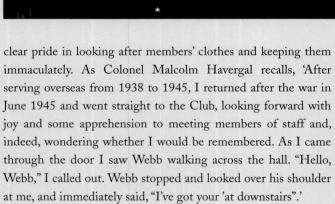

clear pride in looking after members' clothes and keeping them immaculately. As Colonel Malcolm Havergal recalls, 'After serving overseas from 1938 to 1945, I returned after the war in June 1945 and went straight to the Club, looking forward with joy and some apprehension to meeting members of staff and, indeed, wondering whether I would be remembered. As I came through the door I saw Webb walking across the hall. "Hello, Webb," I called out. Webb stopped and looked over his shoulder at me, and immediately said, "I've got your 'at downstairs".'

Joe Thompson retired in 1975 at the early age of sixty-five having worked at the Cavalry Club since May 1924. He had been presented with a clock to mark his fifty years' service at the AGM in the previous year.

Monsieur Edgard Bergevin retired in July 1979 as head chef having spent forty-nine years in the service of the Cavalry Club.

George Church was for twenty-nine years a loyal servant of the Cavalry Club, and retired from service at the end of January

Edward Nelson also recorded this incident in his book I want to count the bottles, *though his recollection of the exchange between the 'gently comical' Boote and the 'senior police officer, distinguishable by prominent silver scrollwork to his headgear' differs from that of Major Wootton. When the top brass had told Boote that he was not a member, the response was, 'Then you'd better remove yourself from the Club while I call the Secretary. If you don't, I'll call the police!' He had another memory of the hall porter too: 'When I was sitting beside Boote on the bus returning us from the Grand Military Race Meeting at Sandown Park, he informed me that "it ain't fitting for Club servants to speak to Club members". No further conversation ensued.'*

1995. He had started work as a porter at Buck's Club in November 1934 and remained there for thirty-one years, apart from a break of five years during the Second World War when he joined the RAF and served variously as an air gunner, wireless operator and radar operator. He returned to Buck's after the war and remained there until the death of the founder, Captain Buckmaster. In February 1966, Mr Church joined the Cavalry Club, opening the new ladies' dining room the following year. In 1968 he took over the position of club steward, a job he held for seventeen years. From 1985 until his retirement he was head porter, with a particular responsibility for coordinating the maintenance of the building.

My brother-in-law John Browne-Swinburne, a member of the Club in 1963, assures me that the following tale is absolutely true. He was standing at the urinals when a Colonel in the next bay passed out and died on the cloakroom floor. JBS summoned the hall porter, Boote, who advised him to 'cover him up with paper towels' while he, Boote, summoned the ambulance. JBS was busy unfolding said paper towels and spreading them neatly over the colonel when Boote appeared. 'Christ, not the clean ones', he said.

ANTONY SNOW

Philip Summers joined the Club in 1974 and was the Club steward for ten years from 1985 to 1995, when he left having bought the freehold of the Crown and Anchor public house at Ramsbury, near Lambourne, which he intended to run with his partner, Marina Marcolongo, who had also been on the Club's staff for twenty-three years. A former 11th Hussars corporal, he started in 1975 as assistant steward, taking over Thompson's Bar. From the cellar to the ladies' dining room, he had stints in every nook and cranny before assuming the august mantle of senior steward a decade later.

Over the years he coped with all manner of potential dramas. When the last permanent live-in member passed away on the

premises, he did so behind his *Sporting Life*. 'Mr Summers, I think you ought to come and have a glance at the Major', squeaked a concerned junior. 'He looks a tad peaky.' When Summers arrived the Major was as dead as a hammer, but still had a grip on his paper on the greyhounds page – his own dog actually won that same night! 'I had to take the paper out of his hands,' Summers recalled. 'As he was so reluctant to let it go, I realised there must be something to it and I've read it ever since.'

With a ready wit and keen sense of fun, Summers was a natural in clubland, but it was his intuitive understanding of the membership that gave him the edge at 127. A gifted communicator, he equally made a young Sandhurst cadet, a senior member on two sticks or a lady member feel at home. On retirement he said, 'I must confess it's been twenty years of brilliant fun. It started out as a job, but it turned into a way of life for both of us.'

Geoffrey Price was born and brought up in Feltham. His father, Ted Price, an ex-Grenadier Guardsman, was employed by the Guards Club as a butler working in the smoking room and card room. In 1949 Geoffrey, aged fourteen, joined his father at the

One afternoon in 1960 when I was working at the ladies' annexe in the Guards Club, Colonel Clarke and his wife arrived for afternoon tea following a little shopping in nearby Bond Street. Mrs Clarke asked for a pot of tea, but Colonel Clarke demanded a whisky and soda, which was something I had never before served in the afternoon.

Having served the tea, I placed the whisky glass carefully on the low table in front of the Colonel, and he requested me to put the soda into the drink. Nervous and unsure, I pressed the soda siphon firmly – and the resulting jet shot across the top of the glass and straight into his lap! Needless to say, he was less than amused – but his wife could not stop laughing and the memory of it continued to make her laugh for years to come. Strangely, the Colonel never appreciated the reminder of his visit to the ladies' annexe.

CAROLE PRICE (WIFE OF GEOFFREY PRICE)

Right: The Secretary with the Heads of Department.

I have many memories of my years at the Guards Club and then the merged Cavalry and Guards Club. I remember two members sitting in the bar of the Guards Club and bemoaning the fact that the Club would close soon if more members could not be found. They were then joined by the former Prime Minster, Sir Anthony Eden, who said that the Club would never close, but would probably end up amalgamating with the Cavalry Club. How right he turned out to be!

One of the unwritten rules of the Guards Club was that members were never in the Club should a lady telephone – and most certainly not when that lady was the member's wife! This led to many confusing and humorous incidents over the years – made more difficult on at least one occasion for the Club staff when, having been told that her husband was not at the Club, the lady in question arrived in a cab at the door some ten minutes later and demanded to see the member who was 'hiding' in the bar! The 'invisibility' of Club staff was never more appropriate than at those times, when we all made a hasty exit!

Members have been known to come into the bar at the Club with the most incredible of stories – none more so than when a very red-faced Colonel Fergus Forbes came dashing in to tell the gathered members that he had been shot at by the police! Slowly, as he was downing a resuscitating pink gin, the story emerged that the police had in fact been chasing another car down Piccadilly when the shots were fired – and that the bullets, having luckily just missed our fortunate Colonel, had lodged themselves in a nearby shop window from where they were later retrieved to be kept framed by the owners – perhaps to remind the Colonel of his lucky escape!

GEOFFREY PRICE

Guards Club and was employed as a coffee boy, serving members in the card room and later working in the dispense bar assisting Fred Peto, the wine waiter. It was not unusual in those days for five or six tables of bridge to be on the go in the afternoon. Geoffrey collected three shillings from each player and wrote their names in a book.

Two years later, the assistant barman departed abruptly. To meet this emergency the Secretary gave instructions to 'put the boy in', and Geoffrey became assistant barman to Johnny Strike, serving drinks at the age of sixteen. So life continued for the next two years. In his spare time Geoffrey, a very accomplished soccer player, played for Hounslow West and was put on the books at West Ham. At the age of eighteen he left for two years of National Service. He had planned to follow his father into the Grenadiers but, due to a foot problem caused by long hours standing on the wooden duckboards behind the bar, he could not join the Foot Guards. He was therefore snapped up by the Royal Army Ordnance Corps who were always on the lookout for high class footballers and boxers.

On returning to the Guards Club he became the second barman in the cocktail bar and well remembers the amazing endurance of a group of wartime friends who met on most weekdays. Pink gin at noon. Claret at lunch. Then the port. At 3pm Johnny and Geoffrey would go off duty. At 5pm the barmen returned whereupon, without a pause, the gathering would switch from port to whisky and soda.

In 1962 Geoffrey married Carole Jones, a charming and very pretty young lady who was a waitress in the ladies' dining room. Then in 1975, when Johnny Strike retired, Geoffrey became head barman and when shortly afterwards the Clubs amalgamated he moved to 127 and took over as head barman, stamping his own style on the job and making it the bar we know today as 'Geoffrey's Bar'.

As Colonel Malcolm Havergal writes, 'I have been lucky enough to have known Geoffrey for most of these fifty years, in good times and in bad for both of us. He remains the same upright, helpful, charming and good-looking character I remember in those far-off days. His beautiful manners have made him a myriad of friends all over the world, all of whom know they can rely on his complete discretion. One of the real pleasures in life is to receive Geoffrey's understated welcome after a long absence.' Geoffrey finally retired after nearly sixty years' service in December 2008.

When I joined the Cavalry Club early in 1949, having for many years been dumped on the sofa in the hall waiting for the school train or for my father to refresh himself, the army – and the cavalry – were in a very different state from the present. Most cavalry regiments were family regiments, which meant that the Club also tended to be a family affair. We all knew each other and knew our brother officers' fathers too, who were often in the Club, making it all rather like going to a well known country house. We knew the staff of old and they knew us. If a backwoodsman from the Welsh marches came on his quinquennial visit, you would see several members of the staff in a huddle poring over the members' list to work out who he was.

My paramount memories of the 1940s, 1950s and 1960s are of the wonderful staff working at the Club. We now have Geoffrey's Bar, and are lucky indeed to have enjoyed his long service, but he took over from Thompson, who joined the Club as a fourteen-year-old boy and, I think, ran the bar from demob until he retired. Then there were the hall porters, Boote and Grey, and Brownie who ran the telephone exchange and carried most members' private numbers in her head. In the Coffee Room, Staples was the head waiter – and a bit frightening to tipsy young officers – and after him Markie. There were many delightful waitresses, some of whom retired only a few years ago. There was also Pat who ran the bar on the ladies' side for many years and stood in for Thompson on occasions. Upstairs were the valets. I always stayed on the fourth floor and the valet there was Lawes. I suspect he had forty years' service when he retired. The smoking room was the preserve of Stringer and Stewart who, like Thompson, knew what we liked to drink and were quick to dispense it. When my father was dying in hospital in London, Stringer asked me whether it would be all right for him to visit him – a visit which meant more to my father than any other. We members must be grateful and proud of the service and friendship we have enjoyed over the years.

CAPTAIN G S HEDLEY

FROM THE BARBER'S CHAIR

The Club has always had the benefit of a traditional barber's shop, located in the basement and providing a much needed service for all those military haircuts.

In the early days this service was provided by Mr Hicks, who retired in August 1959 at the age of seventy-five, having come to the Club in 1934. Some members still remember one of his successors, Mr H W Dobbs, who joined in 1967 and retired in September 1983 after seventeen years. The current barber is Mr Philip Kyriacou (opposite), who writes as follows:

I joined the Club in January 1988. I was headhunted (no pun intended) by Mr David de Pinna, then the Club Secretary. My twenty years as the Club barber have been a happy affair and I've met some really nice people who, and I hope I'm not being presumptuous, have become friends. I consider myself very lucky.

My army experience was two years' National Service with the RASC or, in army parlance, the 'jam stealers'. This consisted of three months' basic training at Blandford Forum, and the remaining time in Paris at SHAPE headquarters. Little did I imagine then that years later I would be telling Generals and Field Marshals to get their hair cut. But then, as I politely point out, in my barber shop I outrank everyone!

I enjoy chatting to the older members, for they all have a story to tell. One member, who lived in Scotland, came to have his hair cut prior to going on holiday. He had been with the LRDG and was subsequently sent to Yugoslavia to fight with the partisans. The group were betrayed and he spent the next two years in Colditz Castle as a prisoner of war. He told me he was driving to Yugoslavia to try to recover some booty which he had hidden. On further questioning he admitted that this was a cache of sovereigns and precious stones which had been 'liberated' and hidden in a cave in the mountains, and that he was determined to try to find them. The problem was that, alongside the treasure, were five dead German soldiers, and if they had been discovered so probably had the booty. He thought it worth the effort. Sadly, I never saw him again so I never knew the outcome. What really struck me about that incident was that he was in his seventies, but he still had the mentality of someone in his twenties. Being a bit of a romantic, I rather hoped that he had indeed recovered his treasure and was seeing out the last few years of his life on some tropical island. I'll never know.

The stories about Boote, head porter at the Club (and the scourge of the younger members), are many, but one tale which I consider worthy of passing on concerned the practice of never disturbing members when a wife telephoned the club. On this occasion a female rang and asked to speak to a very well known member. The usual form was that Boote would say to the caller, 'I'll check to see if he is in the Club', and after a few minutes he would tell the caller that he could not find him and replace the phone. A couple of days later the member asked Boote if he had taken a call from a lady asking for him. 'Yes,' says Boote. 'Well, why didn't you fetch me?' he asked. 'I never do, Colonel,' he replied. 'You don't want to be disturbed by women when you're here in your Club, do you?' The member then told him that Her Majesty was somewhat put out by not being able to speak to him because she knew he *was* in the Club!

127 Piccadilly

'Cries of triumph, mingled with happy sighs of relief, rose from the Hyde Park Corner end of Piccadilly this year when the committee and members of the Cavalry and Guards Club saved their beloved house, number 127, from the threat by its new purchasers to convert it into a hotel.'

J N P Watson, *Country Life*, November 1987

Although the financial rollercoaster that is so typical of London club life has been the cause of numerous headaches for committees over the many years since the purchase of the original lease of 127, one of the positive aspects of this has been that the Club has never had sufficient funds to undertake the sort of major works to the building that could have drastically altered its appearance. Indeed, it is well recorded in minutes of committee meetings held in the 1960s that the Chairman considered that the building was probably going to be demolished at the end of the lease in 1988, and was therefore not worth capital investment at that time.

We must be grateful indeed for this short-sightedness. More appalling would have been a fate like that which befell the Army and Navy Club, who decided to modernise and, flush with financial gains from property, pulled down their beautiful Palladian house in Pall Mall and replaced it with 1960s modernity. They were not the only club to make this mistake, though they were fortunately able to survive the error – unlike the Junior Carlton who, having modernised, failed to find support and closed in 1977.

So although when anticipating the purchase of the Club in 1987 the committee were dismayed to find how much work needed to be done – dilapidations had been estimated in excess of £1.5 million – they can rejoice in the fact that there existed a building on Piccadilly that was true to its architectural creation. Indeed, writing in 1986 to support the upgrading in listing to Grade II*, Anthony Blee of the Sir Basil Spence Partnership wrote, 'We find that in all the significant details the building has remained unaltered since the major remodelling exercise (1908/9) was carried out'.

Piccadilly was not always the fashionable area it has since become, and only 400 years ago was still a semi-rural area on the edge of London. It takes its name from a sixteenth-century draper who lived there and made his fortune from a type of support for the Elizabethan ruff known as a 'pickadil'. People still shot snipe along the hedgerows as late as 1633, when *Gerard's Herbal* recorded that 'small wild flowers do grow upon the drie dytche banks about Pickadilla'.

The first recorded building on the site of 127 was occupied by a watchmaker named Abraham Isaacs, known to have been in residence in 1715 and possibly for some years before that. Although the art of watchmaking was highly regarded in the eighteenth century, Isaacs was little more than a middleman; a contemporary source noted, 'the steel pinions are drawn at the mill so that the

Horse-drawn traffic on west Piccadilly, c 1890.

watchmaker has only to file down the points… The springs are made by a tradesman who does nothing else, and the chains by another. The works are given to the finisher, and the gilder adjusts it to the proper time. The watchmaker puts his name on the plate… though he has not made in his shop the smallest wheel belonging to it.'

By 1759, Horace Walpole could find himself amazed at the rapid development of a neighbourhood which he remembered as the haunt of livery stable keepers and the purveyors of leaden figures: 'I stared today at Piccadilly, like a country squire. There are twenty new stone houses. At first I concluded that all the grooms

Devonport, losing his seat only when Lord Salisbury's Conservatives were ousted by the Liberals under Gladstone in 1892. When Sir John moved from 127 to an apartment in Whitehall Court about 1881, he sold the building to Walter Shoolbred (born 1842), formerly a Captain in the 13th Middlesex Regiment, who also owned a country estate at Wyvis, Ross. Then at some time prior to 1890 it passed into the hands of Captain Weatherall who was to be present at the first committee meeting of the Cavalry Club. How he came to offer it as a home for the Club is unclear, but from that moment its place in the history of London clubs was assured.

The original Club occupied only 127 Piccadilly itself, and was therefore much smaller than the present Club building which also takes in the previous houses at 125 and 126 Piccadilly. The layout of the original building was not very different from the west section of the Club today. There was a much smaller hall, and the morning room was the principal room facing Piccadilly, with two smoking rooms to the rear of the building and gentlemen's lavatories opposite the principal staircase. On the first floor was a somewhat smaller Coffee Room overlooking Piccadilly, with a committee room and a library to the rear. There is no record of what specific use the rooms on the second, third and fourth floors were put to, but from the original plans all of these rooms were of a generous size. A small building to the rear of the Club (and approximately one half of the existing mews/annexe buildings) was for the use of staff and was linked only at basement level. The basement comprised the kitchens to the rear of the building and other rooms identified as steward's room, housekeeper's room, larder and servants' hall.

So the alterations in 1908/9 were not so much to change the layout of the building, but rather to expand and enhance it. This exercise was skilfully accomplished by Charles Mewes and Arthur Davis, the renowned Edwardian architects. We are indebted to a 1915 issue of the *Architectural Review* for an appraisal of their work (see box overleaf). It is this building that the Club is fortunate to occupy today, very little changed in the ensuing years, although individual rooms have had new functions from time to time. Perhaps the room that has seen more changes than any other is the one at the front of the Club originally referred to as the morning room. After the 1909 refurbishment, it became the waiting room where male guests of members were expected to await the arrival of their hosts; then it became the tape room, then the card room and then, when demand for gaming dropped, an administrative office in 1976. It was rescued from this unbefitting fate in 2005 when it was returned to members' use as a library and business room. ▶ 118

that used to live there had got estates and built palaces.' And by 1796 the auctioneer James Daniels lived in the building where 127 now stands, followed in 1823 by one William Gunstone who used the premises as a lodging house; this business was afterwards acquired by Mrs Isabella Moffat and then by William Yates, who ran it until the demolition of the building in 1875.

The new dwelling then erected on the site by the architect A Croft was sold to Sir John Henry Puleston (1830–1908), one of HM Lieutenants of the City of London, Constable of Caernarfon Castle and Chairman of the City of London Conservative Association. For eighteen years from 1874, Puleston sat as MP for

Messrs Mewes and Davis were called in as architects to carry out an extension which embraced two houses on the eastern side of the original Club premises (125 and 126 Piccadilly).

It was decided to leave intact the old front of the building and to follow the same design in the new portion, though we could have wished that Messrs Mewes and Davis might have recast the whole facade, which would then have been stamped with the graceful and scholarly character which distinguishes their work. In carrying out the alterations a bay window was added to the design at either end, below the first floor balcony, and the portico was extended so that the entrance door came in the centre.

The interior of the Club is of considerable architectural interest. The decorative work of Adam character is very pleasing. The walls of all the principal rooms bear panels formed by plaster mouldings, and by way of enrichment there are well designed friezes and appropriate chimneypieces; soft tones of colouring being adopted throughout.

From the vestibule one enters the outer hall, where the new work embracing marble columns and pilasters and a floor of black and white marble squares is clearly distinguishable. This leads into a large staircase hall. Here is a prominent relic of the old Georgian house (sic), in the form of a delicate balustrading in wrought iron with a mahogany handrail. This staircase extends up to the third floor (sic), but the original appearance has been seriously altered by the nineteenth-century changes in its embellishments which embrace an ill-digested arrangement of square columns, figure panels of 'sugary' character and over all a clumsily contrived skylight. The staircase at the Cavalry Club is thoroughly strong yet extremely light and it has a pleasing effect. To the right of the vestibule on the ground floor is the morning room, and on the left beyond the outer hall is a pleasant little writing room, while the whole of the rear portion on this floor is apportioned to three smoking rooms. Of recent years the Club has provided accommodation for ladies, and it will be observed from the ground-floor plan that there is a separate ladies' entrance on the east side, leading into a hall where a lift gives access to the dining and sitting rooms on the second floor. It is a point worth mentioning that the architects have contrived a fine architectural shape in this hall, the treatment being repeated in the lobby above, where medallions of classical figure subjects surrounded by garland wreaths have an excellent decorative effect on the walls.

Proceeding to the first floor of the Club, we find here that the whole front is occupied by the Coffee Room, at either end of which are two carved pine chimneypieces of William Kent style. The other main rooms on the first floor are the library, wherein hangs Mr Dollman's picture of Captain Oates. Adjoining the library is the private dining room (used for regimental dinners of the Club) where one may note three fine glass chandeliers, two of which were in the original Georgian house, the third having been added at the time of the recent extension.

The Club does not offer any spectacular effects… but good taste is noticeable in the architectural treatment of all the rooms and much ingenuity has been displayed by the architects in so adapting the plan that their extension does not give the impression of an addition, but embodies a homogeneous arrangement for the entire building.

ARCHITECTURAL REVIEW, VOL 37, 1915

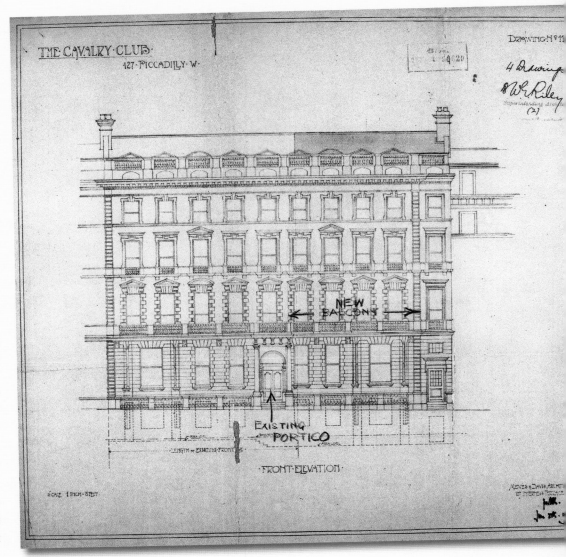

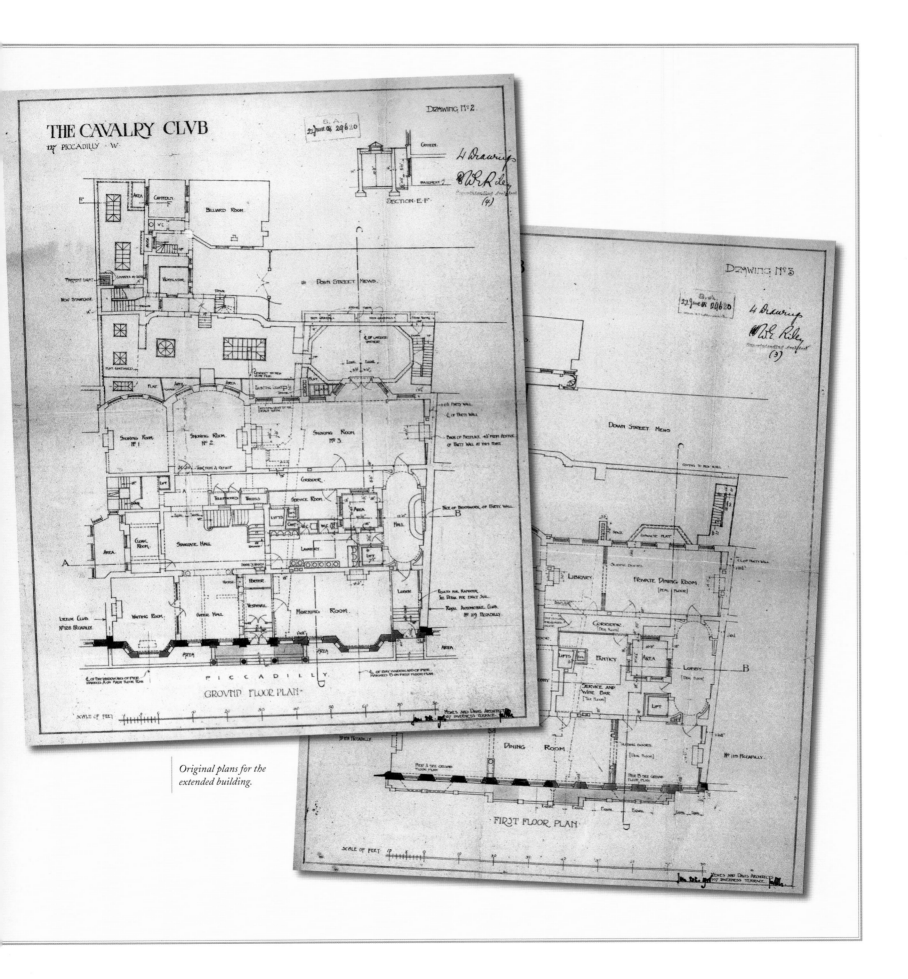

Original plans for the extended building.

THE UNDERGROUND AND DOWN STREET STATION

In the last years of the nineteenth century, when the Cavalry Club was still in its infancy and settling into its home on Piccadilly, attention was diverted from the day-to-day problems associated with the formation of a new – and popular – Club to matters which, while close to home, also had wider implications for the expanding capital city.

The Club's concerns related to plans for the running of a railway beneath Piccadilly to facilitate the expansion of the embryonic 'tube' system. As early as 11 February 1897 it was noticed with some alarm that 'It would appear from the Sutton Estate petition that the back entrance (of the Club) is likely to be stopped up or seriously affected. We imagine that the possession of a back entrance is of vital importance to the Club.' The 'evil of the existence of a station at the back of the Club' would have to be contemplated.

Much of 1897 was spent in petitioning against the Brompton and Piccadilly Circus Railway Bill, with the Trustees making the case that 'a very considerable sum of money has been expended upon the Club premises in altering and adapting them for the purposes' as justification for demanding that their calm on Piccadilly should not be disturbed. In the event, the Brompton and Piccadilly Circus Railway Act 1897 did indeed contain a clause for the protection of the Cavalry Club (section 68). Some of the concern was therefore alleviated, although it was still noted that the proposed line ran 'just inside the railings of Green Park, some twenty-five yards from the Club's entrance'.

However, and perhaps because it was such a major project, the mechanics of Parliament ran slowly and the whole matter was still being widely debated at the turn of the century. At one time, in early 1902, there were five railways competing for the right to run lines under Piccadilly and the possibility existed that two railway lines would be allowed (the second being the Central London line running from Hammersmith to the City); but this was discounted by the Royal Commission set up to oversee the implementation of the project.

In 1902 the Club accounts show that the not inconsiderable sum of £76 5s 8d was spent by the Club's lawyers, Lee & Pemberton, in petitioning the government to ensure that liabilities for damage were on the table; and much of the beginning of 1903 was taken up with correspondence with various parties, both influential and political, about the proposed new railway running along Piccadilly.

The result was The Great Northern Piccadilly and Brompton Railway (Various Powers) Act of 1903, which took 'certain lands houses and premises being portions of premises known as Nos 23 and 24 Down Street Piccadilly and stables and stable yard situated in Down Street Mews adjacent thereto', to create the station to be known as Down Street. The Act also ensured that 'The Company shall not construct under such premises or any part thereof any tunnel or work of which any part shall be within seventy feet from the surface of the street level... nor shall the Company take or interfere with the user of the cellars or offices belonging to any of the houses Nos 117 118 119 125 126 and 127 Piccadilly.'

The underground line then began construction and Down Street station opened on 15 March 1907, three months after the rest of this section of the Piccadilly line. Its distinctive facade of ox-blood red bricks, designed by Leslie Green, is still in place today. It was never very busy, however, both because it was close to the larger stations at Hyde Park Corner and Dover Street (now Green Park) and because it attracted few users from the wealthy residents of the area. It closed, therefore, in May 1932, and its demise must have been under discussion for some years before this since it never appeared on the Harry Beck tube maps with which we remain so familiar today. These were issued in 1933, but Down Street is missing even from the prototype produced in 1931.

Map of the Underground, 1908.

The closure caused new concerns within the Club about the development of the site; and in 1936 a committee minute records that 'Brigadier General Harbord suggested that enquiries be made with regard to the possibility of using the site formerly occupied by the Down Street tube station for the erection of a squash court'. However, the opportunity had been taken to demolish part of the platform to allow the construction of new sidings, and so the station remained as it was until the onset of the Second World War, when a disused tube station was an obvious location for a deep shelter for use by government offices.

Part of Down Street station was therefore adapted, with the provision of office and bathroom facilities (still there today) and a telephone exchange. It was mainly used by the Emergency Railway Committee, but was also an occasional refuge for Winston Churchill and his War Cabinet when the Cabinet War Rooms were unavailable. Churchill is reported as liking his stays there because he slept well. He was perhaps luckier than some Club members, who even to this day complain that sleep is impossible in the basement bedrooms due to the noisy 'lullaby' of the Piccadilly line. More than once, the Secretary's advice has been that an additional nightcap in the bar might aid the member's slumber – a suggestion which quite a number of members have taken up.

London Transport Executive meeting in a room in the disused Down Street Underground station during the Second World War.

In 1921, with the building of the annexe (3 Down Street Mews), the decision was taken to extend the smallest smoking room and create a bar that would face the terrace, still there and now known affectionately as Geoffrey's Bar. Perhaps fortunately, in view of later developments, it did not link with the new annexe buildings in any other way; though it was frustrating for members, when bedroom accommodation was eventually provided in the annexe in the 1950s, that the only means of access was across the terrace in all weathers, and the only recognition of this was the building of a wind trap outside the smoking room doors in 1954 to prevent draughts in the main clubhouse.

The annexe, 3 Down Street Mews, has its own history. The area of land behind the buildings on this stretch of Piccadilly was originally known as the Running Horse Livery Yard and was connected with the tavern of that name on the site of the current RAF Club. As the buildings on Piccadilly were upgraded into smart town houses, so the area at the rear was used for both stabling and carriage houses, and in the mews dwellings would live the coachmen and grooms, servants of the households on Piccadilly.

Photographs taken of 127 Piccadilly in 1909.

By the early twentieth century the area at the rear of the Cavalry Club was named Down Street Mews, and minutes of a committee meeting in 1912 record complaints that had arisen from the barking of dogs in the kennel in the mews established by the United Travellers and Counties Club, and that steps were being taken by the landlords to obviate the nuisance. Indeed, a later injunction was taken against this club using the premises as a kennel.

In 1914 the committee was asked to consider the advisability of the purchase of the lease of the stables in Down Street Mews. Although this idea was shelved for a couple of years, in 1919 the committee decided to go ahead and hired an architect, Mr Wright, to undertake the rebuilding. These works were completed in 1921 and the Club was now able to house servants over three floors of accommodation, with additional storage in the basement which was to be used for wine.

However, the constant demand for more members' accommodation meant that at various times over the next thirty years some of the bedrooms were used on a temporary basis by members. In 1954 it was decided to formalise the situation and have members' bedrooms put in the annexe. Anthony O'Connor, Club Secretary, recalls: 'Two years earlier the committee said they wanted more bedrooms and I suggested that we might be able to make six bedrooms for members in the staff block. They would be very useful for short stayers at a time when bedroom accommodation in the West End was at a premium. The block was situated behind the main building and obviously built for servants, with barred windows on the ground floor, bare concrete stairways and severe cell-like bedrooms, housing two occupants. I knocked down some walls and created six presentable bedrooms, two bathrooms and two toilets which I thought members would appreciate.'

Rallying cry goes out to old guard

THE Cavalry and Guards Club at 127 Piccadilly, threatened with closure on the expiry of its lease in 1988, will be saved if it can raise £3½ million to buy the freehold of its fine 18th-century building, it was disclosed yesterday.

After months of negotiation the club has struck a deal with the Stockley property group which bought the freehold a year ago and which, many feared, had plans to turn the building into a luxury hotel.

Now the Cavalry and Guards' 3,000 members—both serving and retired officers from the guards and cavalry regiments, are being asked to find the money. Their first deadline comes in March when contracts will be exchanged and the preliminary "substantial" payment will hopefully be transferred.

Yesterday Major General John Strawson, the club's chairman who has led the intensive negotiations with Stockley, told me: "We are delighted that the company has given us the chance to buy the place. Now it is up to the members to find the money. We have written to them all, asking them to respond generously."

Saving the Cavalry and Guards has become something of a *cause célèbre* among the members since Stockley first acquired the freehold. At one stage the help of the Prince of Wales was successfully sought in the members' attempts to keep the place.

Newspaper clipping from the Daily Telegraph, *24 October 1986.*

Thus it was to remain for over forty years, with the number of bedrooms in the 1970s being increased to eleven, with additional and separate bathroom facilities. Then by the early 1990s, and following the purchase of the freehold in 1987, it was apparent that the building in Down Street needed urgent attention if it was not to fall into complete disrepair. But at the same time the Club's many priorities in the main building meant that it was impossible to fund these works. Such financial constraints, however, did not impress the local authorities who considered the staff accommodation almost 'condemnable', and required the Club to spend at least £50,000 in the late 1990s to improve, in a very basic way, this amenity for the staff. Committees continued to be perplexed by the dilemma the building created and still had no funds for the works that were needed. In November 1997, executive committee member Peter Jones tabled a proposal for flats on the site, but concluded that not only would the development costs be prohibitive, but also, in his opinion, the value of 127 would be seriously reduced. The committee also considered the cost of alternative hostel accommodation for the staff, or indeed increasing the Club wage bill to pay a 'live-out type' wage to those staff currently resident; fortuitously, although the staff were not moved out, the latter course was chosen, making an eventual 'eviction' more possible.

Peter Jones went on to advise the committee that no development would give a sufficient return without the need for long leases, and that the possibility of borrowing money to furnish lettings could also be investigated; but the cost of preparing the proposals alone could be in the region of £40,000–50,000. For the present it seemed best to improve and redecorate the accommodation where and when possible.

However, by the early twenty-first century it was becoming increasingly apparent that the luxury of keeping Club staff resident in Mayfair was just that, and a better use for the space had to be found if it was to benefit the Club. At the same time, the Vigors report in 2004 identified the possibility that Club membership might decline precipitately over the next decade, and there was also a growing rumbling among the members that the clubhouse on Piccadilly might be too large for the requirements of a smaller membership. A solution really had to be found.

The committee reviewed several ideas, but it seemed that a sale of the property was the only clear option, which would then provide funds for repaying debt and for undertaking works to the main building. Following the agreement of the membership, obtained at an EGM in January 2006, it was decided to market the site to prospective buyers, and this took place throughout the summer of 2006.

However, there was still one problem to overcome. Over the years the Club had had several opportunities both to purchase the land of Down Street Mews and to improve their access rights, but had been content with the status quo and had not considered the cost to be justified in relation to other more pressing financial demands. Inevitably this now presented a challenge, as the current owners of the mews, Charleswood Estates, woke up to the financial implications of improved access for 3 Down Street Mews. In the end negotiations proved to be a mixed blessing and the cost to the Club was substantial (£1.3m), but the delay meant that the sale took place at the top of a volatile London property market and the final price was £5 million, netting the Club over £3.6 million – more than the purchase price of the entire property some twenty years earlier. So on 31 July 2007 the sale was concluded and the property that had been an integral, though worrisome, part of Club life for nearly 100 years was gone.

Meanwhile, however, the Cavalry and Guards Club had been able to take the momentous step of purchasing the freehold of 127 Piccadilly, thus ensuring that members would continue to enjoy the splendid ambience of their clubhouse for the foreseeable future. The story of the campaign to buy the freehold is a saga in itself (see pages 122–3); and the Chairman who oversaw it all, John Strawson, has his own take on those fraught years (see his 'View from the Chair', page 124). But the result is perhaps the final acknowledgement of the foresight of the members of the Cavalry Club of a century ago when they undertook the extension and refurbishment of their beautiful building. □

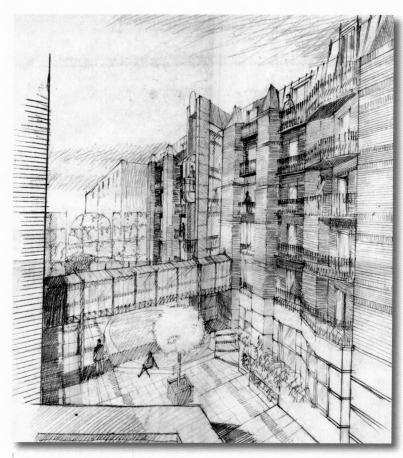

Plan of the proposed hotel development – terrace and annexe building.

THE PURCHASE OF THE FREEHOLD

This account covers the period from Stockley plc acquiring the freehold in the spring of 1984 until the Club purchased the freehold on 30 April 1987. There were several phases in the campaign and they might be described like this:

- discovering the situation and determining the aim, ie what were Stockley's intentions and what were the members' wishes
- an exercise designed to persuade Stockley not to apply for development planning permission, but rather to be prepared to discuss either selling the freehold or renewing the lease
- meetings and negotiations with Stockley to establish their conditions for selling, ie price, how to be paid, over what period
- after agreement on price and timescale had been reached, raising sufficient money from members etc

Throughout this process, the specially formed action group conferred frequently, as did the main committee. It was also necessary continually to consult members and obtain their endorsement of the various proposals. This was done by newsletters, sitreps, special letters and Annual and Extraordinary Meetings.

Between the autumn of 1984 and June 1985, four significant things became clear:

1. Stockley said they intended to apply for planning permission to develop 127 Piccadilly as a hotel, and they sought the Club's collaboration in this project (possibly with the carrot of a financial incentive)
2. The value of the property used as a Club was judged by the Club's advisors to be in the region of £3m
3. It was plain that a substantial end of lease dilapidations liability would have to be met if the Club were to preserve its right to renew the lease (estimated in early discussions at £1.85 million)
4. Most importantly, at the AGM in June 1985, members expressed the firm wish to remain in 127 Piccadilly and not seek alternative accommodation

The campaign to persuade Stockley not to apply for planning permission but rather to negotiate with the Club lasted from June 1985 until the end of that year. This comprised many activities:

- newspaper and magazine articles by sympathetic diarists etc
- upgrading 127 Piccadilly to a Grade II* listed building (confirmed on 6 February 1986)
- letters and talks to Stockley's top people by influential sympathisers
- discussion with Westminster City Councillors and officials
- preparation of a legal case for objecting to the threatened hotel development
- employing the services of a PR company
- formation of The Cavalry and Guards Property Ltd by guarantee with a view to raising finance for the freehold purchase through the offer of two sorts of debentures

The result of it all was that in January 1986 a meeting was arranged between Stockley's Chief Executive and the Club's Chairman to investigate whether common ground existed which might lead to the sale and purchase of the freehold.

Guards Club share offer

Members of the Cavalry and Guards Club were yesterday given one month to find £3,250,000 to secure the club's future by buying the freehold of its 1760 building in Piccadilly.

The 3,000 serving and retired officers from the Guards and Cavalry regiments will today receive details of an offer to buy shares in a specially formed new company before the lease on the Piccadilly building runs out next year.

The negotiations with Stockley were complicated and prolonged, not least because their initial viewpoint seemed to be that the Club was not a viable player. Elliott Bernerd, their representative, was reported as dismissing, in fairly insulting terms, the Club's ability to pay. During the negotiations the advice and assistance of representatives of Gerald Eve & Co, Chartered Surveyors, were of profound importance and value. Discussions continued from January 1986 until October of that year, when agreement in principle was reached with Stockley to buy the freehold at the end of March 1987 for the sum of £3.25m (down from an original asking price of £4m), payable in three instalments, starting on completion and with further payments on 31 December 1987 and 30 September 1988. The contract would contain provisions as to interest and security.

To raise the money, the Club was fortunate in having the cooperation and participation of the bankers County Ltd. In October 1986 pledges of support were sought from members in relation to subscription debentures, in order to satisfy County Ltd that a debenture offer would be justified. About one-third of the membership pledged roughly £1.4m. This was clearly inadequate, and it was then decided to add an additional security related to the value of the property. In February 1987, after a period of intensive study of a number of legal and tax difficulties leading to the abandonment of the guarantee company and the substitution of a plc (originally registered with the rather appropriate name of Equalgallop plc), County Ltd issued the appropriate prospectus accompanied by notice of an EGM to be held in the Club in late March. By mid-March 1987 half the membership had subscribed about £2m. Stockley was then asked, and agreed, to an extension of one month for completion, ie until 30 April, to allow time to raise more money, but would then require the full, though slightly reduced, purchase price of £3.2m in one payment. This change was endorsed by the EGM, a further appeal to members was sent out and by 23 April £2.4m was available.

Lloyds Bank agreed to a twenty-year secured loan of £750,000 on the basis of certain undertakings by the Club to dispose of some assets and 'to keep the real value of subscriptions in line with inflation', and to an additional short-term facility to allow completion of the freehold purchase on 30 April 1987. In the event, a private loan of £250,000 (repayable over a period of years) received in October 1987 meant that the loan could immediately be reduced to £500,000.

Money was also raised from other sources, including loans from the Grenadier, Coldstream and Scots Guards who all gave £10,000, from the Welsh Guards who gave £4,000 and the Household Division who gave a further £10,000. These loans were for a period of ten years and were paid back in the late 1990s. A sale of pictures carried out in the months after the completion of the purchase helped to reduce indebtedness by netting some £100,000. The pictures sold included *A Portrait of Daniel Mackinnon* by George Dawe (£9,000), *Napoleon's Last Grand Attack* by Ernest Crofts (£26,000) and *A Portrait of Sir Robert Baden Powell* by Sir Hubert von Herkomer (£11,000), which perhaps found a more fitting home in the National Portrait Gallery. Similarly, the sale of the library, which Sotheby's had estimated at around £50,000, realised £57,650 less expenses, and the library bookcases raised a further £10,000.

When it was all in place and the purchase was completed, the Chairman issued the following statement:

'On 30 April 1987, the freehold of 127 Piccadilly and 3 Down Street Mews was purchased from Stockley by 127 Piccadilly plc, a company established by the Club. This milestone in the Club's history was achieved largely by the generosity of members, who subscribed approximately £2.3 million in response to an issue of debentures and preferred shares by 127 Piccadilly plc. The remainder of the purchase price of £3.2 million was provided by donations and loans from members and well-wishers, and by a twenty-year bank loan of £750,000 provided by Lloyds Bank plc.

'The purchase of the freehold of our buildings is a magnificent achievement, which secures the Club's future. The servicing and repayment of the bank loan, together with the future maintenance and improvements of 127, will, however, represent a significant call on Club funds. Your committee believes that it will be necessary, in order to keep the Club's finances on a sound footing, both to raise a limited amount of additional capital through the sale of property, and to increase the subscription income. Accordingly your committee proposes:

1. to set a target for realisations of Club assets of £100,000 to be achieved by September 1987 (this target should be achieved by disposal of books from the library, together with one or two paintings)
2. to increase subscriptions from non-serving members, as explained at the EGM held on March 1987, by 50% from 1 January 1988, and thereafter to maintain the real value of subscription income by means of annual increases in line with inflation

'Your Committee considers that both these measures are essential if the benefits of purchasing the freehold of 127 are to be consolidated.'

VIEW FROM THE CHAIR

MAJOR GENERAL JOHN STRAWSON, CHAIRMAN 1984–7

The story of how the Club acquired the freehold of 127 Piccadilly is told elsewhere in this book, and I will confine myself here to recalling a few memorable incidents during my three years as Chairman.

The first thing I discovered was that I had no chair. There was no Chairman's office, not even a desk in the Secretary's domain. As it was clear that a good deal of letter writing and telephoning would be necessary, this deficiency was corrected by setting up desk, telephone with dedicated line and secretarial help in one corner of David de Pinna's office. It was just as well, for I found that the campaign to retain 127 Piccadilly demanded my presence there more frequently than I had expected.

I recall vividly at my first AGM the disagreeable sensation of having little notion of how to set about the task before me. Happily however, sound advice was forthcoming from Club members who were experts in property, legal and financial matters. The first thing we needed to know was whether Stockley plc, the new freehold owners, would be willing to sell. My first meeting with Stockley's Chief Executive established that they were so willing – but at a price! A figure was named quite beyond our capacity. The problem therefore became one of moderating that figure to a level both realistic from our point of view and compatible with the property world's view of sound business.

Much of the work which our campaign required was undertaken by an action group composed of Tom Hall, John Stanier, Jeremy Stephens, Jonny Hok, Ian Frazer, David Barclay, John Rodwell, Peter Jones, Philip Ward and David de Pinna. We would meet regularly to discuss progress and sometimes lunch together with a guest whose advice we sought. These gatherings were both agreeable and fruitful, and enabled us to report to the main Club committee and obtain their sanction for further action. I found that many Club members offered help by letter, and our guests at lunch included a great variety of experts, ranging from the Governor of the Bank of England to the Chairman of Westminster City Council, and the Chief Superintendent in charge of traffic at Scotland Yard.

So the campaign got under way. With the aid of English Heritage, Westminster City Council and certain manipulators of the media it was possible both to upgrade 127 Piccadilly's listed status, thus restricting its use, and to establish in certain quarters of the banking, property, legal, social and even royal worlds the desirability of the Cavalry and Guards Club continuing to be where it was. A sort of PR offensive was launched and seemed to bear fruit. Meanwhile, further discussions with Stockley eventually yielded agreement as to a figure which would satisfy the dual requirements of realism as to valuation and ability to raise the necessary funds.

Now the crucial business of raising the money began; everything depended on the generosity of Club members, plus the willingness of banks to make good a deficiency should there be one. Our first shot at raising the money did not succeed in producing enough, so a further appeal to members was launched. Happily this time further instalments raised us to the point where banks were able to fill the gap. At this particular meeting I remember that my microphone ceased to function at an important moment and I was obliged to raise my voice, which I trust had some effect on raising the sum of money which members subsequently came up with.

A visit to the City where County Bank confirmed their willingness to fill the gap sticks in my mind as a time of great relief and gratitude to all those who had made it possible for us to remain at 127 Piccadilly. I need hardly add that during all this campaign the loyalty, confidence and efficiency of the Club staff were of infinite value. The successful conclusion of our campaign was celebrated with a cocktail party for our supporters which was graced by the attendance of our President, HRH The Duke of Kent.

Clubs in Piccadilly

Writing in 1920, Arthur Dansent noted that, 'the gradual relinquishment on the part of private owners of once-coveted sites overlooking the Green Park has left less than a dozen private houses between Devonshire House and Hyde Park Corner. These are far outnumbered by clubs, social, political, diplomatic, literary, naval and military, by clubs admitting ladies (and even dogs) as guests.' To the founders of the Cavalry Club, part of the appeal of 127 Piccadilly would certainly have been the neighbourhood in which they found themselves. These were the other clubs that could be found all along Piccadilly.

36 – FLYFISHERS

The Flyfishers' Club, founded in 1884, started its life in the Arundel Hotel, Norfolk Street, before moving to Haymarket in 1899 and then relocating to number 36 (on the corner of Swallow Street), where it remained until it was bombed out in 1941. Since then it

has had a rather peripatetic life, and currently resides with the Savile Club in Brook Street, although in 1994 an approach was made by the Flyfishers' Club, then looking to relocate from Buck's, for a home at 127. Randle Cooke, then a general committee member in charge of 'fishing', oversaw the negotiations, which were seen as an opportunity to diversify the membership base. The Balaclava Room in 127 was suggested as a possible clubroom (with a table for ten separately provided in the Coffee Room), but after brief consideration the discussion came to nothing.

81 – ROYAL THAMES YACHT CLUB

This house was originally the site of Crockford's before his move to 50 St James's Street, and had then returned to use as a private residence before being taken by the RTYC in the early part of the twentieth century. Founded in 1775, the Royal Thames Yacht Club is the second oldest yacht club in the world. It originally had no real clubhouse but was based in the tea gardens opposite Vauxhall, and received its 'royal' appellation when its patron, the Duke of Clarence, came to the throne as William IV. Its first clubhouse in 1857 was at 49 St James's Street (a former home of the Guards Club), and after eight years it moved to Albemarle Street before settling in Piccadilly and then in 1923 acquiring the freehold of Hyde Park House, its current home at 60 Knightsbridge.

85 – THE TURF

Founded in 1861, the Turf Club began life as the Arlington, with premises in Bennett Street, Piccadilly, formerly the town house of the Dukes of Grafton. It was there that members drew up the laws of whist. Members had originally wished to call themselves simply 'The Club' until they discovered that that name had already been claimed around 100 years earlier for the famous dining society founded by Dr Johnson and Sir Joshua Reynolds. It had been suggested in 1963 that the Turf might possibly amalgamate with the Cavalry Club, or that the Cavalry Club might be interested in purchasing number 85; but the building was half the size of 127, with no bedrooms on site, though there were some in a separate building in Clarges Street. So in 1965 the Turf Club moved to its current home at 5 Carlton House Terrace, overlooking the Mall.

Left: A statue from the Flyfishers' Club.

of the richest men in the country, he was a great sportsman and master of the Quorn for many years; he is said to have spent the enormous total of £300,000 on fox hunting during his life. He died at Cambridge House in November 1855, and shortly afterwards the house received perhaps its most notable tenant, Lord Palmerston.

The Naval and Military Club spent over 100 years in the premises before the relinquishment of its lease in 1999, when it moved to 4 St James's Square, which had been the London home of Nancy Astor and her husband. In order to commemorate its previous nickname, the words 'In' and 'Out' still appear on either side of the entrance to the new premises, although there is now only one way in or out of the building.

95 – AMERICAN CLUB

The American Club was founded in 1919 with a membership of 200 London residents of American birth and 100 associate British members. The house, 95 Piccadilly, with its entrance on White Horse Street, had been built in 1883 and was previously the home of Sir Bertram and Lady Falle. Lady Falle was a Boston woman who was glad to sell the remainder of the seventy-seven-year lease to her compatriots.

94 – NAVAL AND MILITARY

The Naval and Military, better known as the 'In and Out' because of the conspicuous signs on its stone gateposts, was the first club to move to Piccadilly. It was founded in 1862 by three officers of the Buffs, because the three military clubs in London then in existence had no further membership capacity. Originally based in Clifford Street, and then in Hanover Square, the club moved to 94 Piccadilly at the end of 1865 and opened in the following April. On the renewal of the lease in 1876, the structure was enlarged with a new dining room, billiards rooms, offices and cellars.

The house had a distinguished history. Built in 1760 for the second Earl of Egremont, it then became home to the Marquis of Cholmondeley before becoming a royal residence when it was acquired by the Duke of Cambridge, a son of George III. On his death in 1850, Sir Richard Sutton, the ground landlord of all this part of Piccadilly, came to live there. In addition to being one

100 – THE PUBLIC SCHOOLS CLUB

The Public Schools Club was formed in 1909 at premises in Albemarle Street before a large membership (with a waiting list of over 2,000) forced a move to larger premises at 19 Berkeley Street. However, no fewer than 800 members were killed in action or died of wounds during the Great War (the highest number of any London club), and it was forced into voluntary liquidation. In 1920 it reopened in Curzon Street where it remained for seventeen years before settling at 100 Piccadilly in 1937 after acquiring the lease of the former Badminton Club.

The building, once the town house of the Duke of Beaufort whose country seat, Badminton, gave its name to both the game and the club, had a fine view overlooking Green Park and a self-contained ladies' annexe with a separate entrance from White Horse Street. In 1972 the gates of 100 Piccadilly closed and the club merged with the East India Club in St James's Square.

105 – Isthmian Club

The clubhouse of the Isthmian at 105 Piccadilly has known many vicissitudes. At one time it was the Pulteney Hotel and after that the abode of Lord Hertford. Subsequently the house passed into the hands of Sir Julian Goldsmid, a noted art collector who remained in residence until his death in 1896. The Isthmian had been nicknamed the 'Creche' since it was originally founded as a club for public school men, some of whom were very young. Originally in Grafton Street, the Isthmian migrated first to Walsingham House (the site of the Ritz Hotel in Piccadilly) and then to number 105.

106 – St James's Club

The St James's Club was first established in a wing of Crockford's former premises in St James's Street under the management of one of the Crockford family, and when it came to Piccadilly in 1869 it retained its old name. Its membership had strong connections with the diplomatic service, and consequently embraced many who had an intimate knowledge of foreign countries. The clubhouse at 106 Piccadilly was formerly the abode of the Coventry Club, a somewhat bohemian institution founded in the early 1850s where there was a good deal of gambling and a free supper for the gamesters. The building and the club took their name from the Earl of Coventry who had bought the house in 1764, at which time it was the only mansion standing to the west of Devonshire House. The Coventry Club, despite the amusements it offered, was short-lived and closed in 1854, after which it became the residence of the French Ambassador before the St James's Club moved in.

During the Second World War the St James's took in the Bachelors' Club, whose own house at the end of Piccadilly, on the corner of Hamilton Place, had been requisitioned; and in 1946 the amalgamation of the two clubs became permanent. This influx of members was, however, not enough to make the club viable, so finally in 1975 the St James's Club merged with Brooks's 'bringing with it the Dilettanti Society (and their fabulous picture collection), its own card accountant and Johnny, the much-loved barman'.

107 – The Savile

The Savile Club had its origins in a group of rebels against traditional Victorian clubland in 1868. Called 'The New Club', it started life in rooms in the Medical Club just off Trafalgar Square. It soon attracted other like-minded members who relished its informality and friendliness, and this growing membership necessitated a

move to larger premises at 15 Savile Row, a location which gave the club its name. Even more space was needed by 1885, when the Savile moved to 107 Piccadilly (shown above), where the club thrived until 1927 when a combination of the need for more space plus the increasingly parlous state of the building prompted another move to 69 Brook Street.

Its varied membership has embraced luminaries of literary London such as Robert Louis Stevenson, Thomas Hardy, H G Wells, Rudyard Kipling, Compton Mackenzie, Max Beerbohm and W B Yeats among others, while Arthur Bliss, William Walton and Edward Elgar have represented music, and science has found its advocates in Lord Kelvin, John Cockcroft and Lord Rutherford.

Rising wage costs are the real bogey. The servant-worm did not turn slowly, he did half a dozen somersaults and demanded wages pertaining to those outside. 'Iniquitous', say the members. 'They are serving gentlemen! Surely that should more than compensate for the difference in pay? After all money isn't everything and do we not look after them when they are old?' 'I think,' says the Club accountant, sitting behind a pile of figures, brows furrowed and nose wrinkled, 'that subscriptions will have to go up!' 'Aha!' shouts a member who owns half a county in the Midlands, 'I knew that was coming up. Always subscriptions, always trying to soak us!' He glares at the accountant who replies meekly, 'That is the only answer'. 'Damned nonsense!' comes a Wagnerian bellow from the body of the smoke-filled room, 'damned nonsense! I'll have to resign if subscriptions go up again. Bloody staff don't know when they're well off!'

In 1952 (sic) the Royal Aero Club gave hospitality to members of the Cavalry Club. They seemed to enjoy the atmosphere, particularly the grouchy old Field Marshal, Sir Philip (later Lord) Chetwode, who was Chairman of the Cavalry Club and had ruled it with an iron but unsuccessful fist. It was fast going downhill. I believe he had been in the chair for seventeen years and none dared suggest moving him. He was out of date with the times.

John Betjeman once told me that, when he became engaged to Chetwode's daughter, a discussion took place as to how he should address his future father-in-law. 'Sir Philip', said the Field Marshal, 'sounds too ponderous, and I could not let you call me Philip. Let's settle for Field Marshal.' 'And,' said John, 'that's how it remained. I never called him anything!'

Bill Allenby told me that he had been on the committee for two years before daring to utter. He eventually prepared a little spiel and stood up at the committee table to have his word. For two minutes he spoke and then sat down. There was no comment, except from the Field Marshal who, ignoring him completely, remarked, 'Well gentlemen, as I was saying!'

Most gentlemen's clubs in the West End practised the false economy of employing retired colonels or retired Navy paymasters as secretaries. They gave them a room in the club, the run of their teeth (sic), made them honorary members and paid them a nominal salary. Very fine for the old commanders and colonels but hopeless for the members!

After a search I found the Club kitchens, brilliantly hidden away in a maze of the subterranean corridors that were so adored by Georgian and Victorian architects. They loved their bellies, but if Nash and his contemporaries got a commission to build an establishment, be it a club or a private house, they first of all dug deep holes and put the staff and kitchens into dungeons that can only be described as halfway to hell and gone.

The Annual General Meeting is an occasion for members to meet their committee and criticise their supervision of Club affairs over the previous year. Balance sheets, agendas and books of rules are in abundance; all must come into the open. The attendance is quite often small if the Club is doing well and in the black but, should there be a suggestion that subscriptions or prices are to be increased, the place is packed. Vociferous members wait with bated breath to voice their protests at the damned unfairness of it all!

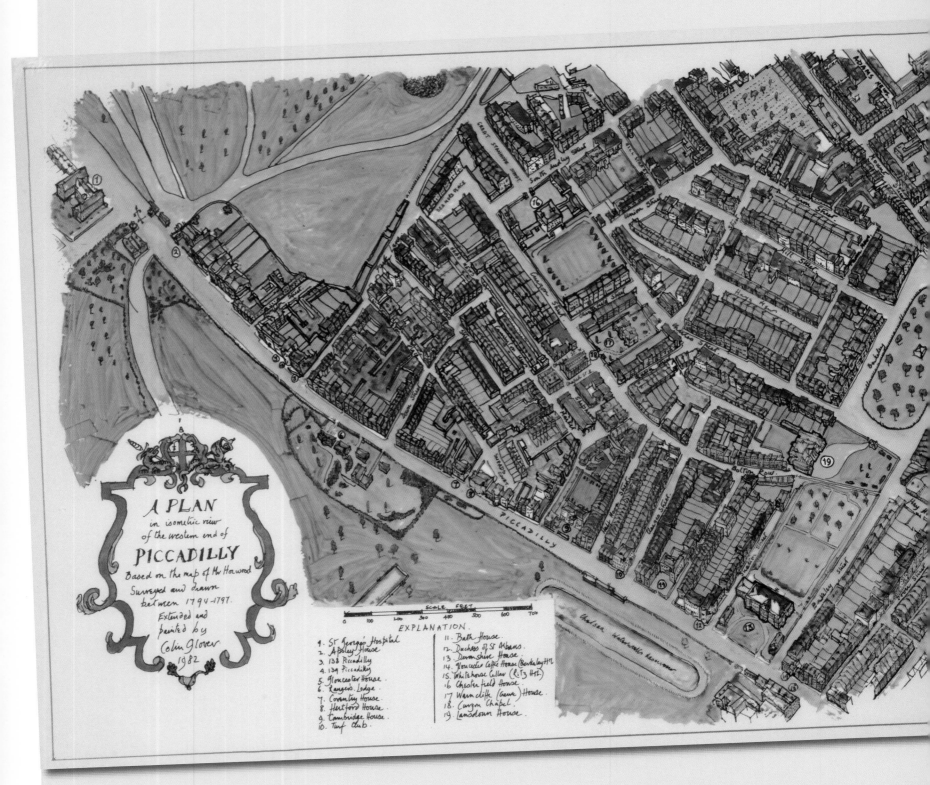

A PLAN
in isometric view
of the western end of
PICCADILLY
Based on the map of Mr Horwood
Surveyed and drawn
between 1794-1797.
Extended and
painted by
Colin Glover
1982

SCALE FEET
0   100   200   300   400   500   600   700

EXPLANATION.

1. St George's Hospital
2. Apsley House
3. 138 Piccadilly
4. 139 Piccadilly
5. Gloucester House.
6. Rangers Lodge.
7. Coventry House.
8. Hertford House.
9. Cambridge House.
10. Turf Club.
11. Bath House.
12. Duchess of St Albans.
13. Devonshire House
14. Gloucester Coffee House (Berkeley Htl.)
15. Whitehorse Cellar (Ritz Htl.)
16. Chesterfield House.
17. Warncliffe (Cuma) House.
18. Curzon Chapel.
19. Lansdown House.

119 – Royal Automobile Club

The Automobile Club, founded in 1897 in four rooms at Whitehall Court, moved in 1902 to the two stone-fronted houses on the west corner of Down Street. King Edward VII agreed in 1903 to become patron of the club, when it added the 'Royal' to its name. In 1908 it acquired the lease of the old War Office in Pall Mall (just along from the Guards Club), and the architects Mewes & Davis constructed what many observers agreed to be the 'last flower from London's great age of club building'. The doors opened to members in 1911.

Relationships with their neighbour in Piccadilly, the Cavalry Club, were generally cordial though a 1908 Cavalry Club committee minute records, 'With reference to a claim by Mr Jenks, owner of the lease of the Automobile Club, for interference with his right of "ancient light", it was decided on the advice of the architect to make him an offer of £1,000'.

119 – The Royal Aero Club

Founded only in 1901 – although the first balloon flight had been as early as 1783 – the club's defined object was 'the encouragement of aero automobilism and ballooning as a sport, and the development of the science of aerial navigation in all its forms and applications'. The concept was a woman's – Miss Vera Hedges Butler.

In 1931 the club moved from Clifford Street to 119 Piccadilly which remained its home until 1961. In December 1940 the premises were hit by a high explosive bomb, which demolished the squash court and fractured the skull of one of the valets. Shortly afterwards a Major Oliver Stewart found himself in trouble with MI5 because, in describing the incident, he had facetiously observed that the bomb had ended up in the lavatory. The War Office regarded this as 'disclosure of information to the enemy'. From Piccadilly the club moved to Fitzmaurice House off Berkeley Square, where it 'wed' with the Lansdowne Club and lodged there from 1961 to 1968, subsequently moving to both the Junior Carlton and the Senior before all but the name disappeared.

128 – RAF Club

On 31 October 1918 the first Lord Cowdray made a gift to provide a permanent building to house the Royal Air Force Club; the present buildings (shown right) were acquired in 1919. The Piccadilly frontage was built in the 1800s, while the rear half, facing Old Park Lane, was stables. Between 1919 and 1921 extensive reconstruction took place, largely financed by Lord Cowdray. The club was fully opened to members in January 1922, although it was not until 24 February that year that it was officially opened by HRH The Duke of York This association with the royal family continues to this day; the club's patron at present is Her Majesty The Queen.

The club operated very successfully during the 1920s and 1930s, and membership rose again with the outbreak of the Second World War. But by 1960 membership had fallen to a level that caused severe financial problems, addressed by a working party of serving RAF officers who designed a plan that substantially increased membership during the 1960s. It acquired the freehold of 128 Piccadilly and 6 Old Park Lane in 1985 and development and refurbishment have continued since then.

THE CAVALRY AND GUARDS CLUB

'In January 1976 the Guards Club was absorbed into the Cavalry. As always, there were difficulties at first, but the two groups of members – who have much more in common than, for example, the members of Brooks's and the St James's Club – seem to be getting on well enough with each other now.'

ANTHONY LEJEUNE, *THE GENTLEMEN'S CLUBS OF LONDON*

The first committee meeting of the amalgamated Club took place on 27 January 1976. Sub-committees were set up with a mix of both Cavalry and Guards Club committee members, and among the very first discussions was the issue of lady members.

By May, 732 Guards officers had joined (of whom 231 were serving) and 156 Cavalry and Guards ladies; though offset against this were the 186 Cavalry resignations following the EGM proposing the increase in subscription rates which would bring the two Clubs into line. It was quickly realised that some enterprising members who had resigned when their wives joined – at considerably lower subscription rates – were continuing to use all the Club's facilities as before; so in July 1976 the motion was carried 'that ladies can only entertain former members of the Club on the second floor and that such former members would not be allowed to use the first and ground floors'.

One immediate result of the merger of the two Clubs was a great increase in the membership: at 31 December 1975, Cavalry Club numbers stood at 2,339, while a year later there were 3,388 members of the combined Clubs, of whom 212 were ladies and 992 serving officers.

In July 1976 the Secretary, Squadron Leader Anthony O'Connor, retired, having given the Club 'twenty-three years of outstanding service and loyalty', and in October that year Miss Joan Mussel, who had been assistant Secretary for a similar length of time, also retired. They then married, O'Connor's wife having died the previous year.

> When I first joined the Club and the staff did not know my name, I would be greeted by 'Good morning, Colonel'. After a few weeks, it must have been thought that I was not Colonel material and I was demoted to being addressed as 'Major'. One day six months later, as I arrived at the Club, the hall porter said 'Good morning, Mr Dudgeon'. The news had spread. I am now, twenty years later, nearly always addressed as 'Mr Dudgeon' – so much nicer than 'Sir'. Any man can be Sir and among the Sirs, Majors and Colonels, I have a name.
>
> PATRICK DUDGEON (MR)

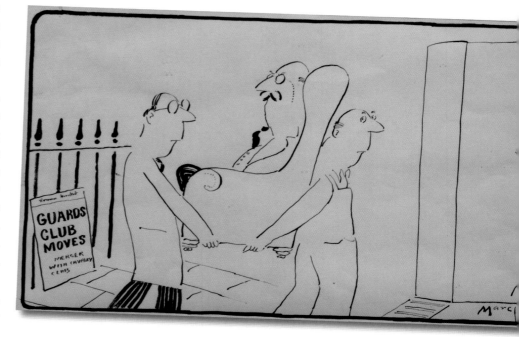

Cartoon by Marc (Mark Boxer).

The matter of improvements to the existing kitchens had become a priority, and the Secretary at the July committee meeting suggested that a 'deep clean' be undertaken, which would postpone the required improvements under the new Health and Safety at Work Act, which had come into force the previous year. The quotation from Rentokil – a company closely associated with pest control – was itself £3,800. Considerable debate ensued, as this meant the postponement of planned redecoration works to the Coffee Room – which were eventually carried out some twenty years later – and some committee members felt strongly that the kitchens needed complete modernisation and overhaul, and that making good of the old represented a waste of money. However, practicalities won the day and an expenditure of £9,000 was planned.

In 1977 the committee decided to put up subscriptions and allowed for 15 per cent resignations – a forecast which to their regret was proved correct. There were no specific celebrations held at the Club for the Queen's Silver Jubilee that year, mainly because of the precarious financial situation but also because the procession was not due to pass down Piccadilly as so many other processions and parades had done in recent years. However, there was enough cash to allow the redecoration of the dining room and the smoking rooms that year.

There was some discussion in early 1978 about the renaming of the function rooms, one of which had already been christened by the Chairman as the Double Bridal Room after one of his horses (see page 97). The other two remained unnamed until 1991, when the small function room became the Waterloo Room and the large the Peninsula Room. In 1978 also, for the first time, the Club stayed open during August, an innovation that proved so successful that the practice has continued ever since; yet three years later, in 1981, the Club closed at Christmas for the first time, as little use tended to be made of it over the festive period.

HRH The Duke of Gloucester, Vice President of the Club.

FIELD MARSHAL HRH THE DUKE OF GLOUCESTER 1900–74

Prince Henry, the third son of Prince George, later King George V, was born at Sandringham and educated at Eton, where his tutor described him as 'cheerful and unassuming but lacking in confidence'. He went on to Sandhurst, followed by a year at Trinity College, Cambridge, from 1919–20, before joining the 10th Hussars. As an outstanding horseman and shot, he enjoyed army life, though he was frustrated at being prevented from serving with the regiment overseas. He was made a KG in 1921 and created Duke of Gloucester in 1928. Thereafter he represented the King on many occasions, including the mission to Japan in 1929 to confer the Order of the Garter on Emperor Hirohito, Abyssinia the following year for Haile Selassie's coronation and a tour of Australia and New Zealand in 1934–5. In November 1935 he married Alice Montagu-Douglas-Scott, daughter of the 7th Duke of Buccleuch. Following the abdication of his eldest brother in 1936 and the accession of King George VI, he became Regent-Designate to the Princess Elizabeth until her coming of age in 1944.

In 1939 the Duke was appointed chief liaison officer between the British and French armies in Europe, and was slightly wounded when his car was dive-bombed in May 1940. In 1941 he became second-in-command of 20 Armoured Brigade. In 1945 he succeeded the Earl of Gowrie as Governor General of Australia, and was popular despite his lack of ready small talk and the growing feeling of independence from Britain among many Australians. He was promoted Field Marshal in 1955, and represented the Queen at the coronations of Kings Feisal and Hussein, and the independence ceremonies in Nigeria and Malaysia. He was Colonel of the 10th Hussars, the Scots Guards, the Gloucestershire Regiment and the Gordon Highlanders.

The Duke was involved in a car crash while returning home from Churchill's funeral in 1965. Although his injuries were slight, his health began thereafter to decline, and he was incapacitated by two strokes in 1968. He died in 1974 and was succeeded by his second son, his eldest having been killed in an aeroplane crash in 1972.

The lease renewal continued to be a concern. The Grade II listed status of the building was helpful to the cause since, as Gerald Eve Chartered Surveyors wrote to the Chairman in 1979, 'Any proposal to use the premises for offices would be very strongly resisted and would have to be the subject of an appeal to the Secretary of State. I can think of no other use except possibly that of a gaming club.' Later that year a meeting with the Managing Director of the freeholder, Sutton Estates, resulted in the Club being notified that, 'while appreciating the position of the Club, the board must consider the interest of the freeholders and these do not permit a decision regarding the lease to be made at the present time, particularly bearing in mind the current unexpired term of nine years'. Sutton Estates continued, indeed, to hold the Club at arm's

It is rather rare that an archbishop is also a military man. It was not surprising, therefore, that within months of his enthronement in 1979 Archbishop Robert Runcie should be guest of honour and speaker at a Club dinner. I remember attending with the late Joe Gurney whose main aim was to fire off the first question following the archbishop's speech: 'Will you defend the Book of Common Prayer, Your Grace?' Without hesitation the archbishop confirmed 'his respect for tradition' and there the matter evaporated into the air in a puff of cigar smoke. How times have changed!

MICHAEL WYNNE-PARKER

(Archbishop Runcie was made an honorary member of the Club in 1981, and remained so until his death in 2000.)

length: during 1983 it was twice suggested by the committee that their Trustees should join them for lunch at the Club, and twice the invitation was declined. Then in 1984 the Chairman advised the committee that he had learned that the freehold of the building had been sold by Sutton Estates to 'a French man living in Switzerland'.

Captains John Compton and Tim Allen, 3rd Carabiniers.

Field Marshal Lord Carver 1915–2001

Born in 1915 at Bletchingley, Surrey, and descended from the Duke of Wellington on his mother's side, Michael Carver was educated at Winchester and had expected to go up to Cambridge. However, his family was severely hit by the Depression, and Carver decided to join the army for a few years before training as a lawyer. He was commissioned from the RMC into the Royal Tank Corps in 1935, and the outbreak of war in 1939 put paid to any idea of a legal career.

Carver, whose name was to become almost synonymous with coolness under fire, won a Military Cross at Tobruk in 1941. By 1943 he was commanding 1 RTR and was awarded his first DSO for a particularly

hazardous reconnaissance at Alamein, where he attracted the favourable notice of General Montgomery. From North Africa his regiment went to Italy, and Carver won a second DSO at Salerno before being withdrawn to prepare for the D-Day landings as part of the 4th Armoured Brigade. The brigade was in action late in June 1944, and when its commander was killed Carver took over, aged twenty-nine, as the youngest Brigadier in the army.

After the war, Carver decided that his prospects of action and promotion justified remaining in a peacetime army. (Field Marshal Montgomery, reporting on him at this time, wrote: 'This officer thinks there is nothing but dead wood between him and the CIGS.') Although not involved in the Korean War, in 1954 Carver became Chief of Staff in Kenya, where the Mau Mau emergency was in progress, and was mentioned in despatches. In 1960 he took over 6 Infantry Brigade Group, and two years later was promoted GOC 3rd Airmobile Division in the Strategic Reserve. He served in Cyprus, where the Eoka terrorist campaign was drawing to an end, first as head of a multi-national truce force and later as Deputy UN Commander.

Carver's next appointment, as Director Army Staff Duties from 1964 to 1967, was one which caused him considerable notoriety. The newly elected Wilson Government demanded defence savings, of which the army was required to bear the brunt. These were achieved by massive cuts to the Territorial Army, overseen by Carver who, regarded as carrying out the distasteful task with unnecessary ruthlessness, made few friends at this time. Nevertheless he became a KCB in 1967 and was appointed C-in-C Far East the same year. He was GOC Southern Command from 1969–71, CGS from 1971–3 and thereafter, as a Field Marshal, CDS until his retirement in 1976. He remained Colonel Commandant of the Royal Armoured Corps until 1977, in which year he was created a life peer and recalled from retirement to become the Resident Commissioner Designate in Rhodesia, with responsibility for overseeing the transition to black majority rule. The appointment was premature, as the Smith government was not yet prepared to concede defeat, and Carver resigned after fourteen frustrating months. He became a life peer in 1977.

He was a prolific author, both during his service and in retirement, with some dozen books to his credit, including *Second to None*, a history of the Royal Scots Greys who had served in his brigade. During his service, Carver had been sceptical about reliance on nuclear weapons in general, and of the need for an independent nuclear deterrent in particular. In later years he was a very vocal critic of the Trident programme, expressing his views most forcibly in the House of Lords, where on one occasion he demanded: 'What the bloody hell is it for?' He also dismissed President Reagan's threats of pre-emptive nuclear strikes as 'either bluff or suicide'. He died suddenly in 2001.

FIELD MARSHAL SIR JOHN STANIER 1925–2007

John Stanier was born in 1925 and educated at Marlborough and briefly at Merton College, Oxford. He was commissioned in 1946 into the 7th Hussars, then equipped with Churchill tanks and based at Palmanova in northern Italy, where life was an idyllic routine of riding, bathing and visits to the Officers' Club in Venice. This all ended abruptly when 7th Armoured Brigade was deployed to Trieste to counter a potential threat of invasion by the Communist forces of Yugoslavia. Lieutenant Stanier, accustomed to receiving orders as laid down in Standing Operational Procedures, was surprised when his squadron leader issued the following: 'You know the Yugoslavs may be coming from Trieste. If they come I suspect it'll be rather like a partridge drive. I think you all know what to do.'

Stanier, who greatly enjoyed anecdotes, particularly ones at his own expense, often recalled an incident from those days when he was briefly ADC to the C-in-C Trieste. There was a dinner party on the evening of his arrival and he was put in charge of the drinks. While assiduously filling the guests' glasses, Stanier did not neglect his own, to such an extent that the following morning he was greeted glacially by the General with the words 'I think we can well do without you', and returned to regimental duty. He subsequently served in BAOR and Hong Kong.

On passing out of the Staff College, Stanier served as Military Assistant to the Vice CIGS, returning to his regiment to command C Squadron. Here he earned what Tam Dalyell MP, who came to know Stanier well and greatly liked him, has described in the obituary he wrote in the *Independent* as 'a fearsome reputation'. He would have been an obvious choice for command, but the amalgamation of the 3rd and 7th Hussars in November 1958 produced a regiment with a surplus of very able officers of his vintage, and Stanier was not selected. As a consequence of this he seriously contemplated leaving the army, and even at one time applied for the post of defence correspondent of *The Times*.

In 1966, however, he accepted the command of the Royal Scots Greys. The advent of a commanding officer from another regiment is never the easiest of times, and Tam Dalyell described his arrival as a 'seismic shock'. His utter insistence on perfection, and the unashamed ruthlessness with which he achieved it, significantly enhanced the fearsome reputation he had earned as a squadron leader. However, after a few heads had rolled, his methods unquestionably produced the desired result, and the Greys achieved levels of efficiency which were the envy of the Royal Armoured Corps.

Stanier was particularly intrigued by the Pipe Band, a novelty to him on his arrival with the regiment. At his first Beating Retreat, he was surprised by the Pipe Major's unsteady gait on parade, but fortunately accepted the Pipe President's bland assurance 'Oh, Colonel, he always walks that way'. Thereafter he developed a particularly cordial rapport with the band, which was invariably in evidence on any important occasion. The Pipe Band frequently played for Stanier long after he relinquished command of the Greys in 1968, and indeed were in attendance for his 80th birthday and golden wedding anniversary in 2005.

After a brief term at the Imperial Defence College, he took over 20 Armoured Brigade the following year, and in 1970 became Director Public Relations, a role in which his clear thinking, phenomenal memory and ability to express himself made him an outstanding success. Tam Dalyell, invited as a Labour MP to debate on nuclear weapons against Stanier at Durham University, and expecting as a politician to have the edge over a mere soldier, received a rude shock. Stanier's ability to memorise a mass of detail was amazing: on occasions he could speak for forty-five minutes without notes, and then handle questions with equal aplomb. His experiences as DPR later became the basis for his book *War and the Media*, published in 1997.

From 1973 to 1975 Stanier commanded the 1st Division in Germany, and from 1975 to 1978 was Commandant of the Staff College. During this time he led the first exchange from Camberley to the Frunze Military Academy in Moscow. His KCB and promotion to Lieutenant General as Vice Chief of the General Staff came in 1978. In 1981 he was appointed an ADC General to the Queen, and took up his final command appointment as C-in-C UK Land Forces. Here he played a leading part in the deployment of troops to the Falklands in 1982 before being appointed CGS (the first holder of that office since the war to have seen no active service), and being made a GCB later that year. His wholehearted involvement in the Falklands War, in which he rightly saw victory as both essential and achievable, were in marked contrast to his equally wholehearted opposition to the invasion of Iraq ten years later. In every role he undertook, the verdict of his subordinates was that he was terrifying but exhilarating to work for if one was up to it. As Tam Dalyell put it, 'He was ambitious, certainly, but ambitious to further what he conceived to be sensible and prudent lines of action, rather than simply climbing a greasy pole'.

Retirement from the army, and his Field Marshal's baton, came in 1985. He had been Colonel of the Royal Scots Dragoon Guards since 1979 and Colonel Commandant of the Royal Armoured Corps since 1982. He became Chairman of the Royal United Services Institute in 1986, relinquishing the post in 1989 and being appointed Constable of the Tower of London from 1990 to 1996. He was also President of the Hampshire Red Cross and a Deputy Lieutenant of the county. He died on 11 November 2007, being survived by Lady Stanier and his four daughters.

Double Bridal Room.

Apart from the tremendous leadership shown by Major General John Strawson in masterminding the purchase of the freehold of 127 Piccadilly, my abiding memory of serving on the executive committee is being asked by the Club Secretary for guidance on the following situation:

Captain Bloggs of the Fleet of Foot was reported by the porter to have entered the Club dressed as a woman, with on his arm a young lady who he claimed was his daughter, both parties then proceeding to a single bedroom on the third floor then reserved for male members only. Mr de Pinna (the Secretary) wanted the committee's advice as to whether

1. Captain Bloggs should be granted a subscription refund as ladies paid less than male members?
2. If 'he' should be redirected to the fourth floor (where mixed accommodation was available)?
3. If 'he' should be kept out of Geoffrey's Bar?
4. If 'he' should be directed to use the 'ladies' rather than the 'gents'?

The Secretary was instructed to take no action, and the Chairman reported the incident to Captain Bloggs' proposer – and needless to say the gallant Captain was not seen again!

PETER W JONES, *EXECUTIVE COMMITTEE MEMBER*

The new owner was a Mr Sopher of ANZAR NV, a company registered in Holland.

Renovation work on the building continued as and when circumstances dictated and finances allowed. Terrorist bombing activity in London necessitated the closure of the ladies' entrance and the installation of mesh over the balustrade at each side of the front door. In 1983 an IBM computer was purchased to handle membership data and staff and salary details, and a new telephone system was installed that would allow a twenty-four hour service and 'a very considerable increase of facility for members staying in the Club who may now make telephone calls directly from their bedroom, using the latest press-button system to virtually anywhere in the world'. But the electrical wiring was still decades old, so in 1984 it was agreed that it should be updated, an exercise that cost in the region of £30,000.

The new landlords were meanwhile flexing their muscles. The story of the Club's purchase of the freehold is told elsewhere (see pages 122–3), and it is clear from the committee minutes of those fraught three years between 1984 and 1987 that the Chairman and committee members spent an enormous amount of time on the impending crisis. It became clear that Stockley, the landlords, were initially in no mood for discussion. Their agent, Elliott Bernerd, used unflattering terms for the Club members. ▶146

WHAT DO THE YOUNG WANT?

(A FEW RAMBLING THOUGHTS AND A CHANCE TO GO DOWN MEMORY LANE)

I joined the Cavalry Club (before it joined with the Guards Club) as a young subaltern in 1968, about two years after leaving Sandhurst. In common with most young officers, I hardly used the Club because it was a somewhat intimidating experience and I was serving abroad.

In 1981 I was posted for the first time to the Ministry of Defence in London. After completing a tour of duty with my regiment in Germany, I was approached by Colonel (later Brigadier the Lord) Nicholas Vivian, a former officer in my regiment who had been my squadron leader in Libya in 1968, about the possibility of my joining the committee of the Cavalry and Guards Club. As I was at the stage of my life when a more regular use of a London club was an exciting prospect, I readily accepted. I was duly selected and invited to attend my first meeting.

In those days, the committee met monthly. Major General Sir Digby Raeburn, a distinguished, approachable and affable man, was the Chairman. The committee numbered at least twenty, including several ex officio members such as the serving colonel of the RAC Officers' Personnel Branch (AG17) in the MoD. It was made clear to me on my first attendance that I was there to put forward the views of the younger members. Indeed, at nearly every meeting in those days, the Chairman would turn to me and say, 'What do the young want?' I was supported by people of similar age, Paul Belcher and John Symons, who had also been recruited to speak up for that age group.

The Club Secretary in those days was Mr de Pinna, an austere, monosyllabic but highly efficient man. As an aside, in this day and age when everyone uses Christian names to such a degree that it is often difficult to discover what the surname is, it is refreshing to realise that I still do not know Mr de Pinna's Christian name [it was David – Eds]. Ian Frazer was then ensconced on the committee as the Honorary Treasurer and is now a fellow Trustee. He must be the longest serving member of the Club's governance, since none of the 1981 committee now remain engaged with the Club's affairs, and Mr de Pinna and Nick Vivian are no longer with us.

The Club was shortly to embark on the challenging exercise of purchasing the freehold of its building, under the leadership of Major General John Strawson. By 1984 I had returned to my regiment and was asked to represent the views of the serving officers in Germany as to whether the purchase of the freehold should happen or not. Most were in favour, but I recall one young turk suggesting that the building should be turned into a car park as that would be a much more sensible use for it. I wonder what he would say now. Colonel Thomas Hall (now the Club's Vice President) was later to make his mark as Chairman, and steer the Club adroitly through the choppy waters of the late 1980s and 1990s, launching key projects such as the rebuilding of the kitchen and the refurbishment of the fourth floor bedrooms and most of the reception rooms.

During my time I have served under eight Chairmen, worked alongside four Secretaries, helped to organise two Grand Military Balls linked to the Sandown race meeting in March and been engaged on numerous sub-committees looking at various aspects of Club life but all concentrating on the members' requirements, especially those of the young. We have considered a nightclub, a bistro, billiards (there was a billiard table once), a fitness centre, a squash court and, of course, access for ladies. In comparison with other clubs, we have emerged relatively unscathed. The Carlton, at the time when Mrs Thatcher was elected leader of the Conservative party in 1975, did not admit ladies as full members. She was offered honorary membership, a dilemma that led to much acrimonious soul-searching. In my early days on the committee, a senior bachelor Major spoke up only once, to remonstrate that he had seen a lady enter the Club through the front door. In those days there was a separate entrance for ladies so that they could reach the second floor unseen via the lift. Hasn't life changed since then?

I am reminded of Groucho Marx's famous quip, 'I am not going to pay good money to join a club that lets in people like me'. Despite the pressure of a contracting army and a more informal society (I have got used to being addressed by young officers as 'Hi, General'), the Club has managed to steer its way successfully through all the changes and yet maintain its standards. It has a vibrant and eclectic membership and many young on its books, as well as a strong lady membership. Harold Macmillan, who belonged to seven London clubs, thought that the ideal composition of membership should be 75 per cent gentlemen and 25 per cent crooks. He reportedly said, 'That is why White's is so fascinating'. I am not suggesting we have the same mix in the Cavalry and Guards Club, but one of its strengths is that we are a healthy mixture of all ages based on our constituent parts: the Royal Armoured Corps, Yeomanry, Guards, Green Jackets and Honourable Artillery Company.

Understandably, the younger members are unable to use the Club regularly due to their many operational commitments, but I know that the time will come, as it did for me, when it becomes for them too a bastion and haven of civilisation in the centre of London: truly 'a London home' – a place to escape to, where one can meet congenial people and relax in the knowledge that there will be a warm welcome and glass of chilled bubbly in Geoffrey's Bar. May 127 Piccadilly flourish for many years to come.

MAJOR GENERAL JONATHAN HALL,
TRUSTEE

VIEW FROM THE CHAIR
COLONEL TOM HALL, CHAIRMAN 1990–6

After serving as Vice Chairman to John Strawson and Philip Ward, I took on the chairmanship in 1990. The campaign to raise sufficient funds to buy the freehold of 127 Piccadilly had been very successful, but we were faced with many fresh problems in our dilapidated building. Following the recent Food Safety Act, an inspection concluded that our kitchens were not up to standard, and we were threatened with imminent closure unless we undertook major renovations.

The appeal to raise funds for the freehold purchase had drained many pockets, but I was faced with going back to the members to ask for further urgent contributions if the Club was to remain open. The cost estimated to the committee by surveyor – and committee member – Peter Jones was £700,000, equivalent to a full year's subscription income. With the help of John Rodwell as Vice Chairman and an amusing cartoon by Simon Dyer, many hundreds of personal letters were written. Contributions slowly trickled in, and eventually only thirty-nine members failed to heed the call, thus enabling us to start work in the basement.

In true Staff College fashion (John Strawson had been my instructor!) I wrote a 'green paper', which examined the

financial and decorative situation of the Club and gave some daunting options as to how members should see the future. Clearly the refurbishment of rooms would add to members' appreciation and enjoyment, which would lend in turn to greater usage and income. So we set about a programme of redecoration, starting with the Yeomanry Room and the former billiard room, now renamed the Balaclava Room. As income slowly improved, we continued the redecorations throughout the fourth floor and eventually the Coffee Room. All the major pictures were cleaned and rehung with the help of a museum specialist, and a location inventory established of over 600 pictures and prints.

Due to the continuing series of amalgamations and reductions in qualifying regiments, the committee decided to undertake a membership campaign organised by Brigadier James Rucker. We widened the catchment areas to include those who had not necessarily served in the army, but who were strongly recommended by a number of members. Sandhurst also played a part by arranging for officer cadets to visit the Club.

Regimental Dinners, Speaker Dinners and other social and business functions continued to contribute to Club activities. Ladies had for many years been welcomed in the Club, but due to the IRA threat to military premises the ladies' entrance had been closed. This gave an impetus to extending the areas of the Club which lady members could use, and the ladies committee, ably run by Anne Curran, started theatre parties and other events. The Club tent at the Sandown Grand Military Race Meeting was reintroduced, though a tent at Royal Ascot was still in the future.

A visit of Sandhurst cadets.

HM The Queen and Colonel Tom Hall.

All these improvements gradually raised the profile of the Club, and this was greatly enhanced by HM Queen Elizabeth The Queen Mother, our Lady President, attending many enjoyable lunches with her Regimental Colonels and the committee.

So in 1996 I was happy to hand over to John Rodwell a thriving Club with great prospects for the future. In this I had been hugely supported by HRH The Duke of Kent, John Stanier, Dick Worsley and all our Trustees, committee, members and staff. It had been a very varied and strenuous six years, which I thoroughly enjoyed.

FROM A LETTER TO THE CHAIRMAN IN 1993
Twenty-five years ago, when I used the Club a great deal, many of us thought it was in terminal decline. If you sometimes feel discouraged, do be assured it is now a thousand times better than in those days.
LT GENERAL SIR ROLLO PAIN

Colonel Tom talking to David Rosier and David Woodd.

143

VIEW FROM THE CHAIR

MAJOR JOHN RODWELL, CHAIRMAN 1996–2002

Although I had been Vice Chairman to Colonel Tom Hall, I was genuinely taken by surprise when he suggested, in 1996, that I might take over from him. I was aware that this was controversial in that I was only forty-nine and, in military terms, very junior. As a letter from an indignant elderly member expostulated, 'The chairmanship traditionally goes to an officer of General rank; a Major is less than an esquire!'

My chairmanship lasted from 1996 until 2002, during which time I was extraordinarily fortunate to have Ian Frazer as my Vice Chairman. In those days the Club was run by a large committee of some thirty members, with an executive committee which made proposals to the main committee for their discussion and decision. Robin Kernick, John Rothwell, Peter Jones and James Rucker, in particular, provided Ian and me with constant and loyal support in respect of food and wine, the law and the Club rules, the property and its fabric and the membership and recruitment respectively. I could not have managed without them.

The main committee was quite daunting for a young and 'junior' Chairman. I was determined, at the end of my first committee meeting, to ask everyone, by name, if they had any other business to discuss. They had been very gentle with me up till then. I did remember all the names and finally came to the Secretary, from whom I did not expect any comment. 'Chairman, I do need some advice from the committee on the subject of the central heating system,' he said. 'I am having trouble with the old boilers.' A rapping from the far end of the table by an elderly Brigadier introduced the comment, 'In these days of political correctness, Chairman, this is no way for the Secretary to refer to the lady members.'

Tom Hall had left me with a fine legacy. The Club had brand new, legally compliant kitchens, and we owned the freehold, but, apart from that, both the 'in' and 'out' side of the building were in a sorry state. The

most daunting problem was probably the outside of the back of the building which became known as 'Jones's rear elevation'. It was to be a further eleven years before this was attended to, but it demonstrated what a robust building we had purchased.

The Club had just experienced two major fundraising efforts and substantial bank borrowings. It needed income, and this had to come from membership subscriptions and operating revenue. Both would be helped by renovating and refurbishing the interior so that we could attract new members and function business. So during the next six years we managed to refurbish all the first floor reception rooms, the Double Bridal Room on the second floor and the main hall and central staircase. The removal of years of staining by cigarette and cigar smoke and electrical rewiring, followed by clever and authentic redecoration and soft furnishing by Zoe Peto, transformed the interior. Somewhat controversially, we opened a business centre with a computer terminal and introduced an electronic point of sale system to the front desk and the public rooms, much to the appalled dismay of Geoffrey the barman; I always felt he regarded this as the ultimate betrayal.

With these newly refurbished reception rooms we developed a programme of events for members, supported and advertised by the introduction of the 127 Gazette, the Club's newsletter. Several polo matches were played against Buck's Club, and two Speaker Dinners were held every year with excellent attendance to hear ambassadors, Metropolitan Police Commissioners, an Old Bailey judge and numerous Chiefs of the General and Defence Staffs and other senior army officers who had just returned from action in different parts of the world. Also popular was the Fathers and Sons Dinner, which soon became even more popular as the Fathers, Sons and Daughters Dinner. It was thought that the twinkle in one or two members' eyes might have been brought on by the fact that they had taken someone else's daughter, not having one of their own. I was certainly guilty!

We were also very aware of the importance of our lady members and their influence. We therefore formed a Ladies Advisory Group, so called because, in those days, any suggestion that ladies should be involved in decision-making or, 'God forbid', on the committee would have been met with H E Bateman-esque gasps from certain sections of the membership. This group was brilliantly led by Anne Curran and became the forerunner of the current ladies committee, which has contributed so greatly to the entertainment and events programme of the Club.

Few Guardsmen had been chairmen of the Club since the amalgamation and I was therefore more aware than most of the need to bring the Royal Armoured Corps and the Brigade of Guards closer together within the walls of 127 Piccadilly. One of the things of which I was particularly proud during my tenure was the commissioning and

John Rodwell and Diana, Princess of Wales.

Major John Rodwell hosts a luncheon for HM Queen Elizabeth The Queen Mother.

so that the custom could be exercised again and so that she could 'toast' the Chairman and committee of the Club. A totally bemused Secretary was despatched, very bothered that by this time the kitchen staff would have gone home for the afternoon but, soon after, a basket of toast appeared and Her Majesty personally passed pieces to all present and we all dipped obediently following her instructions.

At the end of lunch Robin Kernick, then Clerk to the Queen's Cellars, politely rebuked Queen Elizabeth for dipping toast in such good port. 'Ah', said Her Majesty, 'I wouldn't have dipped it in the claret which was even better quality'.

One cannot write about the chairmanship without reference to the Club staff. For many reasons, inappropriate to mention, the staff turnover was greater than one would have liked during my time. Many old faces retired, and I remember having to deal with a furious member who was very angry that we had given early retirement to one of the hall porters. 'It is perfectly monstrous,' he declared. 'He was eighty-one,' I could only reply. But one member of staff must be mentioned by name. I had the pleasure of being Chairman when Geoffrey Price celebrated fifty years' service to the Guards and Cavalry Clubs, and the members presented him with appropriate gifts and return tickets for him and his wife Carole, who had been a waitress at the old Guards Club, to go to Australia to see their daughter and grandchildren.

To have had the privilege of being Chairman of the Cavalry and Guards Club was memorable, exasperating, sometimes thankless, more often enormously rewarding and, on many occasions, joyful. The most important thing for me was that it was so much fun because of the friends with whom one worked. There was usually laughter at meetings, fun and comradeship as well as high points of great pride and pleasure. I will always be grateful to have had the opportunity.

production of a new badge or emblem for the Club, as since the amalgamation we had had two separate badges. The late Sir Colin Cole, Garter King of Arms, was at that time a senior member of the general committee and so I asked him if he would design a new badge for us, combining the two existing ones.

Several weeks later a drawing of a fine new badge arrived, which I rather stupidly sent to the Major General commanding the Household Division and the senior Cavalry Colonel for their approval and comments. How naive I was. The Cavalry complained bitterly that the Guards' influence was far too great, the musket was too pronounced and the Household Division star far too prominent. The Chief of Staff at London District said that the Major General felt that the lances were inappropriate and the cavalry sabre should be straightened to resemble an infantry sword. Again, rather stupidly, I referred these senior comments to Garter King of Arms, who sent a curt note back to me which read, 'Dear Chairman, The badge presented to you by the College of Arms is correct. Yours ever, Colin'. There was nothing more to say. Garter had spoken and we now have the Club badge, which has been well received and adorns much of our Club property and all of our documentation.

One of the most memorable days of my chairmanship was 6 June 2001 when, at the age of 100, Queen Elizabeth The Queen Mother, our Lady President, accepted my invitation to have lunch with the Trustees and senior members of the committee. Her Majesty arrived with her lady in waiting, Lady Margaret Colville, at about twenty minutes to one. Despite having recently injured her leg, she climbed unaided up the front steps and into the lift to go up to the second floor. I apologised for the slowness of the lift but explained that it was very old, to which she quipped, 'I bet it isn't as old as I am'.

Lunch was memorable, and Her Majesty did not drag herself away until after 3.30pm. I had been warned that she had the habit of asking her hosts the derivation of the word 'toast', normally just before hers was drunk. I had done my homework and, having explained the old custom of dipping toast into wine, she called for toast from the kitchen

John Rodwell (right) and his Vice Chairman Ian Frazer.

Bernerd believed that the members were in no position to negotiate, and it was soon learned that extensive plans for developing the building into a 100-room hotel were at an advanced stage.

This was to prove, however, the development that never was. The committee galvanised members with a public relations campaign and went into extremely proactive fundraising mode. As usual at times of trouble, many more members attended the AGMs and urged the committee to take a more belligerent attitude towards Stockley, and when fundraising began in earnest, many of them also put their hands deep into their pockets.

Sir Colin Cole (left), Garter King of Arms, presents the new badge to Chairman John Rodwell.

THE BADGE OF THE CAVALRY AND GUARDS CLUB

Since the Cavalry Club and the Guards Club joined together, all members of the Cavalry and Guards Club have become well acquainted with the regimental-type badges used by each and displayed side by side on the Club's flag and also on items of Club property, menu cards etc.

The Cavalry Club badge, composed of two lances in saltire, with a carbine, cavalry sword and name scroll comprising a 'strap and buckle' or garter, ensigned by a heraldic version of the royal crown, is well suited to stand for members who have been or are serving cavalrymen; and the original Guards Club badge (that of the Household Division), consisting of a similar royal crown within a circlet circumscribed *Septem Juncta in Uno* (seven joined in one) and radiated like an order off the Garter star, is in itself appropriate to represent Club members who are serving or have served in the Household Division, ie in one of the five Foot Guards regiments or the two Household Cavalry regiments.

Placed side by side, however, these two distinctive and very different badges have somehow lacked balance, or at least could be thought capable of improvement; and so it was decided, during the chairmanship of Colonel John Rodwell, that a united Club (as indicated by its name) should have a single badge symbolising the Club's derivation from two and the two main sources of membership.

This unification of the two badges has involved a major exercise in redesign, in which the principal object was to retain as far as possible the familiar elements and devices in the old badges and to combine them in a new badge (not, please, a logo!) in such a way as to preserve their historical significance and ensure the coherence of the whole, with no one element detracting from any other.

By drawing on several heraldic and traditional principles, with the advice of Colonel Sir Colin Cole (formerly Garter King of Arms and Inspector of Regimental Colours) and with the professional assistance of Robert Parsons, one of the artists at the College of Arms, the stated objects (it is submitted) have been achieved. The Club now has a badge which not only demonstrates its history but, it is hoped, will also be regarded in the eyes of the membership in its various categories, civilian as well as military buckled together, as a patent contributor towards the Club's sense of unity, continuity of purpose and confidence in the future.

It was a blow to the landlord when the listing was upgraded to II* in 1986, making it extremely unlikely that a change of use to a hotel would be approved. And eventually a mutually acceptable agreement was reached which allowed the Club to purchase the freehold in April 1987.

During those years the committee had addressed the possibility that such an agreement might prove unachievable, and had appointed a sub-committee to look into an alternative home. The Eccentric Club was one option, and the Crown Estate Commissioners were approached, but none of this came to anything. Not all members, indeed, bemoaned the possible loss of the building. An unidentified commanding officer suggested at one AGM that the Club might consider a move to larger premises incorporating some sports facilities, along the lines of the RAC or Lansdowne Clubs. As he concluded, 'No one feels any real emotional attachment to 127, and so no tears will be shed if we move, provided of course that we remain in the area of the West End'. But he was rather a lone voice and – despite the obvious benefit to them of subscriptions being frozen while the future of the Club remained uncertain – the majority of members threw their weight behind the committee's efforts to remain at 127 Piccadilly.

Club life meanwhile continued. The members' bar and the basement bedrooms were redecorated at this time; and there were increasing numbers of straws in the wind, indicating that the Club's management and members were realising that the changing times dictated new attitudes towards members of all ages and both genders. In 1985 there was a review, under the chairmanship of Captain J N Symons, of the facilities for young members, ie those under the age of thirty-five who made up some 39 per cent of the total membership at this time. The review's recommendations included some changes of facility for lady members, permitting them access through the main entrance and use of the staircase, and unrestricted access to the public rooms on the ground floor with the exception of the members' bar. Further results of the

KRH Amalgamation Lunch with the Colonel-in-Chief, HRH The Princess Royal, 1991.

Cartoon by Simon Dyer referring to the 'Kitchen Appeal', 1991.

review were certain improvements to the catering on offer and the establishment of a 'multi-gym' in the basement.

The same unidentified commanding officer who had suggested a move away from 127 Piccadilly clearly approved of these proposals: 'One of the principal drawbacks to the Club in the eyes of most members, young and not so young, is the fact that women are not made welcome as they come in. All felt that they should be allowed to use the front door, and that they should go straight into the Coffee Room. The other feeling that most of the younger members have is that the place is simply too stuffy. If you go in there wearing anything but a dark suit you are looked at as if the cat had dragged you in. One of them described the place as "being like a country house which has recently suffered a death in the family".'

The sale of the books from the library, necessary though it was to help raise the total needed for the freehold purchase, had caused a certain amount of comment; but more was to follow with the disappearance of the billiards table. One member was deeply distressed in his letter to the Chairman: 'I hear a rumour terrible in its concept, dreadful in execution that the billiard room is to be no more!'

However, one impact of the struggle for the purchase of the freehold was the increase in membership: 363 new members joined during 1987 and 114 rejoined, taking the membership total to 3,244 – the highest it had ever been.

With the freehold theirs and the Club now secure in its occupation of 127, decisions had to be made about the property and about governance generally. The deliberations about the annexe are set out elsewhere (see pages 118–21); and in 1988 Colonel Hall produced the first of a new series of five year plans, which were to come under the control of a new executive committee (renamed the Management Committee in 1990) which would meet on a monthly basis, with a larger general committee meeting every three months.

In 1989 it became clear that 'the next priority must be the modernisation of the kitchens. Designed many years ago to cope with about one-third of the business done today, the kitchens are inappropriately designed for modern needs. Added to this are the very stringent health and hygiene regulations imposed by local authorities. It will be necessary to remodel the whole basement area to take account of these plans. This will have the effect of producing space for better changing, recreation and washing facilities for the staff, which is at present woefully inadequate.' In addition, in response to the insistent demands of a small but vocal section of the membership, 'it will be necessary to locate an excellent billiards room within this area which will, I know, please the many members who miss this facility at the present time'. But these works would have to wait until 1991, when the rapidly approaching need to renew the Club's licence in 1992 – at which

On 6 December 1993 the Club was invited to cater for the Royal Scots Dragoon Guards Annual Dinner attended by Her Majesty The Queen (below and left), which was held at St James's Palace since the facilities at 127 were of insufficient size for the numbers attending. It was noted that 'such was the thorough planning that not even a coffee spoon was forgotten, the only problem that arose being that the parking space promised to the Club for its delivery lorry was occupied by a Bentley belonging to the Prince of Wales'.

point all the regulatory bodies would descend on the basement in force – made them essential.

Membership continued to grow, though the financial results suffered a number of setbacks. Rising costs, especially staff costs and interest charges, eroded the profit margin at a time when many improvements were being made to facilities and accommodation. In 1989 too, the summer rail strikes affected bookings in function rooms and it was necessary to use bedroom space to accommodate essential staff overnight. At the end of June the Secretary reported a shortfall against forecast of £16,000 and it was decided not to go ahead with planned works to the rear elevation of the building; these works were again considered in 1996 and 1998, but it was not until 2007 that they were finally undertaken.

Renovation and improvement continued in small ways during the late 1980s. The ongoing threat from the IRA – which at one time resulted in the Club offering sanctuary to members of the Carlton Club after their building had been bombed – led to a review of security measures, which meant the rebuilding of the porter's lodge and the installation of CCTV in the hall, rather to the consternation of English Heritage. An emergency lighting and fire alarm system was added as well. But these were the years of tensions in the Gulf, on top of financial stringency in the country generally, so the Centenary Ball planned for Balaclava Night

1990 had to be cancelled after too few tickets had been sold. Yet membership thrived, peaking that year at 3,531, and its database was now computerised.

February 1991 saw the announcement of David de Pinna's departure as Secretary. The Chairman's tribute to his tenure stated, 'During his time as Secretary, the Club has taken great steps forward, culminating in the purchase of the freehold. Its reputation as a club is second to none, and this is greatly due to Mr de Pinna's management and dedication to the Club and its staff.' A farewell dinner was held for him on 16 July, and his successor, Nicholas Walford, started work on 8 July.

View from the Chair

Major General Patrick Cordingley, Chairman 2002–4

My appointment was not without controversy. I had never served on the committee and, despite being a member of the Club for some thirty-five years, had not been a frequent visitor. Most controversial was the fact that I was to be an Executive Chairman, employed for two days a week, with an office in the basement. I doubt anyone on the committee foresaw the problems such a change to the Chairman's role would cause. None of us clearly defined my duties and those of the Club Secretary, so inevitably and understandably problems ensued.

The first task for a newly constituted executive committee was to stop the downward slide in the membership. We felt the subscriptions were too high to hold the core member, the 'nearly to be retired' cavalry or guards officer. We devised a simple scheme. We would offer free membership for a year to all eligible officers who had been members in the past. When subscriptions became due in 2004 the rate would be set at £450. The problem was to 'sell' this to the existing membership whose subscriptions were already £750 a year! We felt it should be possible to reduce this to £600. Then the Vice Chairman, David Rosier, came up with the inspired idea of offering 'credits'. The existing member would pay his £600 subscription, but be able to claim back £150 from his dining room or accommodation bill. We hoped everyone would win.

However, to make the plan work we needed 550 new members to sign on after the free year (2003). It was exciting watching the plan unfold. Over 1,000 accepted the free offer; surely over half of them would start paying the following year. We nearly made it, and the slightly reduced membership income was compensated for by the generosity of the existing members who did not claim their credits.

Back to controversy – and the second Gulf War. I had rather publicly announced that I and other cavalry commanders from the first Gulf War were not in favour of backing the Americans' insistence on re-invading Iraq. We felt containment was working and that the leader, Saddam Hussein, would not survive for ever. The feeling among members was by and large conservative, and they approved of further aggression. I worked long hours for the BBC during that hectic month of Operation Telic. Many of my interviews took place in discreet corners of the Club out of necessity, so I could carry out my Executive Chairman role. But members were sensitive and it was difficult to ignore the rustlings of disapproval. I hope, with hindsight, that they will agree that the 2003 invasion of Iraq was, possibly, a mistake.

After a year in office I reverted to a role as non-executive Chairman; the other route was just not working. I hoped in my second year to try to lighten the atmosphere in the Club; to make it perhaps a little more fun, a little friendlier for the younger members and their friends. The executive committee was right behind the plans. But in this, and other matters, I did not have the blessing of a minority, but a vociferous minority, of the twenty-four strong main general committee. The position was untenable and I decided to step down.

But before doing so the executive committee set in motion an independent review of the Club's operations. I also did all I could to make certain that I was succeeded by Colin Methven. I knew he had the skills to turn the fortunes of the Club around although he, like me, was not the obvious choice, because of his short length of service on the committee. In this I was successful and handed over to him after the Annual General Meeting in July 2004.

For me it had been an interesting two years. I grew to love the Club – and particularly the faithful staff. I cannot say that about the main committee. It was too large for decision-making. It would not have been a sensible command structure in war. But that has now all changed.

HRH The Prince of Wales and Major General PAJ Cordingley.

The kitchens finally now had to be tackled, and the decision was taken that they should be rebuilt to conform to new standards, at a cost of £800,000. The only way of raising the money was to embark on a new fundraising campaign, with the aim of topping up a £200,000 bank loan with £600,000 from the members.

It was agreed that members would each be asked for a contribution 'equal to a year's subscription' and it was noted that the wording of the request would have to be carefully done to avoid payment of VAT. Approval was given at the autumn EGM in 1991 to make this a levy on members, although the Secretary noted that 'It is the firm intention of the committee not to require a levy, if sufficient voluntary contributions are received by the end of the year, and are redoubling their efforts to encourage members to help in this way'. It was, however, mandated, and was not welcomed in all quarters. One disgruntled member, chased for his payment as late as 1995, wrote: 'The request for additional funds for the kitchens, which itself was preceded by the request for funds to buy the freehold, seemed unreasonable… By insisting on payment of the kitchen fund money you have forced out a number of well intentioned members who were very happy to continue to pay their subscriptions, although they rarely, if ever, used the place, but were not on that basis prepared to pay additional amounts… Only you will know what effect the kitchen fund ultimatum has had on that goodwill.'

The kitchens were duly refurbished, and the food on offer greatly improved. Anton Edelmann, chef de cuisine at the Savoy Hotel, became a food consultant in the early 1990s, a role that was also taken on by Marco Pierre White a decade later. In 1997 the new chef was Keith Stanley, who had previously worked at the Ritz and the Savoy, and it was approvingly noted that 'he has already started to make great improvements to the food while maintaining the essential Club style'. The Coffee Room was refurbished that year too. And an approach was made to Searcy's to see if they could help with the banqueting bookings – harking back some thirty years to an earlier Guards Club initiative.

Meanwhile, the Ministry of Defence's 'Options for Change' initiative heralded a 40 per cent cut in the cavalry and a 25 per cent cut in the Guards. Widening the membership became essential, and the committee considered a 'green paper' on this issue which was subsequently approved at an AGM. Families of a person qualified to be a member would henceforth be allowed to apply for membership, and applications from gentlemen supported by twelve existing members would also be welcome. In addition, one year

It was a beautiful day in September 2001 when I left the Club on my way to Heathrow, to catch my return flight to America. After I had checked in and was in the process of boarding the aircraft, the news came of the attack on the twin towers in New York, and the grounding of all trans-Atlantic flights. Commendably, British Airways handed us all a note suggesting that this emergency would last many days and not to stay in the airport.

It was a strangely quiet centre of London that I returned to that afternoon. Fortunately I was able to get my old room back in the Club. I sat transfixed in the television room as the attacks were replayed. I had moved from the World Trade Center several years before, but had spent ten happy years on the 89th Floor of the North Tower, which I saw take a direct hit. During our tenure in the towers a twisted sense of humour dictated that none of us on the higher floors took part in fire drills, on the assumption we had little chance of survival. Watching it happen was something altogether different.

With 50,000 workers or visitors in each of the towers on an average day, those of us who knew the complex feared for the worst. The greatest blessing was that 'only' 2,700 people lost their lives. There was no hope for the British employees of Canter Fitzgerald, working on a high floor. Equally, the Windows of the World restaurant where we entertained had no survivors. I sat watching it all in a deep armchair, grateful for the quiet haven that the Club offered on a day when the whole world went mad.

John Woods Conlin

transitional subscriptions were approved for those leaving the army; this was subsequently extended to two years and long-standing members were rewarded by having their subscriptions frozen once combined age and length of membership hit 110.

Two years later in 1993, in anticipation of 1994 being the Year of the Yeoman, the committee decided to amend the subscription rates for yeomanry members, bringing them into line with the rates enjoyed by serving regular officers. At the same time it was agreed that the definition of yeomanry would encompass all regiments who were in the Yeomanry Association, as it was recognised that this would potentially be a fertile source of new military members at a time when the Club needed them.

Membership as an issue regularly exercised the committee. In January 1995, under the auspices of Brigadier James Rucker who had been appointed the membership development officer, the Member Gets Member scheme was launched. Nearly four years later, in December 1998, the Chairman reported that the committee was under increasing pressure from members, articulated by prestigious bodies including the Cavalry Colonels, to introduce a two-tier membership structure to offer the infrequent user a reduced subscription. A vital precondition to any decision to establish such a scheme would be the introduction of the integrated IT system linked to Club membership cards to record individual members' total spend.

THE MEMBER WHO SAID, "RALLY? WHAT RALLY?"

The countryside comes to London.

Work to the building continued. Although the services of an in-house painter and decorator had been dispensed with in 1992 as an unjustifiable luxury, an in-house laundry was built and a pool table was introduced outside the barber's shop. But savings still had to be made, for example by the merger of the two dining rooms. Not all changes met with approval: there were many objections when the old television room outside Geoffrey's Bar was upgraded and the television moved to the small smoking room.

Lady members, however, were finding the facilities open to them widening. The year 1993 not only saw a change in membership criteria in that a lady no longer needed to be a family member to qualify, but they were also able to use Geoffrey's Bar after 5.30pm. Two years later, a new Ladies Advisory Group started under the chairmanship of Anne Curran, and the ladies' involvement in the Club has gone from strength to strength, particularly in the arrangement of social activities.

In 1998, however, the Chairman, John Rodwell, announced to the committee that he was unhappy with a number of aspects of the Club's management. These included the general standard of maintenance within the Club, an apparently high staff turnover, the cost of various services within the Club to members (particularly in the bars and dining rooms), overt commercialism within the Club, the lack of attention to detail and the balance between the number of supervisors against 'foot soldiers'. Lord Vivian and Robin Kernick

volunteered to carry out a management review with the Secretary to look at the organisational structure.

John Rodwell's views were insightful. At the turn of the century and during the opening years of the twenty-first century, it was becoming increasingly clear that the Club needed a tighter management structure and a more modern and professional approach to the challenges of developing and maintaining an

Chairman's Dinner, 2006.

institution which both revelled in its history and traditions and needed to offer a thoroughly up-to-date service if it was to keep the loyalty of its members.

Many members of the committee recognised this too, and when Patrick Cordingley succeeded as Chairman in 2002 it was with a new executive role and a defined two days a week presence; but this was to prove contentious, since it inevitably resulted in tensions between his job and that of the Secretary, with the lack of a clear division of roles proving difficult to manage. It also exposed differences of opinion within the Club committee, and when Cordingley decided to resign after two years in office to leave the way clear for a new broom, the challenge was taken up by Colin Methven, who saw clearly that there had to be fundamental changes in governance. The matrix within which these could be achieved was fortunately in place, since Patrick Vigors had been commissioned in 2004 to undertake a further review, whose wide-ranging suggestions were now keenly embraced by the new Chairman.

The process of change was, as ever, a bumpy one, and resulted at the end of 2004 in the departure of the Secretary. Fortunately Patrick Vigors was available to take on the role in the interim before a new Secretary could be appointed, and he and the Chairman worked closely together to implement the fundamental changes he had suggested. Many of these involved improved facilities for members within the new electronic age, but perhaps the most notable were changes in the size and operational arrangement of the committee, resulting in a structure which fostered clear and

swift decision-making. The appointment in May 2005 of David Cowdery as the new Secretary was the next step in the ever-speedier gallop towards a more effective and efficient method of running the Club. His background in the hotel business, combined with that of a military family, proved ideal, and the fruitful collaboration between Chairman and Secretary over the following years saw major improvements both in the facilities and services on offer and in the revenue that resulted.

Colin Methven's chairmanship oversaw the difficult business of selling the annexe building, as well as many alterations and refurbishments in the main building. Membership had been boosted by a number of initiatives during the first years of the century, and other modernising ventures were bringing the Club up to date – not least the final acceptance of ladies on the committee. Younger members found their voices listened to more carefully as well, and the larger than expected profit from the sale of the annexe left the next Chairman, David Rosier, in the happy position of being able to pay off debts, redeem debentures, fund building and renovation work and yet leave a healthy sum in the bank to pay for future improvements.

So it is that the Cavalry and Guards Club can now celebrate its two centenaries secure in the knowledge that its home is both safely in its own ownership and in an excellent state of repair and functionality. Its members can look forward to the future with confidence and belief in their Club as a vigorous and flourishing institution, fit for purpose for the next century of its existence. □

VIEW FROM THE CHAIR
COLIN N F METHVEN, CHAIRMAN 2004–7

As the most junior member of the committee in early 2004, I think my appointment as Chairman in the middle of that year came as a surprise to many members. Indeed, until Patrick Cordingley announced he would be retiring at the AGM that year, it hadn't crossed my mind that I might find myself at the steering wheel; nor, I might add, had it crossed the mind of any other committee member.

So how did this strange state of affairs come about? There were a number of different reasons, but to me the most important of these was that the affairs of the Club had reached a watershed.

John Rodwell (left), Colin Methven (centre) and Lord Carrington.

For decades the Club had not been generating enough revenue to keep 127 up to the high standards with which it was built 100 years ago. Indeed, at the time we were negotiating to buy the building in 1987, our landlords served us with a dilapidation charge of £1.5m. The subsequent acquisition of the freehold was a fantastic achievement. However, the dilapidations needed to be addressed and the cost of the freehold included borrowings on which interest had to be paid.

My predecessors did a gallant job, making best use of tight funds to renovate most of the main rooms. However, pressure was brought to bear on members to make 'donations' for the modernisation of the kitchens, while a few years later the committee decided to borrow money to repair and modernise the hall and staircase, and again to renovate the second floor dining room and drawing room. The Club was thus vastly improved, but our borrowings started to accrue and by 2004 our bankers were understandably not enthusiastic about lending us any more money.

Nevertheless, more money was badly needed. The exterior of 127 was crying out for repair, and the third floor was starting to give us some serious headaches as well. In addition, a number of the improvements which had been made during the previous fifteen years would soon need updating again. In late 2003, under the chairmanship of Patrick Cordingley, the committee had asked an independent consultant, Patrick Vigors, to undertake a review and advise what steps it could take to assure the Club's future. Patrick delivered a very comprehensive report, which included proposals for fundamental change.

The committee agreed the recommendations of the report in principle, though it must be said that the degree of enthusiasm varied between individual committee members. More importantly, disagreement emerged as to how these recommendations should be implemented. While this was going on, Patrick Cordingley announced that he wanted to stand aside to allow a new Chairman a fresh start to tackle the challenges that lay ahead.

Unfortunately, the disagreement mentioned above had opened up a split within the committee. My personal view was that the time had come for fundamental change and that bold action, rather than the more cautious approach favoured by some of my colleagues, was

needed. I therefore put my hat in the ring to be Chairman, subsequently winning an election by a small margin.

One of the key recommendations of the report was to reduce the size of the committee in order to facilitate clear and swift decision-making. My first change, therefore, was to reduce the committee from twenty-four members to a maximum of twelve, and to hold monthly meetings, rather than quarterly as had been the case. We also established an advisory council of up to thirty members. These changes set us up to cope with the challenging two years that lay ahead.

From the first meeting of the new committee we started to plan the way forward. I was much helped by David Rosier, Vice Chairman, who was very supportive from the start. I also worked closely with the Club Secretary and started to discuss some of the changes I was planning with him. This worked well at the beginning, but as the weeks marched by it became clear that the Secretary and I had different views on a number of issues. In particular, I wanted to raise service standards in order straightaway to make the Club more attractive for members, thereby encouraging them to use it more. I was also determined that we should set ourselves challenging budgetary targets and involve our senior staff in that process. This difference of views was holding up the process of change, and was to lead to a parting of the ways, with the Secretary leaving us at the end of 2004.

It was logical that Patrick Vigors should become acting Secretary, and we were fortunate that he was available. He did a marvellous job of holding the fort, and he and I worked closely together as we started the process of change. During the next four months we published the first of our quarterly newsletters, recreated the porter's box opposite the front

Colin Methven with The Duchess of Cornwall and Mrs Sandra Nelson, Chairman, Ladies Committee.

door and, through my son's introduction, appointed Marco Pierre White as a consultant to help us improve the standard of our food. We also started a new ladies committee, led by Sandra Nelson, and also a younger members committee. We then asked the chairmen of both these groups to join the committee.

My next urgent task was to find a new Club Secretary. It seemed likely that a senior hotelier would be the most suitable solution, and I was very fortunate to be introduced to David Cowdery by Tim Royle, a member of the Club. In April 2005 the committee approved his appointment as our new Secretary, and he joined us in early May. With his long career in the hotel business, he brought invaluable experience and was quick to get his feet under the table. His professional management immediately made its mark, with efficiency levels rising and his friendly manner creating a welcoming atmosphere in the Club. During his first weeks he oversaw the dismantling of the old porter's desk, thereby returning the hall to its former glory.

With David Cowdery on board, the process of change continued apace with the opening of the new library or business room on the ground floor, the start of a comprehensive programme of events organised by the ladies committee and, with the arrival of an additional barman, the ability to keep the bar open until 11pm. These various changes seemed to be appreciated by the members, who started to use the Club more, and as a result the operating surplus at the end of 2005 increased from £100,000 to £165,000 – and that was after we had spent £30,000 more than the previous year on improvements to the building. I was particularly pleased that our focus on improving the quality of the food in the dining rooms, thanks to help from Marco Pierre White and the hard work of our kitchen and dining room staff, led to more business there.

Also in 2005 the committee had been giving careful consideration to the future of the annexe. This building was in a much worse state of repair than 127, with one of the four floors closed up because it had been condemned. Many ideas were considered, but apart from a sale all of them would have involved the Club in an outlay of at least £500,000 to bring the building back to just a basic standard; indeed we later on realised that this figure would be closer to £1 million. We were also conscious that the eleven bedrooms could be replaced by making better use of the basement and third floors of 127 and that the annexe was otherwise surplus to our needs.

So, recognising that the backlog of repairs to 127 had to be our first priority, we sought professional advice as to the saleability of the annexe, conscious that access through Down Street Mews would be vital and that this would need the agreement of its owners. The advice we received was that a sale might raise between £1.5 and £2 million, and the question of access was left to us to resolve; it was only some months later that we found this would be more difficult than we then realised.

The committee decided to proceed with the sale in principle, but to seek the support of the members by holding an EGM. This duly took place on 18 January 2006 and, although there was a heated debate, the committee's decision was supported by a large majority.

Away from the annexe, at the beginning of 2006 change was still continuing at 127 with the renovation of Geoffrey's Bar and the creation of additional bedrooms in the basement, and with increased use of the Club by members the financial results got off to a flying start to the extent that I was able to report to the AGM in June that we had made a £100,000 surplus during the first five months, compared to £50,000 in 2005. It was truly exciting to see the changes we had introduced in 2005 paying off so well. That busy year finished on a high note, with a surplus in excess of £300,000, and at last we were in a position to repair the external elevations of 127; the work was undertaken in 2007.

As far as the sale of the annexe was concerned, 2006 was a frustrating year. Having made the decision to sell early in the year, we had been unable to reach agreement with the owners of the mews for access. Nevertheless, the delay played into our hands as the commercial property market continued to improve, and when we eventually exchanged contracts in April 2007 the agreed price of £3.6m (after paying for the access) was double the original estimate of only fifteen months earlier. Furthermore, it was only three months later that the market started to falter. We were extremely fortunate, and owe a huge debt to Ian Frazer and David Cowdery for their hard work.

I retired at the AGM in June 2007 after three challenging but rewarding years. Much important work still lay ahead, but I felt that the building blocks for a more prosperous Club were in place. I was delighted to know that David Rosier would be in charge, assisted by the committee, our able Secretary and our hard-working staff.

Colin Methven with his wife at the Waterloo Ball, 2008.

VIEW FROM THE CHAIR
DAVID ROSIER, CHAIRMAN 2007– PRESENT

After four years as Vice Chairman and eleven years on the committee, I took over from Colin Methven as Chairman in June 2007. What a marvellous legacy he had left me. We had a Secretary who, as a former hotelier and the son of a soldier, knew how to manage our Club, the Club was trading more profitably than for many years and, most importantly, members were enjoying using it.

In addition, a contract had been signed to sell the annexe, which would not only get rid of a costly liability but also provide the Club with much needed funds. I therefore spent the first two months of my chairmanship waiting anxiously (in a falling property market) for the deal to complete, which it did on 30 July 2007.

From the sale we received £3.6m after all costs, but before tax of some £650,000. In order to decide what should be done with this windfall, which technically belonged to 127 Piccadilly plc, the company which owns the Club's buildings, I set up a small committee consisting of Ian Frazer, David Floyd (both directors of 127 Piccadilly plc), John Rothwell and myself.

We concluded that our top priority was to reduce the Club's debt. We immediately therefore paid off the Club's long term bank debt of some £500,000 and also decided to redeem the subscription debentures five years early at 31 December 2007 which cost a further £700,000 or so. The only outstanding debt remaining was that of the capital debentures. Here we agreed to earmark a sum of money to buy the debentures in if the Club was offered them by holders.

As I write, the remaining £1.5m is on deposit in the bank. Much of this will be used in 2009 to pay for the planned refurbishment of the third floor, where it is intended that each bedroom will have a shower and lavatory en suite, and the first stage of installing a new cooling and heating system, 'comfort cooling', in the Club.

A happy outcome of the decision to redeem the subscription debentures is that the money set aside to repay the debenture holders in 2012 has been put into a contingency fund to be used for emergencies and to add to the Club's collection of pictures and silver.

I was lucky to inherit a strong committee from my predecessor and to have as Vice Chairman Christopher MacKenzie Beevor, who not only 'led the charge' on Cavalry & Guards: A London Home – this book to mark the centenary of 127 Piccadilly – but also, as befits one who was Colonel of

Above left: David Rosier (right) and Christopher MacKenzie Beevor, 2007.

the QDG, gives me sound advice and steadfast support. Thankfully, long-term stalwarts Willy Peto and John Rothwell agreed to stay on and give me great support as well as many laughs. Sandra Nelson, who also chairs the ladies committee, has been responsible for the Club's excellent and varied entertainment programme including the spectacular Waterloo Ball in June 2008. Two long-term committee members, James Rucker, who led on membership matters, and David Floyd decided to retire from the committee. Happily, to replace them, I persuaded Simon Brooks-Ward, Ewen Cameron, Martin Pocock, Peter Scrope, Buzz West and Christian Yates to join the committee. All contribute enormously to the discussions at our meetings.

The first year of my chairmanship saw several improvements made to the Club's fabric. After many years of waiting, the front and rear elevations have been cleaned for the first time since 127 Piccadilly opened for business in 1909, revealing some most attractive stonework. The cleaning of the brickwork at the rear of the Club overlooking the garden terrace encouraged us to give the terrace – something unique and precious in clubland in the new no-smoking era

order to move with the times, in the summer of 2008 the Balaclava Room was returned to the library it formerly was, providing another room where members could work with their laptop computers.

I have mentioned our excellent Secretary, David Cowdery, already. He is ably supported by the Club staff, many of whom have been with us for some years. I cannot mention all the staff by name but Jay Jogia, our financial controller, Paul Farmer, our chef, Mark Beasley, our functions manager, Pietro Petronella, our dining room manager, Julio Alvarez, our sommelier, Alix King, our banqueting coordinator, Arletty Jooron, our housekeeper, Frances Watt, our membership secretary, and Soran Marshall, David Cowdery's PA all make a huge contribution to the successful running of the Club.

As a 'five year wonder' in 1st The Queen's Dragoon Guards who never got above the rank of Captain, I never dreamt, when signing up for the Club on joining my regiment in Londonderry in March 1974, that some thirty-three years later I would become its Chairman. It is a great honour and privilege – as well as enormous fun – to be Chairman of this marvellous Club at a time of such change and when members are using the Club more and more.

Above: The refurbished terrace, 2008.

– a facelift by refurbishing and moving the original Edwardian glass canopy and purchasing new furniture. This allowed us to cock a snook at the government of the day by holding a cigar and port dinner on the terrace on the first anniversary of the no-smoking law.

The front entrance to the Club has also been enhanced by refurbishing and repositioning the two Russian mortar shells that had stood at the entrance to the Guards Club and had languished on the terrace in a poor state of repair since the amalgamation.

There has also been a large amount of change below stairs and behind the green baize door, prompted by the vacation of the annexe. The finance and membership office has been moved to a newly-created office and the Chairman's office dispensed with, thus allowing us to bring four of the original bedrooms in the basement back on stream; staff changing rooms have been created, further improvements made to the kitchens and wine cellars created in the old coal cellars under the pavement. Finally, the ladies' lavatories on the second floor and the gentlemen's lavatories on the ground floor have been refurbished, not before time! And in

Right: David Rosier listening to The Princess Royal, 2007.

Sporting Occasions

Both the Cavalry Club and the Guards Club enthusiastically supported a variety of sporting occasions over their history, as the merged Club still does, whether through active participation or through providing venues at the events offering hospitality to members. Club tents with catering facilities for members wishing to partake of luncheon and tea have been, and still are, features of race meetings and cricket matches, though they have also been victims of the need for cost-cutting from time to time and were suspended during both twentieth-century world wars.

ETON V HARROW MATCH

The annual cricket match between Eton and Harrow is the longest running regular sporting fixture to be held at Lord's cricket ground; the first recorded match was played in 1805 at the Old Ground (where Dorset Square now stands), and the first match on the current ground was in 1818. Both the Cavalry and the Guards Clubs erected tents at the ground for the fixture when the cost could be justified (see pages 162–3 for a fuller account of the occasion).

The committee meeting minutes regularly record debates about whether or not the tent could be afforded, such as on 20 March 1922 when the question of a Guards Club tent at the Eton/Harrow Match was discussed. The previous year had seen considerable congestion, so it was decided to proceed that year on different lines. Three years later, in 1925, the records show that 792 luncheons and 1,122 teas were served at the match.

In 1950 the Guards Club tent lost approximately £160 on the venture, and so the following year arrangements were made to share with the Cavalry Club. The Carlton Club were also partners in the 1960s, though they were dropped in 1966 in favour of the Old Etonian Association and by 1969 both the OEA and the Old Harrovians had given up their tents.

ETON V HARROW,
LORDS, JUILLET, 1898.

MENU.

POISSONS.
Truite Saumoné S^{ce.} Remoulade.
Mayonnaise de Saumon.   Mayonnaise de Homard.

ENTRÉES.
Petits Aspics de Crevette.
Suprême de Volaille à l'ivorie.
Côtelettes d'agnead à la Santiago.
Chaudfroid de Caille à la Strasbourg.
Kari de Mouton à l'Afridi.

GROSSES PIECES.
Jambon d'York.   Langue de Bœuf.
Aloyau de Bœuf, S^{ce.} Raifort.   Quartier d'Agneau S^{ce.} Menthe.
Poulet découpé au Cresson.   Pâté de Pigeon à l'Anglaise.
Terrine de Foie Gras.
Asperges en Branches.
Salade de Pomme de Terre Nouvelle.
Salade de Saison.   Salade de Tomate.

ENTREMÊTS.
Gelée Klondyke.   Meringues à la Parisienne.
Macedoine de Fruits.   Petits Gateaux Française.

DESSERT.
Glace Victoria.
Café

Eton v Harrow menu at Lords, 1898.

THE GRAND MILITARY RACE MEETING AT SANDOWN

The Grand Military Race Meeting is held each year on the Friday before the Cheltenham National Hunt Festival at Sandown Park racecourse, in Surrey. It has been held since 1841 and hosted at Sandown Park since 1881, and it would appear that the Cavalry Club has been involved in some way with the meeting since 1890. As early as 4 March 1895, committee minutes noted that 'owing to the uncertain weather it was decided not to have a luncheon tent at Sandown for the Grand Military Meeting, and notices were placed in the smoking room and front hall to that effect'. The Guards Club also supported the event, with its own tent.

The reason for the Clubs' involvement is that this unique race meeting provides an annual opportunity for servicemen, and women, to ride under the rules of racing, as amateurs, at one of Britain's most prestigious National Hunt racecourses. There was strong historical precedent. In the past, when horses accompanied cavalry officers around the world, military racing

Left: Cavalry Club members outside the Club's tent at Sandown, 1920s.

Right: Inside the Club's tent at Sandown.

Below: A Sandown menu, 1894.

was an important part of military life. Racing in India, for example, still harks back to these origins. Military racing was an opportunity for horses and riders to hone skills and reactions while also providing a social event for military personnel serving abroad.

The Grand Military can boast a long and distinguished list of past riders, including Cavalry Club member Captain Lawrence Oates, the pony man on the ill-fated expedition to the South Pole, who was a keen supporter of military racing. Oates' horse, Angel Gabriel, won the Grand Military Handicap Steeplechase, as the Grand Military Gold Cup was then known, in 1907 and finished second in the two following years.

In those early years, the Club marquees were basic affairs, set in the centre of the course, but due to the competition from regimental tents, use of them was erratic.

In 1923 a discussion took place in the Guards Club committee as to the advisability of having the usual tent at the Grand Military Meeting. The figures relating to the losses sustained for the years 1920, 1921 and 1922 were considered, and it was unanimously decided that no tent could be provided for that year. There is no record as to whether it was ever revived.

The Cavalry Club, having also decided that their own tent was not sufficiently successful in the years after the Second World War, took refuge first within the general facilities provided in the grandstand and, in 1956, secured a section of the members' restaurant for the sole use of Club members. Attendance was sporadic, however, and by 1965 the number using the coach to the course provided by the Cavalry Club had declined to two, so it was discontinued.

During the 1970s and 1980s the space allocated to the Club in the Paddock Bar regularly shrank, which generated scores of complaints from members who were annoyed at the lack of comfort and the poor standard of service. As a consequence, the Club decided to hire their own marquee for 1991 in the hope that the situation would improve, which unfortunately it did not. ▶ 164

BLUE ON BLUE: ETON V HARROW AT LORD'S

As so many members of Eton and Harrow cricket teams later served in cavalry or Guards regiments, and because the Club for many years had a tent at the annual match, it seems appropriate to include a short note about this perennial encounter.

The first cricket match between Harrow and Eton is believed to have taken place in 1800, but no records of the results survive. The first game to take place at Lord's (then situated in Dorset Fields) was a one-day match on 2 August 1805. The most celebrated member of either team on this occasion was Lord Byron, a Harrovian, who may have been responsible for issuing the original challenge to Eton. Byron appears to have played at his own insistence and against the wishes of the Harrow captain. Having a club foot, Byron was permitted a runner, but as he only achieved seven runs in the first innings and two in the second his runner was not unduly taxed. As Byron put it, Harrow were 'most confoundedly beat', Eton winning by an innings and two runs. The two sides later went to the Haymarket Theatre and caused a considerable disturbance. An Etonian poet's fair if not entirely magnanimous comment on the result ran: 'Adventurous "boys" of Harrow School, of cricket you've no knowledge. Ye played not cricket but the fool with "men" of Eton College'.

Although some matches are believed to have been played in the years following 1805, the next one for which records exist took place in 1818, by which time Lord's had moved to its present site and two-day matches had been instituted. The Eton side was severely depleted as the match was arranged at the end of term, by which time all but three members of their First XI had gone home. Harrow won by thirteen runs, captained by a former Etonian, Charles Oxenden, who having been expelled from Eton for a minor mutiny took a carriage to Harrow and was admitted there the following morning. Matches at that date began at 10am and play continued until 7.30 or 8pm, regardless of the weather. Bowling was underarm, wickets were rough and unpredictable and no match ended in a draw until 1860. Cricket was played in breeches and tall hats, at least until 1830, and Eton's light blue was adopted the following year.

Eton v Harrow cricket match at Lord's, 1864.

In 1841 Eton won the match by the highest-ever margin of an innings and 175 runs, largely thanks to the batting of Emilius Bayley, whose score of 152 remained a record until 1904; no Harrovian achieved a century against Eton until 1860. At one point in the mid-1840s, Harrow numbers were down to sixty-seven, and as Eton then had some 600 to choose from, it is remarkable that Harrow went on to win four of the matches in that decade.

One of the Harrow team in the 1841 match, William Nicholson, was later to be instrumental in saving Lord's cricket ground from property developers, when in 1866 he lent the MCC £18,355 to purchase the freehold. At that date, the Eton v Harrow match had not acquired its later prestige as a social event, and the only spectators were normally boys and a few of their relatives. One of the diversions in that era was an annual fight between two cads, traditionally instigated by the Eton pug with the comment: 'All the good I see in 'Arrow is that you can see Eton from it, if you go into the churchyard'. In later years a more seemly alternative spectacle was the real tennis match between Oxford and Cambridge.

Left: Lord Byron (1788–1824).

Admit One for ETON v. HARROW TO MEMBERS' ENCLOSURES

Ist. DAY

JULY 8TH, 1938.

This does not admit at the gate and must be worn so as to be seen by attendants.

No. 8565

In 1852, John Wisden, later the founder of the *Almanack*, became the cricket professional at Harrow, and Harrow's distinctive blue-and-white striped cap dates from the same year. By this time, protective clothing was in use, and on the Lord's billboard for the 1854 match there is an advertisement for Dark's 'newly-invented leg-guards, also his tubular and other India rubber gloves, spiked soles for cricket shoes and cricket balls'. Rather surprisingly, the Eton XI did not wear white boots until 1891. At that period there were no boundary ropes, and every hit had to be run. If the ball happened to go into a group of hostile spectators, they might well make it difficult for a fielder to retrieve it in order to give the batsmen more time to run.

No match was played in 1856, as the headmaster of Eton refused to allow it to take place at Lord's, and Harrow refused his offer to hold it at Eton. Fortunately the match returned to Lord's in 1858, and in 1860, no doubt due in part to the advent of railway travel, it drew a large crowd for the first time. By 1864, when 16,000 spectators, including the Prince and Princess of Wales, attended, the event had, according to *The Times*, become 'the Derby Day of the cricketing year'. In the same year, overarm bowling was authorised by the MCC, and boundary ropes were introduced. A boundary counted for three runs, prompting the words of a Harrow song in which Queen Elizabeth, having granted a charter to the school's founder, allegedly announces a great decree that 'Hits to the rail shall count for three/And six when fairly over'. By the time the song was composed in 1875, the 'great decree' was already obsolete, as boundaries had been increased to four runs in 1870. In that year crowd levels reached such a record figure that the takings for the two days amounted to £1,450. As a consequence, for the first time no one was allowed into the ground on horseback, although this did not of course prevent spectators' carriages being parked around the boundary, a practice which continued until well after the Second World War.

A succession of drawn games in the mid-1890s led to a proposal in 1897 that the match should be extended to three days. This was turned down by the headmaster of Eton on the grounds of disruption to academics (hardly a strong argument in those blissful days before the advent of A levels), and of the equal importance to Eton of Henley. In 1900, the closest ever finish was recorded when Harrow won by one wicket, and in 1904 D C Boles of Eton established the highest score ever achieved in this series with 183 runs. In 1910, by which time spectator levels had reached 20,000 per day, the event described by *Wisden* as

the most remarkable turnaround in the history of the match took place. In this game Harrow, needing 55 to win and with all wickets standing, suffered a catastrophic collapse when eight members of the team succumbed to the devastating bowling of R St L Fowler (later 17th Lancers). The last pair, which included the future Field Marshal Alexander (later Irish Guards), put on thirteen runs, but when Alexander was finally caught in the slips for eight, Eton won by nine runs. This was particularly disappointing for Harrow, as they thereafter failed to achieve a single win between 1909 and 1939, although in 1913 G Wilson recorded Harrow's highest ever score, with 173 runs.

No match was played in 1915, and in the remaining three years of the Great War the matches were played at Eton or Harrow rather than at Lord's. In 1923, Eton achieved the highest innings score in the history of the match, with 502, though to no avail as the game ended in a draw, aided by a record last wicket stand of 92 by Harrow in their first innings.

Despite the one-sided nature of the encounters in the inter-war years, Lord's remained a most fashionable event, 30,000 spectators being recorded in 1932. Although no matches were played there during the Second World War, the occasion had resumed much of its former splendour by the early 1950s, with carriages still parked around the boundary and most spectators, other than boys, in morning dress. In the 1960s a gradual relaxation began in the formality of the occasion, with morning dress eventually disappearing. County cricket became totally professional in 1962, effectively ending the progress of those who had played in the Lord's match into first class cricket after leaving school or university. Despite becoming a one-day single-innings event in 1982, Eton v Harrow at Lord's remains a popular item in the sporting calendar.

Right: Club tent at the Eton v Harrow match, 1909.

ROYAL ASCOT

The world's most famous race meeting dates back to 1711 when Queen Anne made the decision to purchase a plot of land close to Windsor Castle, believing it would be a suitable location for holding races. The land was purchased by the Crown for the princely sum of £558, and the first races were held in August of that same year. The very first race held at the course, Her Majesty's Plate, carried a purse of 100 guineas and was open to mares, colts and geldings over the age of six. It was also something of a handicap event, with each horse required to carry twelve stone. Seven horses competed in that first event, with the winner decided after three heats of four miles. As time passed the event gradually expanded to include more races, with the first four-day meeting held in 1768.

From the beginning of the nineteenth century the race meeting grew in popularity among the aristocracy, in terms both of the racing and of the social events that came with it. In 1813 Ascot racecourse was made the subject of an Act of Enclosure which guaranteed public access to the land while ensuring that the racecourse remained the property of the Crown. The oldest of Royal Ascot's Grade 1 races came into existence in 1807, with the first running of the prized Ascot Gold Cup. The race, held on Ladies Day at the

HM Queen Elizabeth The Queen Mother presents the Grand Military Gold Cup to B Munro Wilson at Sandown Park, March 1981.

However, after a meeting with the caterers, the facilities provided in 1992 proved to be much more successful, and have continued in a similar format ever since.

In conjunction with the racing, the committee decided in 1992 to hold a Grand Military Ball at the end of the day, which was a great success and was therefore repeated in1993. But in 1994 there was insufficient interest and so it was cancelled.

Between 1970 and 2002, HM Queen Elizabeth The Queen Mother was the much valued patron of the meeting, running her horses in the military races as often as possible and with much success. She won the Grand Military Gold Cup on no fewer than five occasions – with Special Cargo in 1984, 1985 and 1986, The Argonaut in 1990 and Norman Conqueror in 1996. A statue of Special Cargo stands as a permanent memory to this at Sandown, in front of the weighing room and overlooking the winners' enclosure.

The Club's marquee at Royal Ascot, 2008.

Left: Ascot Royal Enclosure, 1895.

meet, proved to be a massive success and marked the occasion on which modern Royal Ascot came into existence.

Within the next fifty years the majority of the races now contested at the annual Royal Ascot meeting were established, including the Queen Anne Stakes and the St James's Palace Stakes. By the turn of the twentieth century, Royal Ascot had earned the reputation of being easily the most popular and prestigious flat racing meeting in Britain. In 1913 the Ascot Authority was established by virtue of an Act of Parliament to administer the racecourse and the races. Until 1939 Royal Ascot was the only meeting held there.

The involvement of both Clubs goes back many years. The Club tents were all originally on the heath side of the course, facing the small grandstand and the winning post. Along the rail would be the many four-in-hand coaches that conveyed racegoers to and from the course, and behind them a number of tents provided lunch and tea for Club members.

The Guards Club in 1925 charged 17s 6d for luncheon, with 1,388 served, and 2s 6d for tea, with 1,136 served. Interestingly, in 1932, the committee minutes record that, 'it was decided to make White's Club honorary members of our tent at Ascot'.

As the Secretary of the Cavalry Club, Anthony O'Connor, noted in his book *Clubland*, 'Pre-war, it was a much more leisurely performance. The Club closed for a week and all the staff went to Ascot, taking with them two hundred cases of champagne, one hundred cases of brandy, fifty cases of gin, fifty cases of whisky, fifty cases of port, five hundred pounds of beef, sixty hams, one thousand quails in aspic, three hundred pounds of fresh salmon and an arrangement for a daily delivery of fresh lobsters and crabs from a firm at Staines. You could, an old waiter told me, eat and drink yourself silly for ten bob! That was the all-in price for the whole day!'

After the Second World War the Club arranged to share a refreshment buffet tent with the Carlton Club, charging 5s per person per day for the use of the tent, with all drinks and meals paid for at the counter. By 1966, however, with the rearrangement of the

MENU DE DEJEUNER.
ASCOT, JUIN, 1894.

POISSONS.

Saumon à la Tartar.   Salade d'Homard.
Homard S^{ce} Mayonnaise. Crab Dressé. Filets de Sole Bagration.
Crevettes en Karie.   Suprême de Truites à la Jardinière.

ENTRÉES FROIDES.

Chaudfroid de Caille favorite.   Medaillons de Foie Gras.
Salades de Poulardes à la Louis.   Ballontine de Volaille.
Petites Pâtés à la Strasbourgeoise.   Côt. d'Agneau Connaught.
Chaudfroid de Volailles.   Pain de Mauviettes Printanieré.
Galantine de Dinde en Belle Vue.   Sandwiches Varieés.

GROSSES PIECES.

Rond de Bœuf Mameluke.   Hure de Sanglier à l'Ancienne.
Quartier d'Agneau S^{ce} Menthe.   Bœuf Pressé.
Aloyau de Bœuf au Raifort.   Pâtés de Volaille à la Française.
Jambon d'York.   Langue à l'Ecarlate.
Pâtés de Pigeon de Bordeaux.   Poulet Rôtie Deconpeés.
Asperges en Branches.   Salade de Saison.

ENTRÊMETS.

Gelee aux Frûits. Bavaroise Panachés. Meringues à la Vanille.
Tartes de Frûits Assortis. Patisseries Varieés. Fraises à la Crème.

Petworth Park, courtesy of the Earl of Egremont, but when that capricious nobleman did not renew the invitation in 1801, the Duke of Richmond came to their rescue by laying out a course on that part of the Goodwood estate known as the Harroway.

So pleased was the Duke with the popularity of that first two-day meeting that he organised a three-day meeting under Jockey Club rules the following year. On the first day he won with a horse called Cedar, but on the third day Cedar was beaten by Trumpator, owned by the Prince of Wales, later King George IV. To accommodate the more distinguished guests the Duke had a small wooden stand erected.

Goodwood's popularity as a venue for racing began to grow rapidly, particularly after the Second World War during which time there had been no racing on the course. In 1953, 55,000 spectators were there for the Tuesday of the July meeting (still at that time the only fixture staged at Goodwood; an August meeting had been held from 1946 to 1948, but had then been dropped from the programme), with no fewer than 21,000 on the slopes of Trundle Hill. That figure has never been surpassed, though the meeting continues to attract a good crowd each year.

Ascot Menu, 1894.

course, the decline in popularity of the tents and the building of a new grandstand, the Cavalry Club discontinued its presence: 'Very few of our own members have used the tent in the past two years, and with the vastly increased amenities in the new stand, the demand for a tent is insufficient to warrant the work and cost involved'.

In the early 1980s the now combined Club committee suggested that a tent be re-established at Royal Ascot; but having considered the idea, and been offered only a location on the heath side, the committee deemed it unlikely to make sufficient profit, particularly since the location was 'too far distant from the amenities and unpopular with Royal Enclosure members'. So it was not until 1998 that a Club tent was re-established, at first sharing with Buck's (a previous partner in 1955 after the Cavalry Club had given up their tent). Originally adjacent to the parade ring in Green Yard, the marquee has moved several times, and following the building of a new grandstand in 2005/6 now forms part of a 'Royal Enclosure Garden' with other clubs – White's, Turf, Buck's and the Garrick.

GOODWOOD

The third Duke of Richmond introduced racing to Goodwood out of a sense of obligation to the officers of the Sussex Militia, of which he was the Colonel, rather than any devotion to the turf. For many years the officers had held their annual races in nearby

Charles Lennox, 3rd Duke of Richmond and Lennox, by George Romney.

GOODWOOD, 1894.

MENU.

POISSON.

Saumon, Sauce Tartare.   Mayonnaise d'Homard.

ENTRÉES.

Cailles Farcies à la Perigord.
Côtelettes de Mouton en Chaudfroid.
Petits Pâtes Variées.
Sandwiches de Foie Gras.   Petits Aspics de Volaille.

GROSSES PIECES.

Pontets Rôtis au Cresson.   Quarter d'Agneau Rôti.
Langue de Bœuf à la Gelée.
Bœuf Braize.   Jambon de York.
Salade.

ENTREMÊTS.

Genoise Glacé.
Meringues à la Crême.   Bonchées aux Amandes.
Dessert.

Above left: Goodwood menu, 1894.

Above right: A painting of the riders preparing to start a race at Goodwood, 1836.

As with Ascot, the Clubs attended in a similar fashion, providing tents and catering facilities for their members, but things did not always proceed smoothly. In June 1908 a letter was received from Mr Dundas, the Duke of Richmond's agent, stating that the Cavalry Club would be required to employ Messrs Bertram & Co to cater for lunch at Goodwood. The Secretary was instructed to write and inform Mr Dundas that, if the Duke's decision was final, 'the Club would not require the space reserved for them on the lawn'. His Grace's decision stood and the Club did not go; but in 1909 he relented and the Club was allowed once again to 'find its own luncheon'. For how much longer is not known, as it is not recorded when the Clubs discontinued this fine tradition.

POLO

One sport with which the cavalry has been particularly associated is, of course, polo. The British cavalry drew up the earliest rules while in India in the 1850s, and in 1869 the first polo match was played in England on Hounslow Heath between the 10th Hussars and the 9th Lancers.

In 1874 the first polo match was played at Hurlingham in London, and a year later Hurlingham became the headquarters of polo and the Hurlingham Polo committee drew up the first

English rules. In 1903 the Hurlingham Polo committee was retitled the Hurlingham Club Polo Committee and expanded to include representatives on the Council from the services, the County Polo Association (formed in 1898 to look after the interests of the country clubs and to run the County Cup Tournaments, and which amalgamated with the HPA in 1949), the three London polo clubs – Hurlingham, Ranelagh and Roehampton – and all associations within the empire where polo was being played. In May 1904 permission was given to the Hurlingham Club Polo committee to hold its meetings at the Cavalry Club.

In 1925, the Hurlingham Club Polo committee was redesignated the Hurlingham Polo Association (HPA), but at the outset of war in 1939 polo was played at Hurlingham for the last time. The grounds were turned over to agricultural use and after the war they were subject to a compulsory purchase order for building. No polo was played in London during the Second World War, and it was not until 1952 that polo restarted in England with the HPA based at Cowdray Park, West Sussex. During the 1950s a Social Club Polo Cup Tournament with a cup presented by Buck's Club was devised, and involved regular participation from the London clubs.

A specific annual match involving the Cavalry and Guards and Buck's did not materialise until the 1990s, held first at the Guards

THE WESTCHESTER AND THE CORONATION CUPS

The following account by Colonel David Woodd was published in *127 Gazette* in spring 2003:

For many years the Westchester and Coronation Cups have languished in a strongroom, and the Hurlingham Polo Association, or HPA as it is more usually called, is delighted that the Cavalry and Guards Club has agreed to put the cups on display.

The Westchester Cup (right) represents the famous international series between America and England. Commissioned from Tiffany and Co by the Westchester Polo Club in Newport at a cost of $1200, or £240, the cup was first played for in 1886 when Hurlingham travelled to Newport, Rhode Island, to play the Americans and won both matches. In all, twelve Westchester Cup series were played between then and 1939, with the Americans winning nine times.

The Coronation Cup (below) was first presented and played for in 1911 to mark the coronation of King George V. From then until 1939 it was played for by the winners of the Inter Regimental and the major open tournaments at Hurlingham, Roehampton and Ranelagh. Until 1939, most of the leading players held a military rank and there are many famous names engraved upon both cups, many of whom served in either the Household Division or the cavalry: players such as Henry 'Mouse' Tompkinson who commanded 1st (Royal) Dragoons, Frederick 'Rattle' (his nickname the result of breaking so many bones falling off) Barrett, 15th Hussars, rated at ten goals from 1912 to 1920, Vivian Lockett, 17th Lancers, ten goals from 1912 to 1921, Noel Edwards, 9th Lancers, who died from gas poisoning during the Great War, Lesley Cheape, who was also killed in the war, and many others.

After the Second World War, England could not match America in player or pony power at the high goal level, but in 1970 Michael Butler, producer of the hit musical *Hair* and then governor of the United States Polo Association, was playing in England and, along with Lord Patrick Beresford and Ronald Ferguson, approached the HPA and USPA with an alternative to the Westchester series: the two countries would play an annual one-day International at a goal level suitable for both. The two associations agreed, and so was born the HPA's International Day.

The HPA chose as the trophy the historic Coronation Cup, English polo's most coveted high goal prize until 1939. The first International was held at Cowdray Park Polo Club in 1971, but moved the next year to the Guards Polo Club. In 1975, the HPA changed the format of the day to include teams from other countries, and over the years the challenge has been taken up by Mexico, Argentina, Brazil, Chile, South Africa, New Zealand and composite teams representing North and South America, Australasia and the Rest of the World.

In 1992, and again in 1997, International Day came full circle from its conception as an alternative to the Westchester Cup series; in 1992, the venerable trophy was played for again, with America winning, but in 1997 at the Guards Polo Club England won for the first time since the Great War.

The Hurlingham Polo Association's International Day has grown to be the world's biggest polo event. In 2002, in recognition of Her Majesty the Queen's Golden Jubilee, England played the Rest of the Commonwealth. In one of the most exciting matches in memory, the Rest of the Commonwealth won in the dying seconds. This year (2003) England will play Mexico at the Guards Polo Club, and it is hoped that we will play America for the Westchester Cup in the near future.

The HPA holds many of its meetings in the Club and those involved have certainly appreciated seeing both these wonderful cups on display. It is hoped that they will also be enjoyed by the members. Given their history, I am sure that both cups feel very much at home in the Club.

Cavalry and Guards Club polo match v Buck's Club at Cirencester Polo Club, May 1997.

Polo Club on Smith's Lawn, Windsor Great Park, and then, in its fourth year in 1997, at Cirencester Polo Club, with HRH The Prince of Wales included in the C&G team which was beaten by Buck's 8 goals to 3½. It is sad to record that, due to a lack of support from Club members, it did not continue, but there are constant hopes that this splendid fixture may be revived.

Short history of polo tournaments and cups

1876 The Champion Cup inaugurated at Hurlingham

1878 Inter-Regimental and the Oxford v Cambridge University matches inaugurated

1911 Coronation Cup presented on the coronation of King George V, when it was won by the Indian Polo Association. Thereafter it was played for by the winners of the four major Open Cups, until 1939. The Coronation Cup was first contested as an International Match in 1951 and 1953 and yearly since 1971.

1955 Polo ended at Roehampton. The Roehampton Cup was moved to Ham, now the only London polo club, and the County Cup to Cirencester Park Polo Club.

1956 Cowdray Park Gold Cup inaugurated

Other sports

Involvement on a smaller scale has been key to some of the Club's sporting occasions. For example in 1960, a race was held in conjunction with the Household Brigade Saddle Club on the course at Crowell, sharing a tent with the Guards Brigade, and in later years it was organised with the Grafton Hunt at Tweseldown. By 1965 however, only four runners had entered the race and the Club had incurred a debt of £73, so it was decided that it would not be run in 1966. A short, sharp burst of energetic involvement!

The involvement in sailing seems to have been similarly sporadic. As early as 1939 there is the suggestion in committee minutes of a Cavalry Yacht Club, though presumably nothing more was done due to onset of the Second World War. It was not until 1995 that the Club entered a team for the first time in the Royal Armoured Corps Yacht Club Regatta at Seaview, Isle of Wight. The Club team, ably skippered by Captain Simon Jacobs with Captain Alan Healy and the Club Secretary, Nicholas Walford, were a close second to the Armoured Trials and Development Unit.

In the following year, 1996, the Club was able to enter two teams, and the A team, consisting of Patrick Lort-Phillips, John Ross, John Prince and Robin Wilson, won the Ironside Trophy. But sadly committee member Major Robin Wilson, who was a driving force behind this success, was to die later that year in a tragic accident while moored in the Royal Yacht Squadron in Cowes, and consequently the Club's involvement in this sport waned.

Some sports have survived the changing patterns of Club life – and golf is one such sport. As early as 1910, the Cavalry Club committee records a motion to sanction the appointment of a committee for the regulation of golf competitions among members; and similarly in 1921, the Guards Club minutes note that 'the entrance fee for members representing the Club in the Inter-Club Golf Competition should be provided from the Club funds'.

In April 1933, annual accounts record, 'It is hoped that members who play golf, and who have not yet done so, will join the Cavalry Club Golfing Society. No charge is made.' A very smart suggestion book with the title 'Cavalry Club Golfing Society' has only one entry dated 12 May 1934: 'When more than 32 players – an eliminating round be played on Sat morning – match play against par – reducing the numbers to eight'. A pencilled note states that this was put to a General Meeting and not carried.

The Inter-Club Ski Race, 1994.

No records exist of golfing activities in the immediate post-war years but in 1979 efforts were made by the Chairman to revive the Golfing Society, with some little success. Nowadays an annual Cavalry and Guards Club golf match against the Royal West Norfolk is held at Brancaster, and teams regularly represent the Club in the Bath Club Cup which is an inter-club tournament played at Woking Golf Club.

Finally, a footnote to mention skiing, a sport enjoyed by many Club members but rarely presented on an organised basis. The exception to this was an Inter-Club Ski Race which took place in St Moritz on 12 February 1994 between the Cavalry and Guards, White's, Boodle's, The Turf, Brooks's, the Clubino in Milan and the Corviglia Ski Club. A hugely enjoyable occasion!

The Kadir Cup

This is probably one of the better known silver cups in the Club and has a fascinating history. The famous pig-sticking contest was first held in India in 1869. In 1873, Mr W A Forbes of the Indian Civil Service presented a cup to the winners of the competition, which was run after pig, first spears to count. The contestants were divided by lot into parties of not more than four and rode to spear in heats, continuing until the winner emerged from the final run. Each competitor could enter two horses and the cup was won by the horse, not the rider. The event was traditionally held at Sujhmana, near Meerut, where the Indian Mutiny started, in the Ganges Kadir (riverine) country. In 1922, a new and larger silver cup was presented by the Royal Calcutta Turf Club as a challenge trophy, and this is the one now on display in the Club. In addition, the winning owner received the sweepstake money for the purchase of a sealed-pattern cup, which he kept. The list of winners, whose names appear on the plinth of the Kadir Cup, can be found in Appendix B.

The Kadir Cup competition was not held after 1939. Its winner that year was Major (later Brigadier) P H J Tuck RA, who would originally have kept it for a period of one year. However, after the outbreak of war and a transfer to Egypt, he placed it in the RA mess at Meerut and reclaimed it after the war, when the Calcutta Turf Club decided that its final winner should hold it until his death. Several years later Brigadier Tuck was persuaded to lend it to the Indian Army Museum at Sandhurst for display in the Indian Army Memorial Room, and there it stayed until it was removed from display in the mid-1980s when, with the agreement of the National Army Museum and the Royal Calcutta Turf Club, the Kadir Cup was accepted on permanent loan by the committee of the Cavalry and Guards Club.

'Pig-stickers, Beware!',
1878.

Below: Elephants carrying officials and spectators ready for the start of a pig-sticking competition in the jungle outside Mutta in the United Provinces, India. 20 September 1934.

Members' Suggestions

That the Cavalry Club has a tent at the Royal Agricultural Show each year, 5 October 1948

That the roof be repaired so that raindrops do not drop on the heads of members when weighing themselves. 12 October 1948

In view of the improved sugar position would it not be possible to provide two lumps at breakfast? 25 January 1949

Somebody seems to have made an awful balls of the beer situation with the night porters tonight. 3 June 1951

Would it be possible to have the automatic cigar and cigarette lighters repaired in the smoking room and hall? 18 December 1951

This club appears to have stamped notepaper with the address in the top LEFT corner. Pardon! 26 March 1952

The rhubarb tart today was full of ants. Could some enquiries be made in the kitchen, please? 22 February 1953

May we have some fish inserted in the fish cakes for the snack bar as at present they are potato cakes, 26 February 1953

One table in the card room should be marked '2/6 or more', 25 February 1953

Now that spring is here, could not the paper flowers in the ladies' room be replaced by something more akin to nature? 1 April 1954

Would it be possible to arrange with the bank to have some CLEAN CURRENCY EVERY DAY to replace the filthy dirty pieces of paper now available? 24 April 1955

How about floating soap in the bathrooms? 12 June 1958

Would it be possible to have something on which to rest newspapers on the dining room tables? 1 June 1962

Could the breakfast bacon be cut much thinner? 4 April 1963

Could the game be hung (properly) before appearing in the Coffee Room? 13 February 1964

Would it be possible to keep a bottle of Kummel with the night porters for alcoholics? 6 December 1971

That the Club servants once again wear LIVERY – at the moment they are dressed like attendants at a low class gambling club, 18 June 1975

The two sausages that are currently being served at lunch are now considerably smaller than in the past. May I therefore suggest that we are served with either three small sausages or two sausages of former dimensions?
28 September 1978

That without disrespect to ladies it be possible to dine here without their chatter, 12 July 1979

So far as I can see, the Club flagpole has lost its 'bobbles' and also the rope. Is all in order for the royal wedding? 14 July 1981

Death to the RUBBER PLANT in the hall. This is not a suitable PLANT for this Club. May it be REMOVED, 12 JANUARY 1982

Why does a glass of whisky cost £1 in Geoffrey's Bar but merely 95p in the ladies' sitting room? Is this sexual discrimination? March 1982

I don't like the coffee sugar, of uniform size, that we now get in the smoking room; could we not revert to the former variety of variable size and shape? 14 October 1982

The lumps in the mashed potato served in the snack bar get larger and more plentiful every time they are served to me! 24 May 1985

That there be a bootjack suitable for hunting/polo boots which could be kept downstairs in the changing rooms, 17 March 1988

Oh when will we see the return of the snooker table? 20 September 1988

No more girls' schools parties at lunch time, please! 10 March 1992

Denims and baby bouncers are the giddy limit. Are we in competition with the Hard Rock Caf? 9 September 1993

I would not dream of complaining that the staff in the dining room so assiduously command us to 'enjoy (our) meal' and 'have a nice day'. Indeed it is quite charming of them. But oh, how I wish they wouldn't! 7 August 2001

A cull of the pigeons who have taken over the patio, 12 June 2003

The British Army

This appendix traces in outline the origin and development of the regiments whose officers have been eligible for membership of the Guards and Cavalry Clubs, and of the combined Cavalry and Guards Club.

THE REGULAR CAVALRY

After the restoration of the monarchy in 1660, the British cavalry consisted of three troops of Horse Guards (later to form the Life Guards), supported by three troops of dragoons (which at that date were mounted infantry) entitled Horse Grenadier Guards. The other cavalry elements were the Royal Regiment of Horse (later the Royal Horse Guards), a Cromwellian regiment disbanded at the Restoration but immediately reformed, and the Tangier Horse, raised in 1661 for garrison duty in Tangier but recalled to Britain in 1684 as a dragoon regiment (later the 1st Royal Dragoons). A second dragoon regiment (later the Royal Scots Greys) was formed in the late 1670s.

In 1685, the Duke of Monmouth's rebellion gave James II a pretext to increase the standing army, and seven new regiments of horse were raised. These were numbered 2nd to 8th, the 1st Horse being the Royal Regiment of Horse, whose title shortly afterwards became the Royal Horse Guards. Two more dragoon regiments were also raised in 1685, later numbered the 3rd and 4th Dragoons.

Between 1689 and 1715, ten more dragoon regiments (5th to 14th) were added to the establishment. In 1746 the 2nd, 3rd and 4th Horse were converted to dragoons as an economy measure, since dragoons received less pay, although they now fought mounted rather than as infantry. To acknowledge their previous status these three regiments were numbered in a separate line as 1st, 2nd and 3rd Dragoon Guards, titles which in the case of the 1st and 2nd were unchanged for over 200 years. The remaining horse regiments became the 1st to 4th Irish Horse until 1788 when they too became Dragoon Guards (4th to 7th).

The requirement for light cavalry for reconnaissance, vedettes, escorts and similar duties led to the formation of a light troop in each of the dragoon regiments, and from 1759 all new regiments (the 15th to the 18th) were raised as light dragoons. By the end of the eighteenth century all the existing dragoon regiments except the six senior ones had also been converted to light dragoons.

During and shortly after the Napoleonic Wars, five regiments of light dragoons (the 7th, 8th, 10th, 15th and 18th) were retitled hussars, although the 18th were disbanded soon afterwards, and the change of title had sartorial rather than tactical implications. The 11th Light Dragoons became a hussar regiment, with Prince Albert as its Colonel, in 1840.

In 1817, lancers were introduced into the British Army by conversion of the 9th, 12th, 16th and 23rd Light Dragoons. The 23rd, having just had time to purchase their exotic new uniforms, were disbanded the following year; the 19th Light Dragoons replaced them as lancers, only to be disbanded themselves in 1821, when the 17th became a lancer regiment.

In 1818 the 3rd and 4th Dragoons were converted to light dragoons, leaving only the Royals, Greys and 6th (Inniskillings) as heavy dragoons, the 5th having been disbanded for mutiny in 1799. And in 1820 the status of the Royal Horse Guards as

The 16th Lancers (British School, nineteenth century).

Household Cavalry, on a par with the Life Guards in all respects, was officially confirmed.

After the Indian Mutiny and consequent disbandment of many native cavalry regiments, the 18th Hussars were reformed, and in 1861 the 5th Dragoons were also revived as the 5th Lancers. The last remaining light dragoon regiments were converted in the same year to become the 3rd, 4th, 13th and 14th Hussars.

The final addition to the order of battle as it stood at the formation of the Cavalry Club was the transfer in 1861 of three Bengal European cavalry regiments to the British army as the 19th, 20th and 21st Hussars. Thereafter, the only change in the cavalry establishment before the first tranche of amalgamations after the Great War was the conversion of the 21st Hussars to a lancer regiment in 1897.

The mechanisation of the cavalry began in 1928 with the conversion of the 11th Hussars to an armoured car regiment. By 1939 most regiments had been incorporated, with the Royal Tank Corps, into the Royal Armoured Corps. The last mounted regiment, the Greys, was converted to tanks in mid-1941. Six additional cavalry regiments (22nd and 25th Dragoons, 23rd and 26th Hussars and 24th and 28th Lancers) were raised during the Second World War but disbanded shortly after the end of the war.

THE YEOMANRY

The first yeomanry forces were raised in 1794, to counter the threat of a French invasion. The early units were mainly of troop strength, and had a long and complex history of disbandments and re-raisings before eventually being formed into county regiments. There were some forty yeomanry regiments in existence at the outbreak of the Boer War in 1899. Since their terms of engagement did not permit them to be sent overseas, those who volunteered for active service in South Africa were designated Imperial Yeomanry, a title which lasted until the formation of the Territorial Army in 1908.

Some seventeen more yeomanry regiments were raised during the Boer War, and all were heavily involved in the Great War. Thereafter many of them were re-roled as artillery or signals units; most of those who retained their horses were deployed in 1939 to Palestine, where they served until they could be mechanised.

The history of the yeomanry since the Second World War has been one of drastic amalgamations and reorganisations. As at 2008, four regiments (the Royal Yeomanry, Royal Mercian & Lancastrian Yeomanry, Queen's Own Yeomanry and Royal Wessex Yeomanry), all composed of squadrons representing their

former regiments, remain part of the Royal Armoured Corps, and many other regiments still exist as elements of other corps. The yeomanry has played a very significant part in operations in Iraq and Afghanistan.

THE FOOT GUARDS

The history of the Foot Guards, compared with that of the cavalry, is relatively straightforward. The 1st Guards were raised by a commission dated November 1660 to a Colonel Russell (an ancestor of the Duke of Bedford) to raise twelve companies of 100 men each. This regiment was reinforced in 1665 by a previous royal guard which had served Charles II during his exile in the Netherlands and had subsequently formed the Dunkirk garrison. In 1815 the regiment was granted its present title of Grenadier Guards for its defeat of the French Imperial Guard at Waterloo.

The 2nd Guards were a Cromwellian infantry regiment recruited at Coldstream in the Scottish borders. The regiment accompanied their Colonel, General Monck, in his march to London in January

UNITS OF THE FOOT GUARDS

Grenadier Guards

1st Battalion

Nijmegen Company

Coldstream Guards

1st Battalion

No 7 Company

Scots Guards

1st Battalion

F Company

Irish Guards

1st Battalion

Welsh Guards

1st Battalion

1660 to negotiate the restoration of Charles II, and became the Lord General's Regiment of Foot Guards in 1661. The Coldstream title dates from 1670.

The first companies of the Scots Guards were raised at the same date as the 1st Guards, for service in Scotland. In 1666 the regiment was noted as having the same status as the two English Guards regiments. Their title became the Scots Fusilier Guards in 1831 but reverted to its present form in 1877.

The Irish Guards were formed in 1900 by recruiting volunteers from the Irish line regiments. The Welsh Guards were raised by a similar process in 1915. The Machine Gun Guards were also formed during the Great War but disbanded in 1920. All five Foot Guards regiments now have one battalion. However, as at 2008, the Grenadiers, Coldstream and Scots Guards each have a separate incremental company, representing their former Second Battalions. The Guards Division has also had, since 2004, a Territorial Battalion formed by the London Regiment.

Winners of the Kadir Cup, 1869–1939

YEAR	RIDER	REGIMENT	HORSE	EXTRA INFORMATION
1869	Lieutenant Bibby's	4th Hussars	THE DOCTOR	
1870	Lieutenant Stewart's	11th Hussars	TIPPOO	Two horses in final
1871	Captain Phillips's		JURHAM	
1872	Captain Studdy's	20th Hussars	CATO	
1873	Captain Studdy's	21st Hussars	CATO	
1874	Lieutenant White's	15th Hussars	HINDOO	Two horses in final
1875	Lieutenant Jeffries'	RA	BOBBY	
1876	Captain White's	15th Hussars	JOE	
1877	Captain St Quintin's	10th Hussars	VIVIAN	
1878	Lieutenant Grant's	4th Hussars	KATE KEARNEY	Ridden by Captain Hutchins
1879				No contest - Afghan War
1880				No contest - Afghan War
1881	Lieutenant Grenfell's	10th Hussars	MAIDAN	
1882	The Hon G Bryan's	10th Hussars	GREY DAWN	Ridden by Lieutenant Bishop
1883	Lieutenant Baden-Powell's	13th Hussars	PATIENCE	
1884	Lieutenant Kier's	RHA	JOHN O'GAUNT	Ridden by Mr Robinson
1885	The Maharana of Dholpur's		RED PRINCE	
1886	Mr Rees's		JACK	
1887	Major Clowes's	8th Hussars	KHEDIVE	
1888	Lieutenant Mahon's	8th Hussars	CORNET	Two horses in final
1889	Captain Le Gallais's	8th Hussars	PHILLIPINE	
1890	Captain Hanwell's	RA	LUCY'S KNOT	
1891	Lieutenant Oakes's	5th Lancers	JINKS	
1892	Lieutenant West's	5th Lancers	DANCING MASTER	
1893	Captain Blane's	RHA	SCOTTIE	
1894	Captain Fanshawe's	Ox Lt Inf	BYDAND	
1895	General Gurdit Singh's		SYLVIA	
1896	Mr Edwards's	ICS	OUTCAST	
1897	Lieutenant Gillman's	RHA	HUNTSMAN	
1898	Lieutenant Dunbar's	5th Dragoon Guards	LOLA	
1899	Lieutenant F Allhusen's	9th Lancers	SANTOZA	
1900	Mr Clementson's		FOREST KING	
1901	Lieutenant Warre-Cornish's	17th BL	HERMIA	
1902	Colonel Seeva Singh's		GOVERNOR	
1903	Captain Cameron's	CIH	MOUSQUETAIRE	
1904	Lieutenant Livingstone-Learmonth's	15th Hussars	ELDORADO	

YEAR	RIDER	REGIMENT	HORSE	EXTRA INFORMATION
1905	Lieutenant R Grenfell's	9th Lancers	BARMAID	
1906	Lieutenant Richie's	15th Hussars	BOBS	
1907	Major Vaughan's	10th Hussars	VEDETTE	
1908	Lord Kensington's	15th Hussars	TWILIGHT	
1909	Lieutenant Vernon's	60th Rifles	FIREPLANT	
1910	Lieutenant Paynter's	RHA	THE HAWK	
1911	Lieutenant Bromilow's	14th BL	BATTLEAXE	
1912	Captain Gatacre's	11th BL	KARIM	
1913	Lieutenant Sherston's	11th BL	MAGISTRATE	
1914	Captain HE Medlicott's	Skinner's Horse	DROGHEDA	
1915				No contest - The Great War
1916				No contest - The Great War
1917				No contest - The Great War
1918				No contest - The Great War
1919	Mr PW Marsh's	ICS	LADY KATE	
1920	Captain C West's	RHA	MAGISTRATE	
1921	Captain Davison's	2nd Lancers	DOLEFUL	
1922	Captain P Baldwin's	11th/12th Cavalry	BLUE BARROW	
1923	Lieutenant Bates's	RFA	LOVELACE	
1924	Captain J Scott-Cockburn's	4th Hussars	CARCLEW	
1925	Captain J Scott-Cockburn's	5th Hussars	CARCLEW	
1926	Captain KJ Catto's	4th Hussars	JACK	
1927	Captain J Scott-Cockburn's	7th Hussars	CARCLEW	
1928	Captain H McA Richards's	RA	CENTAUR	
1929	Captain HWN Head's	4th Hussars	BULLET HEAD	
1930	Captain H McA Richards's	RA	MANIFEST	
1931	Captain H McA Richards's	RA	MANIFEST	
1932	Lieutenant R Jones's	10th Hussars	HORSE'S NECK	
1933	Captain Hon H Grenfell's	10th Hussars	AUSTRALIAN STAR	
1934	Lieutenant CRD Gray's	Skinner's Horse	GRANITE	Two horses in final
1935	Lieutenant Hon G Hamilton-Russell's	Royal Dragoons	LINDY LOO	
1936	Captain PHJ Tuck's	RA	MANIFEST	
1937	Major JH Branford's	RA	RED TURK	
1938	Squadron Leader Sinclair's	RAF	MISSFIRE	Ridden by Captain G Keighley, 19L
1939	Major PHJ Tuck's	RA	THE SQUEAKER	

Patrons, Presidents and Chairmen

THE CAVALRY CLUB

PATRON
1890–1901   HRH The Prince of Wales KG (later HM King Edward VII)

LADY PATRON
To 2002   HM Queen Elizabeth The Queen Mother

PRESIDENTS
1890–1904	HRH The Duke of Cambridge KG KT KP GCB GCSI GCMG GCIE GCVO
1904–42	HRH The Duke of Connaught and Strathearn KG KT KP GCB GCSI GCMG GCIE GCVO GBE TD
1942–74	HRH The Duke of Gloucester KG KT KP GCB GCMG GCVO
1975–	HRH The Duke of Kent KG GCMG GCVO ADC

VICE PRESIDENTS
1890–1902	HSH Prince Edward of Saxe-Weimar KP GCB GCVO
1890–1904	HRH The Duke of Connaught and Strathearn
1904–08	Lieutenant General W T Dickson
1909–20	Colonel The Viscount Valentia CB MVO MP
1920–50	Field Marshal The Lord Chetwode GCB OM GCSI KCMG DSO
1950–55	Brigadier The Right Honourable The Earl of Gowrie VC GCMG CB DSO
1955–67	General Sir Richard McCreery GCB KBE DSO MC
1968–89	Field Marshal Sir Richard Hull KG GCB DSO
1976–86	General Sir Rodney Moore GCVO KCB CBE DSO
1990–2003	Field Marshal Sir John Stanier GCB MBE
2003–07	General Sir Richard Worsley GCB OBE
2007–	Colonel T A Hall CVO OBE

CHAIRMEN
1890–95	Major General Sir Baker Russell KCB KCMG
1895–1909	Lieutenant General W T Dickson
1909–27	Colonel The Viscount Valentia CB MVO MP
1927–50	Field Marshal The Lord Chetwode GCB OM GCSI KCMG DSO
1950–53	Major Sir Digby Lawson Bt
1953–56	Brigadier Sir Henry R K Floyd Bt CB CBE
1956–59	Major General R B B B Cooke CB CBE DSO
1959–62	Lieutenant Colonel V A B Dunkerly DSO JP
1962–65	Brigadier A H Pepys DSO
1965–68	Colonel G W C Draffen DSO
1968–71	Lieutenant Colonel Sir Douglas Scott Bt
1971–74	Lieutenant Colonel Sir Richard Verdin OBE
1974–75	Colonel K E Savill CVO DSO DL

THE GUARDS CLUB

PATRONS

1810–30	HRH The Prince Regent (later HM King George IV)
1830–37	HM King William IV
1865–1910	HRH The Prince of Wales (later HM King Edward VII)
1910–36	HM King George V
1937–52	HM King George VI
1952–76	HM Queen Elizabeth II

CHAIRMEN (no records exist prior to 1919)

1919–21	Major General J Ponsonby CB CMG DSO
1921	Major General The Hon J F Gathorne-Hardy CB CMG DSO
1922	Major General Vesey J Dawson CVO
1923–32	General Sir Ivor Maxse KCB CVO DSO
1933–35	Brigadier General W H V Darell CB CMG DSO
1936–46	Brigadier General Francis G Alston CMG DSO
1946–50	General Sir Andrew Thorne KCB CMG DSO
1950–51	Colonel P L Reid CBE
1951–53	Colonel W B N Roderick OBE
1953–58	Lieutenant Colonel W H Kingsmill DSO MC
1958	Captain Ralph Howard (elected but died within a month)
1958–60	Lieutenant Colonel J L Campbell
1960–68	Captain E Algernon Asprey
1968–69	Major General C M F Deakin CB CBE
1969–75	Captain P N Railing

THE CAVALRY AND GUARDS CLUB

CHAIRMEN

1975–80	Major General Sir James A D'Avigdor-Goldsmid Bt CB OBE MC
1980–84	Major General Sir Digby Raeburn KCVO CB DSO MBE
1984–87	Major General J M Strawson CB OBE
1987–90	Major General Sir Philip Ward KCVO CBE DL
1990–96	Colonel T A Hall CVO OBE
1996–2002	Major J F M Rodwell
2002–04	Major General P A J Cordingley DSO
2004–07	C N F Methven Esq
2007–	F D S Rosier Esq

Club Secretaries

THE CAVALRY CLUB

1890–91	Wm Redston Warner
1891–98	Captain F A Sargeaunt RN
1898–1931	Major Henry Read Darley DSO OBE (died in office)
1931–42	Captain P G Davidson (died in office)
1942–44	Sub-committee
1944–53	Major W Guy Horne
1953–76	Squadron Leader Anthony O'Connor

THE GUARDS CLUB (no records exist prior to 1919)

1919–20	Captain Stuart C Grant OBE
1921	Major Ralph W Maude DSO (retired due to ill-health; died 1922)
1922–23	Captain Rowland A Hill
1923–37	Captain Harold J Fletcher MC
1937–39	Lieutenant Commander B R Brasier-Creagh RN
1940	Captain Charles Gordon
1941–49	Major Otho V Thomas OBE
1949–52	Lieutenant Colonel T P M Bevan MC
1952–53	Major E W Hylton
1954–68	C E Buss Esq
1968–75	A P Blackie Esq
1975–76	J E Savage Esq

THE CAVALRY AND GUARDS CLUB

1976–91	L David de Pinna Esq
1991–98	Nicholas Walford Esq
1998–2004	Commander Ian Wellesley Harding RN
2005–	David J Cowdery Esq

by George Belcher 1926.

THE SECRETARY
of the Cavalry Club
taken from Life.

Major H. R. Darley D.S.O. O.B.E.

List of Subscribers

This book has been made possible through
the generosity of the following subscribers:

Colonel James Aarestad
Philip J Adams
Captain Sir Rudolph Agnew
Sir Alastair Aird GCVO
Ian Albert
Major Tim Allan
Andrew T Allen
C J Allen
Jacqueline M Allen
John C Anderson
Ronald Albuquerque Andjel
Ambassador André Mernier
Colonel P J Andrews OBE
Guy Appleton
Captain Geoffrey Archer
T C R Armstrong-Wilson TD
Alain Arnot
J G Aspinall
Captain R T H Ayton

Captain Thomas R Bailey
M Bannister
Ian Hunter Barbour
J R Barkes
Colonel A J Bateman
P R Baty
Lieutenant Colonel Ewart Baxter
William A Beaumont
Captain David Bellamy
Count Bernadotte
Major R P A de Bernière-Smart
John Bettinson
Basil Bicknell
James Biggart
Lieutenant Colonel Jonathan Biggart MBE

Robert Biggs
Tim Black
Anthony Blackburn
R Boggis-Rolfe
A R Bolitho
Major R C H Boon
Captain W R Boulter
James Bouskell
Captain Tom D L Bowden
Major J R I Bower
Sir Neville Bowman-Shaw
Tim Brocklebank-Fowler
Major Johnny Brooke
Major G G Brown
Sir George Bull
M T C Burkitt
The Lord Burton

Colonel E G Cameron TD
Captain Peter Cannon
A R P Carden
Lieutenant Colonel Kenneth Carhart CD
Consul Anthony Carlbom & Mrs Anthony Carlbom
Captain P A Carr
Sir Ralph Carr-Ellison
J H L B Carter
George Carter CBE & Anne Carter DL
Colonel D S Casstles TD DL
G R H Chamberlain
Nicholas Chamberlin
Colonel Simon Chapman
Major Adrian Charman TD
Captain J H Chatfeild-Roberts
John E Chisnell
Colonel G V Churton MBE MC TD DL
Captain Charles D Clark
N L Clifford-Jones
R Paulin Clinton

Viscount Coke
Major J R Compston TD
John Woods Conlin
R T Constable-Maxwell DL
Major Jollyon Coombs
John B Cooper
P E Cooper
Captain T A Cooper
Captain M Cooper-Evans
Simon Copley
Major General Patrick Cordingley
Lieutenant General Sir Roderick Cordy-Simpson KBE CB DL
Michael Corkery QC
Major General Walter Courage
James A Coutts CM
Colonel Richard Coxwell-Rogers
Major J N A Crichton-Stuart MBE
L J Cubitt
J CM Cuthbert

N H D'Oyly
R Dalton Holmes
W D Dane
M W Daniel
Clendon Daukes
Brigadier M J Debu
Lieutenant Colonel J D Deykin
Colonel R G Dixon
Richard Dixon-Warren
Mathew Dobbs
C A R Dobrzynski
Major Dominic Dobson
David Dodd
Captain Sir Ralph Dodds Bt
Michael Donnelly
Colonel & Mrs D Donnithorne-Tait
Gawain T A Douglas DFC
A R Douglas-Nugent

Timothy Drabble

Nancy and Joseph Dryer

Colonel Andrew Duncan

J D Graham Duncan

J Alan B Dunlop

S Dustnal

Alastair Eadie

HRH The Duke of Edinburgh

P Owen Edmunds

Captain E C N Edwards

Captain Peter B Edwards CD

R D K Edwards

Brigadier James Ellery CBE

Julian Ellis

Major C M R Elmhirst

Colin Elwell

Major Robert F Erith TD DL

Philip Erskine

Captain Brett Erskine-Naylor

Lieutenant Maxim Erskine-Naylor

John Ewart

The Honourable P J W Fairfax

Angus Fanshawe

G J O Farage

H J P Farr

Lieutenant Colonel T H F Farrell

C A K Fenn-Smith

P T Fenwick OBE

S Z de Ferranti

Sir Francis Ferris

William Fisher

General Sir Robert Ford

Alistair Forsyth Yngr of that Ilk

A R G Frase

Major Mike Fraser

Ian Frazer

Michael H Freericks Oberstlt DR

Major E J S Frost-Kell

Anthony Gaddum

Charles Garnett

James Gasson-Hargreaves

Captain Philip Gay

C B Gibson

Zafar Ali Gilani

Mr Giles

Colonel G A G Gilhead

Colonel A P Gilks

H R Gillespie

Colonel W F Gillespie OBE TD JP DL

Barry Gillions

Robert Glossop

T W Glover TD

Hugh Godber

G V Goodey

Sir Brian Goswell

Guy Gribble

J D Griffiths-Eyton MBE

Dr M van Grondelle MSc PhD

Brigadier Khutab Hai

The Earl Haig

C J W Haines

Major General Jonathan Hall CB OBE

Mrs Mariette Hall

Colonel Tom Hall

Dr Nabil Hamami

Major Christopher Hanbury

Mrs Peter F Hanbury

Henry Hanning

Captain M J Hanson

D L Harland

General Sir Jack Harman

Major G R Harris MBE

Major J D Harris

Captain William Fielding Hatton

Colonel Malcolm Havergal CVO OBE

Mrs R G T Hawkins

C F R Hayes

O E Hayes

Sir Robert Hayman-Joyce

Major Peter Headey

Major E Hempsall

D R Hill

Douglas Hill

W B Hill

R K B Hitchcock MC

Reverend Toddy Hoare TD MA

Frank R D Holland

Keith Holland

Lieutenant Colonel T J D Holmes

Lieutenant J R Hood

George A Hope

Major Philip Hope-Cobbold DL

A T Hopkinson

Peter Hornby

Peter Horsburgh

O C Howard

Major Edgar Hutchings

T R Illingworth

David A Innes

Major D J Innes-Lumsden

Captain A A J Innes-Whitehouse

Rob I A Ireland

Alexander W Jackson

David Jacobs

J L Janssen van Raay

Captain Hugo Jee

Peter J L Jenkins

Robin Jenkinson

Major I Dalzel Job

Wynford Johns

Colonel Neil Johnson OBE DL

P W Jones

Ole Kai-Christensen

Lieutenant Colonel J R S Kaye

Michael J St G Kelton

Major P D Kennerley TD

Robin Kernick CVO

R Graf Kerssenbrock

I C A King-Holford

Colonel Richard Kinsella-Bevan

R W Krefting

Mark Krieg

Philip Kyriacou

Christopher L'Estrange

M E Lapping

Robin Laurence

Captain E J P Lawrence

Major J D Lawrence

J M R Lee

Lieutenant Colonel Gerald Lesinski

I T Lewis

N S Lewis

James Lister

Major Henry Llewelyn-Usher

C A R Lockhart

Lieutenant Colonel I D Lonsdale TD

Captain Martin Lowe

Colonel Sir Charles Lowther Bt

Captain P M Luttman-Johnson

Captain Guy Lyster DL

Peter H Lyster

R F Macaire

Michael MacCallan

Captain Conn Jeremy MacEvilly

Colonel Christopher MacKenzie-Beevor

Dr K S Mackenzie

R S Mackenzie

Richard D L Maclure

Major J J Macnamura TD JP

Lieutenant Colonel D A G Madden MBE

Mrs M Magan

Major S P Maggs

Allan Mallinson

Right Reverend M A Mann KCVO

Captain N A Marsh

Colonel Alastair Mathewson

Keith McIntosh

David McLaren

Capt D "Sandy" McLennan Fordyce

Lieutenant Colonel J-D von Merveldt

C N F Methven

Captain Christopher J Miles

Colonel Branko Milovanoviç

Captain the Lord Monteagle of Brandon

Richard J E Moore

S P Morant

Christopher Morgan

Major Mickey Morrissey

Robert Morton

Brigadier L J R Nash

J A S Neave

Edward S Nelson

C D Newton

M M Nicholson

Colonel John R Nickell-Lean TD

R G H Noel

R A Noone

R L D J More O'Ferrall

Nils Opperman

Captain Nicholas Orr

Brigadier J D Osborne OBE

Dr David Otton

Nicholas Oulton MA

R A B Ouwens

R R Paling

Mrs R R Paling

David V Palmer DL

Neil Palmer

J G Payne

David Peake

Frederick E Pearson

Lady Peat

Major Miles Pennett

Captain Christopher Percival QVRM

Major W G Peto

Zoe Peto

Colonel John Pharo-Tomlin

Peter W Phillips

Major Frederick Pidcock TD

George Richard Pinto

Lieutenant Colonel Hugh Pitman

Major M D A Pocock

Captain S G M Portal

Brigadier John Pownall

J L C Pratt

Captain D L Prebble

Ambassador Frank Pringle CD

John R Purvis CBE MEP

Rupert Pusey

Charles Pybus

Mark H J Radcliffe

Alexander Raven

Sir Roy Redgrave

W A L Reid

Major General Sir Desmond Rice

Michael Ritchie

Brigadier Clive Robertson CVO DL

C W Robinson

J Michael Robotham OBE

J E Robson Esq MC

Major John Rodwell

J A Roll Pickering

Mrs A L Rook

Tamara Rosenberg

Captain F D S Rosier

John Rothwell

Captain S J Rought Whitta TD

A J Rundell OBE

Honourable William Russell

Major R K Ryan TD

A F Sabin

Colonel Hugh Sandars

Peter B Sangster

S N J Schilizzi

Major David Schofield

Captain O N G Scholte

Andrew Scott

Major J R Scrivener

Major P Scrope

John Seagrim

Captain R L Seaman

Lieutenant Colonel Karl Albert Senn

B H Shepherd-Smith

Major P M Shires TD

Major N C Shuttleworth

Mrs Susan Simpson

C J Simpson Gee

Nicholas Simunek

Captain P Sinclair- Knipe

Roy Smalley

Captain Kempley M A Smith

Peter Angus Smith

Antony Snow

Colonel A W A Spiegelberg

John and Ros Stace

John L Stacie

Colonel N M T Stafford

Leslie V Stell

Captain J A H Stephenson

Mrs Penelope Stevens

D W Stilwell

Major Peter R Stone TD

Dermot Strangways-Booth

Major General John Strawson

C W David Sutcliffe OBE DL

J M B Sutcliffe

Major General Sir John Swinton

Sir John Swire CBE

Daniel P T Thomas

Major J W Thomas

Lieutenant Colonel Sir Christopher Thompson Bt

Colonel D R B Thompson

Colonel Ian C Thompson TD

Jeremy Thorman TD

Rupert C Thornton

Count Tolstoy-Miloslavsky

Major Milan Torbica

Major G H Trew

Edmund Truell

Lieutenant Colonel N J Tuck

G W Tufnell

Brigadier J W Turner

Captain Robert Turrall-Clarke

Lieutenant Colonel D W Utting

Major R I Vallance DCM MBE

M van Grondelle MSc PhD

Major J C Varley TD

Christopher Vaughan

R F Venn

Patrick Vigors

T F Villiers-Smith

John P D Walker

Michael G N Walker CBE

Major Malcolm Wallace

R F Wallis

Sir Henry Warner Bt

Lieutenant Colonel C I P Webb

Peter S Wells

Buzz West

Lieutenant D A Wheatley

Colonel Rupert Wieloch

Christopher Willy

W S Wiley

Frederick H P H Wills

Jane Wilson

Thomas Wilson

E J F V Wiltshire

Colonel R F M Windsor CBE DL

Robert Winterton

Major N H Woellwarth

Lord Wigram

Major General Henry Woods

Major T P Wootton

Captain R J S Wright

Dr Trevor Wright

Michael Wynne-Parker

Christopher Wysock-Wright

Major C J Yates

C J K Yates

Captain William Yates

Lieutenant Colonel D J Younger

Index of Names

Abadie, Colonel H 54

Alexander, Colonel 100

Alexander of Tunis, Field Marshal, Earl 31, 36, 40,

Allen, Tim 136

Allenby, Viscount Bill 58, 60, 83, 129

Allhusen, Colonel Frederick 82

Allhusen, Michael 82

Allhusen, Nick 82

Alston, Brigadier General Francis G 181

Alvarez, Julio 159

Anne, HRH Princess, The Princess Royal 148, 159

Arabin, Lt Colonel John 33

Asprey, Captain E Algernon 45, 181

Auchinleck, Claude 36

Baden-Powell, Major General Lord 63, 81

Balfour, Sir Arthur 28

Barclay, David 124

Barclay, Gurney 20

Barnby, Lord 76

Bateman, H M 32

Bayley, Emilius 162

Beasley, Mark 159

Belcher, Paul 140

Bell, Arthur 45

Beresford, Lord Patrick 168

Bergevin, Monsieur Edgard 104

Betjeman, John 129

Betlem, J 75

Bevan, Lt Colonel TPM 182

Birdwood, Field Marshal Lord 68, 72, 93

Blackie, A P 182

Blewitt, Major 43

Bloggs, Captain 139

Boles, Colonel D C 84, 163

Boote, E R 103, 105, 108

Brasier-Creagh, Lt Commmander B R 29, 182

Brooks-Ward, Colonel Simon 158

Browne, General Sir Sam 54, 56

Browne-Swinburne, John 105

Bruxner, James 95

Buller, Sir Redvers 66

Bulter, Michael 168

Burns, General Sir George 45

Buss, C E 182

Byng, Field Marshal Lord 60

Byng, Lady Hester Joan 28

Byron, Lord 162

Caledon, Earl 36

Cambridge, HRH The Duke of 14, 54, 55, 80, 180

Cameron, Colonel Ewen 158

Campbell, Lt Colonel J L 181

Carleton, Lt Col the Hon D M P 46

Caroline, HM Queen 19

Carr, Henry 31

Carver, Field Marshal Lord 28, 137

Charles, HRH The Prince of Wales 151

Chetwode, Field Marshal Lord 83, 88, 90-91, 102, 129

Chetwode, Lady 90

Church, George 104

Churchill, Horace 19

Churchill, Sir Winston 87, 94

Clarke, Colonel 106

Clarke, Mrs 106

Clive, Lt Colonel Windsor 26

Cole, Colonel Sir Colin 145, 146

Colville, Lady Margaret 145

Compton, Captain John 136

Connaught, HRH The Duke of 80, 87,180

Cooke, Major General R B B B 180

Cordingley, Major General Patrick 151, 154, 156, 181

Cornwall, HRH The Duchess of 156

Cowdery, David 7, 157,154, 159, 182

Craik, Sir Henry 93

Crockford, William 18

Curran, Mrs Anne 49, 142, 144, 153

D'Avigdor-Goldsmid, Major Gen Sir James 45, 95, 96, 97, 96, 181

Darell, Brigadier General W H V 181

Darley, Major Henry Read 82, 182

Davidson, Captain P G 87, 182

Dawson, Major General Vesey J 181

Dayell, MP Tam 138

de Pinna, David 108, 139, 140, 150, 124, 182

Deakin, General 96

Deakin, Major General C M F 181

Deverell, Sir Cyril 31

Dickson, Lt General W T 180

Dickson, Major General 54

Dobbs, H W 108

Draffen, Colonel G W C 180

Dudgeon, Patrick 134

Dudley, Captain the Earl of 54

Dunkerly, Lt Colonel V A B 180

Dyer, Simon 142, 149

Eden, Sir Anthony 107

Edinburgh, HRH The Duke of 94

Edmund, Hillary 94

Edward VII, HM King 20, 74, 76, 180

Elizabeth II, HM The Queen 94, 143, 150

Elizabeth, HM Queen, The Queen Mother 46, 145, 164, 180

Everett, C J 102

Farmer, Paul 159

Ferguson, Ronald 168

Fitzgeorge, Colonel G 54

Fletcher, Captain Harold J 182

Floyd, Brigadier Sir Henry R K 95, 96, 180

Floyd, David 158

Foot, Sir Hugh 40

Forbes, Colonel Fergus 107

Forbes, W A 171

Fowler, R St L 163

Frazer, Ian 98, 124, 140, 144, 157, 158

French, Field Marshal Sir John 58, 59, 61,63, 66, 83,

Gathorne-Hardy, Major Gen The Hon J F 181

George V, HM King 24, 102, 135

Gilbart-Denman, Major S V 41

Glanusk, Lt Colonel Lord 26

Gloucester, HRH The Duke of 87, 135, 180

Godwen-Austen, General 40

Gordon, Captain Charles 182

Gordon, General 66

Gore, Captain 54

Gort, Field Marshal Lord 30–31, 32, 36

Gough, Brigadier General Hubert 90

Gowrie, Brigadier, The Earl of 180

Grant, Captain Stuart C 182

Graves, Charles 53, 81, 102

Greville, Mrs Ronald 29, 32, 62

Grey, Mr 108

Gronow, Captain 14, 17, 18

Haig, Field Marshal Earl 30, 58-9 66, 83

Hall, Colonel Tom 49, 124, 140, 142-43, 144, 181

Hall, Major General Jonnie 7, 140, 144

Hall, Mrs Mariette 49

Hamilton, Sir Ian 68

Harbord, Brigadier General 117

Harding, Lord 36, 40

Hardinge, Sir Henry 19

Harrison, Henry 20

Havergal, Colonel Malcolm 104, 107

Hayman, G 76

Healy, Captain Alan 170

Hedley, Captain G S 108

Hedley, Ken 96

Heseltine, Captain Herbert 75

Hicks, Mr 108

Hill, Captain Rowland A 182

Hillary, Sir Edmund 94

Hoare, Reverend Toddy 96

Hoby – bootmaker 19

Hok, Jonny 124

Hore-Belisha, Sir Leslie 31

Horne, Major W Guy 87, 182

Howard, Captain Ralph 181

Hozier, Colonel Sir H M 102

Hull, Field Marshal Sir Richard 100, 180

Huntingfield, Lord 87

Huntley, Commander 98

Huth, Lt Colonel Henry 95

Hylton, Major E W 182

Jacobs, Captain Simon 170

Jeffries, General Sir George 38

Jones, Peter 121, 124, 139, 142, 144

Keate, Dr 14

Kent, HRH The Duke of 7, 43, 124, 143, 180

Kernick, Robin 92, 144, 145, 163

King, Alix 159

King, F 103

King, Thomas 73

Kingsmill. Lt Colonel W H 42, 181

Kyriacou, Philip 108

Lawes, Mr 108

Lawrence, Colonel T E 83

Lawson, Major Sir Digby 180

Lejeune, Anthony 133

Lennox, Charles 166

Levett, Major B 25

Lloyd, Fred 42, 102

Lort-Phillips, Patrick 170

Lutyens, Sir Edwin 75

Lycett, Major 100

Macduff, Earl of 80

MacKenzie, Colonel Phillippe 54

MacKenzie-Beevor, Colonel Christopher 7, 158

Mackinnon, Colonel Daniel 14, 16

Maclean, Colonel Allan 54

Macmillan, Harold 44

Marshall, Soran 159

Martel, Peter 93

Massey Shaw, Capt Sir Eyre 20

Maude, Major Ralph W 182

Maxse, General Sir Ivor 27, 181

McCalmont, Colonel H 54

McCalmont, Major D 81

McCreery, General Sir Richard 180

McEwan, William 29

Metcalfe, Major Fruity 81

Methven, Colin N F 49, 151, 154, 156-7, 181

Montagu, Col the Hon O 54

Monteagle, Lord 7, 43, 44-45.

Montgomery, Field Marshal, Lord 137

Moore, General Sir Rodney 45, 180

Moore, T 19

Morley, Robert 78

Morton, Marie Evelyn 60

Murray, Sir Archibald 61, 90

Mussel, Miss Joan 134

Napier, Major the Hon J 54

Naylor, Major General D M 33

Nelson, Edward 105

Nelson, Mrs Sandra 49, 158

Nevill, Ralph 22

Newton, Captain Christopher 99, 103

Nicholson, William 162

Norton, Brigadier General CEG 88

O'Connor, General 40

O'Connor, Squadron Leader Anthony 119, 129, 134, 165, 182

O'Moore Creagh, Sir 58

O'Rorke, Lt Colonel Brian 48

Oates, Captain Lawrence E G 69, 161

Oxenden, Charles 162

Pain, Lt General Sir Rollo 143

Palin, Mildred 61

Parsons, Robert 146

Patterson, Ralph 23

Pepys, Brigadier A H 180

Peto, Fred 107

Peto, Major William 7, 158

Petronella, Pietro 159

Plumer, General 28, 68

Plymouth, Lord 26

Pocock, Major Martyn 158

Ponsoby, Major General J 181

Portal, Major M E B 86

Portal, Simon 86

Pownall, Brigadier John 94

Poynter, Lt Colonel J 54

Price, Chelsea Pensioner 102

Price, Geoffrey 42, 106, 197, 144, 145

Price, Mrs Carole 106, 145

Prince, John 170

Probyn, Sir Dighton 56

Purbrick, Reggie 42

Quick, Mr 38

Raeburn, Major General Sir Digby 45,140

Raggett, George 17

Railing, Captain Peter N 41, 44, 181

Reid, Colonel P L 181

Reynolds, Sir John 44

Richardson, Colonel J J 87

Roberts, Lord 56, 66, 80

Robertson, Sir William 61

Roderick, Colonel W B N 181

Rodwell, Major John 124, 142, 144-5, 146, 146, 153, 156, 181

Rosier, David 143, 151, 154, 156, 158-9, 181

Ross, John 170

Rothschild, Lord 20

Rothwell, John 144, 158

Royle, Tim 157

Rucker, Brigadier James 142, 144, 152

Runcie, Archbishop Robert 136

Russell, Major General Sir Baker 54, 55, 180

Rutherford, Colonel John 73

Ruthven, Lord 27

Sargeaunt, Captain F A 182

Saroop, Major Narindar 93

Savage, J E 45, 182

Savill, Colonel Kenneth 'Kate' 98, 108

Saxe-Weimar, HSH Prince Edward of 54

Scott, Captain 69

Scott, Lt Colonel Sir Douglas 180

Scrope, Peter 158

Shelley, Sir John 19

Smith-Dorien, General 61, 66

Snow, Antony 98, 105

Spencer-Churchill, Lady Henrietta 47

Stanier, Field Marshal Sir John 138, 124, 143, 180

Stanier, Lady 138

Stanley, Keith 152

Staples, Mr 108

Stapleton, Major the Hon M 54

Stapleton-Cotton, Hester 90

Steel, Air Chief Marshal Sir John 81

Stephens, Jeremy 124

Stewart, Mr 108

Stewart, Sir Herbert 66

Strawson, Major General John 121, 124, 139, 140, 142, 181

Stringer, Mr 108

Summers, Philip 105

Surtees, Robert 30

Sutton, Sir Richard 73

Swaine, Major C 54

Symons, Captain John 140, 148

Talbot, Jack 14, 15

Thomas, Major Otho V 182

Thompson, Joe 104, 108

Thorne, General Sir Andrew 181

Todd, Brigadier George 92

Tonga, Queen of 94

Trenchard, Lord 60

Tuck, Brigadier P H J 171

Valentia, Colonel The Viscount 84, 85, 180

Venables-Llewellyn, Charles 26

Verdin, Lt Colonel Sir Richard 180

Vereker, Corinna 30

Vesci, Viscount 26

Vigors, Patrick 154, 156

Vivian, Brigadier The Lord Nicholas 140, 153

Vivian, Hon Dorothy 58

Walford, Nicholas 150, 170, 182

Ward, Major General Sir Philip 124, 142, 181

Wardrop, Colonel F 54

Warner, W Redston 54, 182

Warner, Sir Edward 29

Watt, Frances 159

Weatherall, Captain H A 54, 55, 56, 57, 113

Webb, Lt Colonel Charles 7, 103

Wellesley-Harding, Commander Ian 182

Wellington, The Duke of 14, 16, 19

West, Buzz 158

Weston-Smith, Captain Ian 33

White, Sir George 66, 90

Willey, Lt Colonel F V Willey 81

Wilson, Major Robin 75, 170

Wilson, Sir Henry 28, 61

Winch, Colonel G B 81

Winter, Jeffrey 42

Wisden, John 163

Wolseley, Lt General Sir Garnet 66, 80

Wood, Colonel E 54

Woodd, Colonel David 143, 168

Woods, Conlin John 152

Woodward, Rear Admiral Sandy 48

Wootton, Major Tony 105

Worsley, General Sir Richard 143, 180

Wynne-Parker, Michael 136

Yates, Christian 158

York, TRH The Duke and Duchess 28

Ypres, Field Marshal Earl of (see French) 76, 90